THE SPANISH TRAGEDY

broadview editions
series editor: Martin R. Boyne

THE SPANISH TRAGEDY

Thomas Kyd

edited by Patrick McHenry

broadview editions

BROADVIEW PRESS – www.broadviewpress.com
Peterborough, Ontario, Canada

Founded in 1985, Broadview Press remains a wholly independent publishing house. Broadview's focus is on academic publishing; our titles are accessible to university and college students as well as scholars and general readers. With over 600 titles in print, Broadview has become a leading international publisher in the humanities, with world-wide distribution. Broadview is committed to environmentally responsible publishing and fair business practices.

The interior of this book is printed on 100% recycled paper.

© 2016 Patrick McHenry

Library and Archives Canada Cataloguing in Publication

Kyd, Thomas, 1558-1594, author
    The Spanish tragedy / Thomas Kyd ; edited by Patrick McHenry.

(Broadview editions)
Includes bibliographical references.
ISBN 978-1-55481-205-9 (paperback)

    I. McHenry, Patrick, 1961–, editor II. Title. III. Series: Broadview editions

PR2654.S6 2016   822'.3   C2016-901638-2

Broadview Editions
The Broadview Editions series is an effort to represent the ever-evolving canon of texts in the disciplines of literary studies, history, philosophy, and political theory. A distinguishing feature of the series is the inclusion of primary source documents contemporaneous with the work.

Advisory editor for this volume: Denis Johnston

Broadview Press handles its own distribution in North America
PO Box 1243, Peterborough, Ontario K9J 7H5, Canada
555 Riverwalk Parkway, Tonawanda, NY 14150, USA
Tel: (705) 743-8990; Fax: (705) 743-8353
email: customerservice@broadviewpress.com

Distribution is handled by Eurospan Group in the UK, Europe, Central Asia, Middle East, Africa, India, Southeast Asia, Central America, South America, and the Caribbean. Distribution is handled by Footprint Books in Australia and New Zealand.

Broadview Press acknowledges the financial support of the Government of Canada through the Canada Book Fund for our publishing activities.

Typesetting and assembly: True to Type Inc., Claremont, Canada
Cover Design: Lisa Brawn

PRINTED IN CANADA

Contents

Acknowledgements

This project would not have been possible without the institutional support of Columbus State University. Many thanks to Dean Dennis Rome, Angela Johnson, and Jill Carroll of the College of Letters and Sciences, as well as Provost Tom Hackett. It is a pleasure to work with Broadview Press, and I am particularly grateful to Marjorie Mather, Martin Boyne, and Denis Johnston for their patient and expert editorial work.

I appreciate the help and good humor of my colleagues in Columbus and in the Department of English at Columbus State. Special thanks to Susan Hrach and Jim Owen, who read drafts and offered valuable advice throughout the process. Thanks to Shannon Godlove, Pedro Maligo (now of Rockhurst University), Nick Norwood, and Dan Ross, who took delight in helping me find answers to the most esoteric questions, and to Peter Parisi (of Brookstone School) for his Latin translations. I am grateful to the students in my Shakespeare courses in 2014 and 2015 for studying *The Spanish Tragedy* in my draft text and offering their valuable comments.

Thanks most importantly to my wife, Cheryl Yatsko, for her support from beginning to end.

Introduction

Sometime in the mid-1580s, the exact place and time unknown, a London theater audience attended an extraordinary event, the first revenge tragedy on the Elizabethan stage. This play, *The Spanish Tragedy*, went on to be one of the most successful of the era. It was performed repeatedly, published in at least ten editions between 1592 and 1633, and imitated by a generation of playwrights. The most literate in that audience would have noticed a debt to the Roman playwright Seneca, who was revered at the time for his moral tragedies, and to the writers of *The Mirror for Magistrates*, an anthology of verse whose ghosts narrate their own tragic stories. Others would have noticed the dialogue in a powerful verse form, unrhymed iambic pentameter; it had appeared two decades earlier in the static political drama *Gorboduc*, but it had never delivered such viscerally appealing material before. It came to be called "Marlowe's Mighty Line," for Kyd's fellow playwright Christopher Marlowe, who developed it alongside Kyd and made it soar on stage. Others yet would have noticed a strange and pleasing combination of elements, including a supernatural framework, depictions of both aristocrats and commoners, comic episodes in the course of the tragedy, a powerfully self-actualized woman as a central character, scenes of thrilling violence, and a spectacular catastrophe to bring the action to a close.

The Life and Work of Thomas Kyd

Kyd's Early Years

Thomas Kyd was born into a comfortably situated family in London in 1558. The parish register of the Church of St. Mary Woolnoth notes his baptism on 6 November: "Thomas, son of Francis Kidd, Citizen and Writer of the Courte Letter of London" (*Transcript* 9). His father's profession as Writer of the Court, also called a scrivener, required a literate mind and a skilled hand to copy court documents. It was a profession that, at times, invited hostility, and clerks such as Francis were often derided as "Noverints" or "Noverint-makers," after the Latin words that began such documents, *noverint universi*, "Let all men know." Nonetheless, it offered prosperity for Francis and his family, which consisted of his wife Anna and, at least, Thomas's two siblings, Ann and William (*Transcript* 11, 16; Freeman, *Thomas Kyd* 2), and probably household servants.[1] Francis later served a year as churchwarden at St. Mary Woolnoth, another indication of his stable position in the community (*Transcript* xxxvii). If the Kyd family was ordinary, the times were not. In the very month Thomas was baptized, Queen Mary I died. She had reigned since 1553, and her marriage to King Philip II of Spain triggered intense fears of a Spanish takeover. Her heavy-handed effort to restore Roman Catholicism in England, which had moved increasingly toward Protestantism during the reign of her half-brother Edward VI (r. 1547–53), earned her the nickname "Bloody Mary," for the many Protestants she had burned at the stake. That same month saw Mary's younger half-sister, the daughter of Henry VIII and Anne Boleyn, take the throne as Elizabeth I (r. 1558–1603). Elizabeth's Protestant agenda triggered a fundamental shift in foreign and domestic policy. Suddenly, English Catholic families were at odds with the ruling powers; suddenly the pope and his allies in Europe were threats to the English throne. These momentous changes filtered down to the local level very quickly, as the records of Kyd's parish show. In these months, St. Mary Woolnoth paid six shillings and eight pence[2] to "Eton the carpenter and iiij men to help him to take downe the roode," sixteen pence "to iiij men for taking down the altares, and the altar stones," and four pence "for ij laboureres for ij dayes dyggynge downe the altares and conveying out the rubbishe" (*Transcript* xxii).[3] Getting rid of the Catholic crucifix (the "roode") and altar at this church was a small part of a nationwide shift from Catholicism to Protestantism. Tensions between those

---

1 A servant of the Kyd household, Prudence Cook, was buried in 1563 (*Transcript* 187; Freeman, *Thomas Kyd* 2). This is no sign of unusual wealth since even modest households at the time employed servants.

2 At this time, a shilling was equal to twelve pence, and a pound was equal to twenty shillings. To get some idea of the economic value of money, the Elizabethan theater manager Philip Henslowe (c. 1550–1616) records a payment of six pence to a laborer, presumably for a day's work, and six shillings to two plasterers for four days' work, which calculates to nine pence per workman's day (Henslowe 66–67).

3 A common practice at this time was to use the letter j as the final digit in lower case Roman numerals. In this sentence, iiij = 4. At least in handwriting, this makes it more difficult for another digit to be added later.

loyal to one side or the other continued as a fact of life in Kyd's England.

In October 1565, when Thomas was almost seven years old, his father enrolled him in the Merchant Taylors' School (*Register* 9). Why Francis committed as much as five shillings per quarter (Barker lxi) to provide Thomas with a humanist education in Latin and other languages is impossible to know. He may have seen it as a good foundation for a life as a scrivener; he may have gained prestige by having a son in such a school; or he may have recognized that his son excelled in his elementary studies and thought him a good candidate for an advanced education. Whatever the reason, the decision placed Thomas in good company with the sons of other tradesmen, including many merchant tailors, drapers, dyers, haberdashers, and others from England's thriving cloth trade, but also fishmongers, grocers, poulterers, brewers, and the occasional gentleman. Most importantly, as a student of Merchant Taylors', Thomas came under the educational philosophy, and possibly the direct influence, of the school's famous headmaster, Richard Mulcaster (c. 1531–1611).

Even without records specific to Kyd, it is no stretch to imagine that Mulcaster's school had a profound influence on the scrivener's son. He would have found his school days austere and regimented, featuring the study of Latin and other languages, music, and possibly theatrical performance, an experience similar to that of judge and Member of Parliament Sir James Whitelocke (1570–1632), who, in an often quoted passage, remembers his experience as a student at the Merchant Taylors' School just a decade after Kyd first enrolled:

> I was brought up at school under mr. Mulcaster, in the
> famous school of the Marchantaylors in London, whear I
> continued untill I was well instructed in the Hebrew, Greek,
> and Latin tongs. His care was also to encreas my skill in
> musique, in whiche I was brought up by daily exercise in it,
> as in singing and playing upon instruments, and yeerly he
> presented sum playes to the court, in whiche his scholers
> wear only actors, and I on among them, and by that meanes
> taughte them good behaviour and audacitye. (Whitelocke 12)

Mulcaster, who served as the school's "high maister" from 1561 to 1586, was the product of Eton, Cambridge, and Oxford (Wilson 11, 21–22), and he articulated his educational philosophy in two books, *Positions* (1581; see Appendix B1) and *Elemen-*

tary (1582). According to the founding statutes of the school, Mulcaster and three "ushers" would have managed 250 students, many on reduced or free tuition. Statute 27 states, "The children shall come to the school in the morning at seven of the clock both winter and summer, and tarry there until eleven, and return again at one of the clock, and depart at five" (Wilson 17). Statute 31 states that the children should never have "leave to play, except only one in the week" (Wilson 17), a practice that seems to run counter to Mulcaster's philosophy to encourage exercise in the body as well as the mind. As for the students' other needs, the statutes are strict: no food is allowed, and "unto their urine the scholars shall go to the places appointed them in the lane or street without[1] the court, and for other causes, if need be, they shall go to the water-side" (Wilson 17).

What did Kyd learn at Merchant Taylors' School? At the most practical level, we can reasonably assume that he mastered Latin and developed a knowledge of classical writers, such as Virgil (70–19 BCE) and Seneca (4 BCE–65 CE), whom he quotes in *The Spanish Tragedy*; he may have also acquired some French and Italian, which he drew upon to translate works from these languages for publication later in his life. He may have received an introduction to the stage: Chambers lists the Merchant Taylors' School among the child acting companies active in London and cites records of performances in 1572–73 before the Merchant Taylors' Company (2: 75). Whether Kyd, at around age 14, was part of these performances (or even still enrolled), is impossible to say, but staging plays with boy actors was common at this time. Mulcaster himself may have gained a taste for the stage at Eton, where, as Chambers notes, "Christmas plays by the boys had become the practice" (2: 74). It is tantalizing to think that the characters Kyd created in *The Spanish Tragedy* might have been shaped by the values introduced to him in Mulcaster's school: Bel-imperia as a woman of agency, Pedringano as a social climber, Lorenzo as an imperious member of the upper crust. Mulcaster allowed for educating women, "not as preachers and leaders: yet as honest perfourmers, and vertuous livers" (Mulcaster, *Positions* 181). Among Kyd's classmates were children who were apt to learn but of humble origins; perhaps Kyd met many Pedringanos there, ambitious and clever but with no chance of advancement.

---

1 Outside.

Kyd did not attend university. At what age he left the Merchant Taylors' School or what he did in his young adulthood is unknown, but he appears to have been active in the London theater world sometime in his mid-twenties. The theatrical business Kyd would have known in London was organized around companies of players. These profit-seeking enterprises were in the process of professionalizing during the 1570s and 1580s by establishing purpose-built playhouses that provided a base for their operations. The first of these, the Red Lion (1567), was short-lived, but in 1576 the actor James Burbage (c. 1530–97) constructed the first successful playhouse, the Theatre, and so inspired the construction of several more public theaters in the next decades, including the Rose, the Swan, the Curtain, and the Globe, which was built in 1599 from the timbers of the Theatre after the latter was torn down.[1] Another factor in the professionalization of theatrical companies was the Vagabonds Act of 1572, which had the effect of inhibiting independent traveling acts and requiring troupes of players to operate under the patronage of a noble household, an arrangement that had been practiced for a decade but was now all but compulsory. The patron provided the name for the company, such as the Earl of Leicester's Men, for Robert Dudley, the Earl of Leicester (1532–88), who formed a company of players as early as 1559. Companies rose and fell, merged and divided as they competed for talent, patrons, scripts, and, above all, audiences.

It is possible to make connections between Kyd and three acting companies: the Queen's Men, Lord Strange's Men, and the combined Lord Admiral's and Lord Chamberlain's Men,[2] based on the documents that exist and inferences that can be made. Freeman and Erne connect Kyd to the Queen's Men through *A Knight's Conjuring* (1607) by Thomas Dekker (c. 1572–1632), a dream narrative that places groups of English writers in

---

1 Gurr provides an excellent introduction to the evolving theatrical facilities in London, including the development of indoor theaters, which I have omitted here as less relevant to Kyd, who died before indoor theaters flourished (*Playgoing* 13–48).

2 The patrons of these companies were Queen Elizabeth herself; Ferdinando Stanley, Earl of Derby, also known as Lord Strange (1559–94); Charles Howard, Earl of Nottingham and Lord High Admiral (1536–1624); and Henry Carey, Lord Hunsdon and Lord Chamberlain (c. 1525–96) (Chambers 2: 104, 118, 134, 192).

a pleasant underworld garden: "In another companie sat learned *Watson*, industrious *Kyd*, ingenious *Atchlow*, and (tho hee had bene a Player molded out of their pennes) ... Inimitable *Bentley*"[1] (Dekker). If Kyd wrote parts for the actor John Bentley, who died in 1585, then it's likely that he wrote for the Queen's Men (Freeman, *Thomas Kyd* 13; Erne 1). How long Kyd continued and whether he wrote *The Spanish Tragedy* for the Queen's Men is simply unknown. Charles Nicholl concludes that both Kyd and Christopher Marlowe[2] were writing for Lord Strange's Men in 1591 based on Kyd's own comment in his first letter to Puckering (42; also see Appendix B3). This would seem to be corroborated by performances of *The Spanish Tragedy* by Lord Strange's Men noted in *Henslowe's Diary* in 1591–93; Henslowe also notes a performance of *Hamlet*, presumably Kyd's (see below, p. 27), by the combined Lord Admiral's and Lord Chamberlain's Men in June 1594, shortly before Kyd's death (Henslowe 21; see also Erne 153–54), but this does not necessarily mean that Kyd was a member of that company.

The Dutch Church Libel and Kyd's Death

Thomas Kyd's last two years reflect how suddenly early modern lives could veer into tragedy, whether by disease, violence, oppressive authority, or any number of other forces. We can imagine that 1592 looked promising to Kyd. His *Spanish Tragedy* was an audience favorite at the Rose Theatre in London; he was a close associate of London's premier playwright, Christopher Marlowe; he had an aristocratic patron; he had other works planned or in publication, including translations from Italian and French and a poem based on the conversion of St. Paul; he was sufficiently respected for contemporaries to remember him, after his death, as "among our best for tragedy" (Francis Meres), "industrious" (Thomas Dekker), "sporting" (Ben Jonson), and "famous" (Thomas Heywood).[3] In the fall of 1592, a sequence of events

---

1   Thomas Watson (c. 1557–92), London poet, translator, and classicist; Thomas Achelley, poet and playwright with the Queen's Men whom Freeman estimates to have died in the early 1590s (*Thomas Kyd* 18); John Bentley, an actor with the Queen's Men who died in 1585.

2   London playwright (1564–93) whose *Tamburlaine the Great* (1587), along with Kyd's *Spanish Tragedy*, ushered in the era of blank verse on the Elizabethan stage.

3   Freeman discusses these references to Kyd (*Thomas Kyd* 48). Meres (1565–1647), Dekker (c. 1572–1632), Jonson (1572–1637), and Heywood (1575–1641) were all English authors and/or playwrights.

began that, even though unrelated to Kyd, unraveled his life. Two years later, he was dead at age 35.[1] This dismal final portion of Kyd's life can be pieced together partly from his own writings (two letters and a final dedication; see Appendices B2–B4) and partly from papers mentioned below related to the Dutch Church Libel, although these documents are not enough to reconstruct events in detail.

Late in 1592 an outbreak of the bubonic plague swept into England, claiming thousands of victims in towns and across the country. The Elizabethan government responded by investing local justices with new powers, ordering dead bodies to be inspected before burial, requiring the sick to be quarantined, and raising new taxes to cover the expenses caused by the plague (*Orders Thought Meete*). The outbreak was followed by unemployment and general social unrest in London. Playhouses were ordered closed and remained so throughout 1593 (see Chambers 4: 313–24, 348–49), which cut off performances as a source of revenue for those in the theater business, presumably including Kyd. As the year ended and a new one began, conditions only worsened. Freeman writes, "Spring of 1593 was a grim one in London, with continual plague, rumors of a new Spanish invasion, intensified prosecution of schismatics and recusants, bad weather, and mounting unemployment" (Freeman, "Marlowe" 44).

At this time a new source of social disruption caught the attention of the Elizabethan government: xenophobic anger toward Flemish and French traders in London. London had long been an important center of trade for goods traveling to and from the continent, but war in the Low Countries between Protestants (aided by England) and Catholics (aided by Spain) had driven many traders from the continent to the relative safety of London. In 1593, posters appeared threatening violence against these resident aliens. Elizabeth's Privy Council,[2] following its general disposition to subdue social unrest at all costs, acted to suppress the threats. On 16 April 1593, the Council sent a letter to the Lord Mayor of London to find the culprit responsible for these

---

1 The information in the following three paragraphs has been covered by various scholars, including Boas (lxvii–lxxiv), Riggs (318–21), Nicholl (42–47), and others. Freeman's article "Marlowe, Kyd, and the Dutch Church Libel" is particularly valuable on the topic of Kyd's arrest and death.

2 A cabinet of advisers to the monarch that became particularly influential during the reign of Elizabeth I.

posters: "We thincke it convenient he shalbe punyshed by torture" (*Acts of the Privy Council of England* 24.187). About a month later, one particular poster, a poem now known as the Dutch Church Libel, aggravated the tensions. It accuses "Ye strangers that do inhabit in this land," of undermining market prices, putting local artisans out of work, living twenty to a household, driving up rents, and benefiting from England's soldiers (fighting the Spanish) in France and Belgium, who "die like dogs as sacrifice for you." It accuses the ruling class of being complicit: "With Spanish gold, you are all infected / and with that gold our nobles wink at feats." In the end, it says "our swords are whet, to shed their blood." It is signed, "per Tamberlaine" (Freeman, "Marlowe" 50–51).

The Privy Council's response came on 11 May 1593. It ordered London authorities to round up and "make search and aprehend everie person so to be suspected" and to "enter into al houses and places where anie such maie be remayning, and uppon their aprehencion to make like search in anie the chambers, studies, chestes or other like places for al manner of writings or papers that may geve you light for the discoverie of the libellers."[1] Further, the Privy Council advises putting recalcitrant suspects "to the torture in Bridewel" prison (*Acts of the Privy Council of England* 24.222). While no records exist that implicate Thomas Kyd, he would likely have attracted the attention of the authorities in three ways. First, he had close ties to Christopher Marlowe, whose play *Tamburlaine the Great* had recently been an audience favorite and who was a person of interest to the Privy Council;[2] the libel not only is signed "Tamberlaine," but also seems to make passing references to two of Marlowe's other plays: its mention of "Jewes" and "Your Machiavellian Marchant" refers to the title and the character Machiavell from *The Jew of Malta* (c. 1589/90), and its phrase "paris massacre" seems to refer to *The Massacre at Paris* (c. 1593; Freeman, "Marlowe" 50–51). Second, Kyd was a playwright and capable of writing verse for this purpose. Third, as a scrivener, or at least the son of one, Kyd had the pen-and-ink skills to write the verse on paper.

---

1 Here a *libel* indicates a bill posted publicly that stirs up trouble (loosely in the sense of *OED* 4). This instance of the word *libeller* is an early use, the first noted by the *OED* in 1589.

2 The Privy Council summoned "Christofer Marlow" by name on 18 May and recorded his appearance on 20 May (*Acts of the Privy Council of England* 24.244).

Whatever the reason, around 12 May the authorities arrested Kyd, rifled through his possessions, and found some papers (a fragment of an academic exercise on the topic of Arianism, an early Christian heresy) that triggered a suspicion of atheism. A week later (in records dated 18 and 20 May), the Privy Council brought Marlowe before them. Ten days after that, on 30 May, Marlowe was stabbed to death by political operative Ingram Frizer at a dinner table in Deptford Strand, a dock town outside of London. The crown's coroner, William Danby, wrote that the fight occurred "about the payment of the sum of pence, that is, *le recknynge*,[1] there" (Hotson 32), but the most recent generation of Marlowe's biographers holds that his death was a political assassination, though the precise motive remains unclear.[2] Although some have suggested that whatever Kyd said during his torture led to Marlowe's arrest, it seems unlikely that Kyd revealed anything about Marlowe that the authorities didn't already know, given Marlowe's history of contacts with Elizabeth's spies and underworld figures.

What is clear is that Kyd was broken by the experience and desperate for the protection and resources of an aristocratic patron. This desperation led him to write to Sir John Puckering (1544–96), Lord Keeper of the Great Seal and member of the Privy Council, to ask for his help in regaining his standing with his patron, whom he does not name (see the two letters in Appendix B3). Kyd emphasizes his cooperation by offering up detailed information on Marlowe's transgressions—to no effect, of course, since Marlowe was already dead. In the first letter, he protests his innocence, both of the libel and of atheism, and asserts that his "tortures" were undeserved. He does not specify what he endured, but the Privy Council directed suspects to be tortured at Bridewell prison, where they could have been stretched on a rack or forced to hang from manacles. Nicholl, citing various sources, identifies others swept up in these events who were imprisoned, pilloried, carted, and whipped (351). The Arian fragment, Kyd writes, was "affirmed by Marlowe to be his, and shuffled with some of mine" when they were writing in the same room two years before. In the second letter, Kyd distances himself further from Marlowe by reporting some of the scandalous things Marlowe said, such as that St. John was "our savior

---

1 The bill.

2 See Nicholl for a book-length investigation of Marlowe's death, or Riggs for a concise treatment.

Christ's Alexis" (object of homosexual affection) and that St. Paul was "a juggler" (swindler). Kyd's attempts to regain a patron and clear his name were apparently unsuccessful. The last words from Kyd, his 1594 dedication to *Cornelia*, reveal a physically and emotionally troubled man, who refers to his "misery," "afflictions of the mind," and "privy broken passions" (Appendix B4). Kyd died that same year at the age of 35 and was buried on 15 August. Whether the tortures he suffered contributed to his death is unknown.

Thomas Kyd's Works

About half of Shakespeare's plays, including *The Tempest* and *Macbeth*, would not have survived if they had not been printed in the First Folio seven years after his death. Had Thomas Kyd's works been similarly collected and published, more plays by him would no doubt exist today. Thomas Dekker's description of Kyd as "industrious" is all the more indication that we are missing much of Kyd's canon, since Dekker himself, writer of more than 60 plays, was industrious by any standard. As it stands, Kyd's reputation rests almost entirely on *The Spanish Tragedy*, which was attributed to him only long after his death. Kyd's complete works, to the extent that they are known, remained uncollected until Frederick Boas's edition of 1901, which includes *The Spanish Tragedy*; *Cornelia*, Kyd's translation of a French play by Robert Garnier (1544–90); *Soliman and Perseda*, a freestanding version of Hieronimo's play from *The Spanish Tragedy*; *The House-holder's Philosophy*, Kyd's translation of a pamphlet by the Italian Torquato Tasso (1544–95); *The Murder of John Brewen*, a short prose account that is no longer considered part of Kyd's canon; a discussion of Kyd's lost *Hamlet* (see below, pp. 27–28); and *The First Part of Hieronimo*.

This last play, *The First Part of Hieronimo*, published in a 1605 quarto, could be unrelated to Kyd, or it could be the mangled first part of a two-part play with *The Spanish Tragedy*, as Lukas Erne argues. This puzzle has its source in the diary of Philip Henslowe, who maintained active business interests in theaters and acting companies from the 1580s until his death in 1616. *The Spanish Tragedy* was exceedingly popular, as *Henslowe's Diary* confirms with notes of multiple performances and strong receipts, first by Lord Strange's Men in 1591–92 and later by the Lord Admiral's Men in 1597. Henslowe, like others of the age, referred to the play as *Jeronimo*, spelling it in various ways, after its main character, Hieronimo. He also notes performances in 1591–92 for a "comodye donne oracoe" (among other spellings for *Comedy of Don Horatio*), and *Comedy of Jeronimo*. Whether these are two titles for the same play or two separate plays is difficult to say; whether they are related to the 1605 quarto is also unclear. Boas, writing over 100 years ago, argues that the 1605 play is unrelated to these earlier titles but rather the work of a hack writer seeking to capitalize on a newly expanded version of *The Spanish Tragedy* that appeared in 1602 (Boas xliv). More recently, Lukas Erne argues that the 1605 *Don Horatio* contains fragments of an original play by Kyd that would have formed the first part of a two-part structure with *The Spanish Tragedy*. Erne further speculates that a diptych of *The Spanish Tragedy* and (now mostly lost) *Don Horatio* might have brought two-part plays into fashion (Erne 21–22). By Henslowe's records, the first part of this diptych was unsuccessful and disappeared while *The Spanish Tragedy* on its own became the most successful play of the era.

Thomas Kyd and Elizabethan Literature

Revenge Tragedy

Writers and audiences have always understood the appeal of revenge. The impulse to get even, to exact justice, in the broadest sense, drives Ishtar to set the Bull of Heaven on the people of Uruk in the *Epic of Gilgamesh*, Achilles to kill Hector in the *Iliad*, Rama to battle Ravana in the *Ramayana*, and countless other characters to take action against their antagonists.[1] At some visceral level, this same impulse drives Hieronimo and Bel-imperia to settle the score by killing the killers of their beloved Horatio. As timeless as the impulse toward vengeance is, however, *The Spanish Tragedy* and the revenge plays that followed it were products of the specific time and place of early modern England. Having been printed at least ten times between 1592 and 1633 and revived so often that playwright Ben Jonson complained that audiences want nothing else (Appendix C6), Kyd's play was clearly successful. It is no surprise that other playwrights followed

---

1   *The Epic of Gilgamesh* (c. 2000 BCE) recounts the life of the Mesopotamian king Gilgamesh; Homer's *Iliad* (c. 700 BCE) is the Greek story of Achilles' rage and grief during the Trojan War; *The Ramayana* (c. 300 BCE) is the Sanskrit epic of the hero Rama, avatar of the god Vishnu.

its successful pattern, establishing a set of conventions that became the familiar elements of the revenge drama: ghosts, uncertain revengers, murderers protected from justice by powerful interests, scenes of madness, scenes of humor, clever devices to reveal the murderers, and final bloodbaths that consume a broad circle of characters including the revengers themselves.[1]

At the heart of the revenge tragedy is a thrill ride that leaves the audience in a philosophically uncomfortable position. The thrill comes from seeing criminal characters face the consequences of their actions—all the more thrilling if the characters are corrupt aristocrats, such as the malignant Lorenzo. Kyd allows Lorenzo's specific motivations to be vague, but we understand that he would benefit if Spain and Portugal were united through a marriage of his sister Bel-imperia and his prisoner-turned-guest Balthazar. Lorenzo's power is in manipulation, which perhaps explains why he seems to prefer having his sister and Balthazar in power rather than maneuvering toward the throne himself. His obsession to control his sister's sexual choices adds another layer of moral repugnance and triggers his onstage murder of Horatio—all the more thrilling to audiences accustomed to violent acts being reported from offstage, as the murders are in *Gorboduc* (1561). To cover up his crimes, Lorenzo isolates his sister for several days and plays on Pedringano's misplaced ambitions to manipulate him into killing their accomplice Serberine, a crime for which he is executed. Satisfaction comes when Lorenzo falls into Hieronimo and Bel-imperia's trap and is stabbed to death in front of his own royal family.

However, *The Spanish Tragedy*, and revenge tragedy generally, is not just about the thrill of getting even but also about the moral and psychological discomforts of exacting private revenge, what Francis Bacon called "wild justice" (Appendix C7).[2] Unlike Bel-imperia, who witnessed the crime and is single-minded as a revenger, Hieronimo considers alternatives. First he contemplates suicide: "For if I hang or kill myself, let's know / Who will revenge Horatio's murder then?" (3.12.17–18). After rejecting suicide,

---

1 Bowers discusses two patterns of revenge tragedy, one developed by Kyd as discussed in this paragraph, and a variation that follows Marlowe's *Jew of Malta*, in which the protagonist is a villain and pursues revenge in response to being personally injured rather than taking on the duty to revenge a loved one's death (143–44).

2 Other ways out of the discomfort did exist in Elizabethan society. One alternative thread is articulated by Richard Jones, who sees revenge as a duty and matter of honor (Appendix C4).

he brings his suit to the king, only to have Lorenzo block his access to justice. This drives Hieronimo to extremes. In his soliloquy that opens 3.13, he articulates the dilemma of the revenger: either observe the biblical injunction against private revenge and allow God to "be revenged of every ill" (3.13.2), or follow the Senecan model and "Strike, and strike home, where wrong is offered thee" (3.13.7). Shortly thereafter, Hieronimo, himself a Spanish magistrate and therefore an embodiment of justice, symbolically rejects a judicial remedy by tearing up the written suits the Citizens bring to him: "Then will I rend and tear them thus and thus, / Shivering their limbs in pieces with my teeth" (3.13.126–27). By using the phrase "thus and thus" as he shreds the papers, he audibly aligns himself with the murderer Lorenzo, who used the same words as he stabbed Horatio:

HORATIO: What, will you murder me?
LORENZO: Aye, thus, and thus! (2.4.54–55)

Any empathy the audience might feel for Hieronimo would be undermined by his defiance of the well-known passage in Paul's letter to the Romans: "Dearly beloved, avenge not yourselves, but give place unto wrath: for it is written, vengeance is mine: I will repay, saith the Lord" (Appendix C1).[1] Hieronimo's plan also defies the equally stern injunction against private revenge articulated in royally sanctioned homilies: "And in so going about to revenge evil, we show ourselves to be evil" (Appendix C3). Psychologically, from this point forward, Hieronimo's obsession with revenge results in madness, for instance in mistaking an old man for the ghost of his murdered son Horatio, "from the depth / To ask for justice in this upper earth" (3.13.36–37), proposing a tragedy to be acted in four languages (none of which is Spanish or Portuguese) as entertainment for a wedding, displaying the bleeding corpse of his son on stage after the revenge murders, biting out his own tongue, and committing suicide just after murdering the Duke of Castile, who is not implicated in any of the original crimes.

The discomfort caused by the revenger's dilemma—either leave the revenge in the hands of God or act on the revenge and

---

1 Ronald Broude argues that Hieronimo is not defying the Biblical injunction but in fact is God's agent, fulfilling the providential plan to effect God's vengeance and martyr himself in the process ("Vindicta Filia Temporis" 498–99).

risk madness, death, and damnation—was one of the main drivers as the revenge genre matured over the next 40 years.[1] In that time, dozens of plays appeared that followed the basic pattern established by Kyd in *The Spanish Tragedy*, including *Titus Andronicus* (c. 1592) and *Hamlet* (c. 1600) by Shakespeare, *The Revenger's Tragedy* (1607) by Thomas Middleton (1580–1627), *Antonio's Revenge* (1602) by John Marston (1576–1634), *The Atheist's Tragedy* (1611) by Cyril Tourneur (c. 1575–1626), and *The White Devil* (1609–12) and *The Duchess of Malfi* (1612–13) by John Webster (c. 1578–c. 1626), each a unique addition to the genre. The genre was flexible, and much of the variety was driven by different ways to manage the revenger's dilemma, as the following three examples illustrate.

In 1602, Henry Chettle (c. 1560–c. 1607) offered a cheeky twist on Kyd's pattern in *The Tragedy of Hoffman*. It begins with a reference to the end of *The Spanish Tragedy*, as the revenger, Hoffman, draws a curtain to display the dead body of his father and vows revenge on anyone with any part in his murder. We soon learn that his father was not murdered but judicially executed for piracy. What follows is a killing spree by Hoffman in the name of revenge. By merging the revenger and the villain, audience members are relieved of the revenger's dilemma since they develop no empathy for Hoffman, and justice is served when he meets a violent death in the final scene. A few years later, *The Revenge of Bussy D'Ambois* (1613) by George Chapman (c. 1559–1634) skirted the dilemma in the opposite direction. His revenger, Clermont, is so scrupulous that he refuses to take any illegal or immoral actions to revenge his brother's murder, despite the urgings of several characters, including the ghost of his dead brother, even when the ghost provides Clermont a framework to justify killing his brother's murderer: "What corrupted law / Leaves unperformed in kings do thou supply, / And be above them all in dignity" (5.1.97–99). It is to no avail. As a devotee of stoicism, Clermont remains immune to the passion it takes to consume oneself in an act of revenge. It is only after challenging the murderer to a duel that he finally kills him, and then only within the strict bounds of decorum. Toward the end of the era, *The Changeling*, by Thomas Middleton and William Rowley (c. 1585–1626), shifted the moral hazards typically faced by revengers onto the villains themselves. With its grisly onstage

---

1   The discussion in the next two paragraphs frequently draws on Bowers, which is the most complete work on Elizabethan revenge tragedy.

murders, ghost, and passionate revenger, the play works in the tradition of the genre, except the revenger appears only late in the play. The first four acts concern the initial murders, as Beatrice persuades De Flores to kill the suitor her father prefers, and later her own maid, in order to free her to marry her love, Alsemero. By benefiting from the wicked nature of De Flores, she becomes his moral equal, a fact that neither her high birth nor chastity can change. The revenger, Tomazo, is as obsessed with revenge as Hieronimo of *The Spanish Tragedy*, but before he can kill Beatrice and De Flores and imperil his own soul, they confess their crimes and kill themselves.

The Influence of Seneca

Readers have long noted the influence of the ancient Roman writer Seneca on *The Spanish Tragedy* and on the revenge genre generally. One of Kyd's contemporaries, the writer Thomas Nashe (1567–1601), framed an attack on Kyd (or possibly a group of playwrights including Kyd) around the idea that he was merely rearranging Seneca's plays to appeal to audiences at the time. In "To the Gentlemen Students of Both Universities," which introduces Robert Greene's *Arcadia or Menaphon*, Nashe writes,

> It is a common practise now a daies amongst a sort of shifting companions, that runne through euery arte and thriue by none, to leaue the trade of *Nouerint*, whereto they were borne, and busie themselues with the indeuors of Art, that could scarcelie latinize their necke-verse if they should haue neede.

Nashe is just getting started when he suggests that Kyd should keep his day job as a noverint, the profession his father taught him, and stay away from artistic endeavors. He insults him further by implying that Kyd could not read Seneca's plays in their original Latin, which Nashe no doubt considered among the highest achievements in that language. English translations of Seneca first appeared in the 1550s, but Kyd was capable in Latin. That Kyd could not render his "necke-verse" in Latin, a reference to the prayers that condemned people said before being hanged, is not just to insult his language skills, but also to jab at Kyd's status as a commoner with no university education (unlike Nashe himself, a Cambridge man), summoning up the image of

Kyd meeting the kind of death reserved for people of low social status.

While Seneca constituted an important influence on *The Spanish Tragedy*, the similarities are not especially deep. To use one play as an example, Seneca's *Thyestes* takes as its subject the feuding brothers Atreus and Thyestes of Greek myth. Their grandfather, Tantalus, has cooked and served his son Pelops to the gods at a banquet. The gods resurrect Pelops, who then commits a series of unsavory acts to secure his power as a king. It is Pelops' cursed kingdom, among other things, that his sons Atreus and Thyestes feud over. In the play, Atreus lures Thyestes to a banquet on the pretext of reconciliation, murders Thyestes' three children, cooks them into the main course, feeds them to his brother, and taunts him while showing him the severed heads of his sons. Like *The Spanish Tragedy*, *Thyestes* opens with a ghost and a mythological figure, Tantalus and Fury, who comment on the expected events. It also features an avenger who, like Hieronimo, berates himself for not acting sooner as he becomes obsessed with exacting his revenge in spectacular fashion. The avenger Atreus says, famously, "*Scelera non ulcisceris, nisi vincis*" ["You cannot say you have avenged a crime / Until you better it"] (Seneca, Watling edition, 53–54, and n. 1). Both plays feature a final episode of extreme violence that entangles characters beyond those involved in the original crimes.

While these and other echoes indicate an important thread back to ancient Roman literature, the success of *The Spanish Tragedy* cannot be said to rest on Seneca or any other single precedent. Indeed, comparing Kyd to Seneca (whose plays may not have been meant for performance) highlights the former's genius for theatrical innovation more than his imitation of classical models. Where Seneca's Fury and Ghost of Tantalus provide a prologue then go silent, Kyd's Revenge and Ghost of Andrea remain on stage and connect themselves to the events, and indeed they follow more from Thomas Sackville's "Induction" and "Complaint of Buckingham" from *The Mirror for Magistrates*[1] than from Seneca. Where Seneca provides a platform for his mythological characters to deliver cold meditations on stoicism, Kyd puts the audience in the shoes of the avengers Hieronimo and Bel-imperia, even while their actions are morally disquieting. Where Seneca's characters are royalty

---

1 See Sackville's poems in *The Last Parte of the Mirour for Magistrates*, 1574 (fol. 107–31). Baker discusses these works extensively.

drawn from classical mythology, Kyd's stage is inhabited by royal, middling, and common characters. Where Seneca creates a messenger to describe the central act of violence, Kyd puts the central violence on stage. Where Seneca moves the action inexorably toward the fulfillment of a predetermined fate, Kyd creates a complex tension between fate, as articulated by Revenge, and events that follow from decisions made by the characters. Where Seneca focuses on a single event in the House of Atreus, Kyd allows his narrative to range across space and to transgress social barriers, allowing us access to the royal courts of Spain and Portugal; the trysting space of Horatio and Belimperia; the private garden of the grieving Hieronimo and Isabella; and the sphere of a public hanging, with all of its carnivalesque and comic dimensions.

Kyd and Shakespeare

It is possible that Shakespeare saw a kindred spirit in Kyd, six years his elder. If Shakespeare arrived in London to begin his career in theater in the late 1580s, he would have found Kyd already established as a playwright. Neither came from families of great name or wealth, and neither was university educated, unlike their contemporaries Christopher Marlowe, Thomas Watson (1557–92), Thomas Nashe, and others. They may have contributed to the same company, Lord Strange's Men (later known as the Earl of Derby's Men), for a short time before Shakespeare joined the Lord Chamberlain's Men around 1594 (Chambers 2: 126). Regardless of the precise connection, Kyd's works had a profound influence on Shakespeare, especially through the development of the revenge tragedy and through blank verse, which Kyd and Christopher Marlowe developed as the age's dominant medium of dramatic expression.

Kyd's influence is apparent in Shakespeare's first tragedy, *Titus Andronicus*, which picks up and enlarges upon the pattern, characters, and themes of revenge established in *The Spanish Tragedy*. Shakespeare follows Kyd in setting *Titus Andronicus* against a political background where the revenge plot cuts obliquely across the political divisions; as former political enemies Lorenzo and Balthazar form an alliance, so Saturninus and Tamora, enemies as the play opens, become allies. These unexpected alliances have the effect of bringing the revenge plot into relief. Thematically, *Titus Andronicus* emphasizes the inaccessibility of justice, echoing some of Hieronimo's pleas:

TITUS: And sith there's no justice in earth nor hell ...
(4.3.50)
HIERONIMO: For here's no justice. Gentle boy, be gone, /
For justice is exiled from the earth. (3.13.142–43)

Both revengers, Hieronimo and Titus, start the play as paragons
of justice, Hieronimo as a respected Spanish magistrate, Titus as
a victorious military leader who turns down the emperor's throne
in favor of an orderly transition to the previous emperor's oldest
son, Saturninus. At the end of both plays these paragons have
premeditated and effected violent spectacles of revenge in which
they consume themselves and, as the audience surely sees it, endanger their souls (anachronistically in Shakespeare's ancient
Roman setting). Titus takes the Senecan idea that the revenge is
complete only if it exceeds the original crime to an absurd level,
baking Tamora's two sons into a pie and feeding them to their
mother; but unlike the cannibalistic feast in Seneca's *Thyestes*,
Shakespeare's happens right on stage.

Hamlet, Shakespeare's most celebrated play, also follows the
basic framework of Kyd's revenge tragedy while vastly expanding
its thematic scope. The ghost of Hamlet's father, perhaps inspired
by Kyd's ghosts, tells Hamlet that his uncle, Claudius, has murdered his beloved father and married his mother. In this way the
ghost imposes on Hamlet the duty to avenge his father's murder
by killing Claudius, but *Hamlet* contemplates the same revenger's
dilemma that is central to *The Spanish Tragedy*. Even as Hamlet
learns that his mother is now married to his father's murderer,
the ghost gives him an impossible restriction:

But howsoever thou pursuest this act,
Taint not thy mind, nor let thy soul contrive
Against thy mother aught. Leave her to heaven.
And to those thorns that in her bosom lodge
To prick and sting her. (1.5.84–88)

The ghost urges Hamlet to prevent the act of incest between
Claudius and his wife/sister-in-law, Gertrude, but, in what seems
like a contradiction, to "leave her to heaven" and to her own conscience rather than imperiling his own soul with action. Later,
Hamlet contemplates the idea that the ghost "may be the devil"
who "abuses me to damn me" (2.2.576, 580). Although Hamlet,
like Hieronimo, remains obsessed with the idea of revenge
throughout the play, Shakespeare exploits the dramatic and

philosophical possibilities of never allowing him to formulate a plan of action for the revenge. Though the play has a bloody end, true to the conventions of the revenge, it is not orchestrated by Hamlet the way Hieronimo and Titus plan their revenge spectacles. Whether Hamlet damns his soul when he forces Claudius to drink his own poison is one of the many ambiguities that make *Hamlet* the greatest play in English literature.

Most scholars accept the theory that a play called *Hamlet* existed before Shakespeare wrote his around 1600, and that this *Ur-Hamlet* was most likely authored by Thomas Kyd. The play is lost, and all conclusions about its existence are based on just three tantalizing threads of evidence. The first comes from Thomas Nashe, who, in his 1589 preface to Robert Greene's *Menaphon* (see above, p. 23) complains of writers using English translations of Seneca to churn out bad plays: "yet English *Seneca* read by candle light yeeldes manie good sentences, as *Bloud is a begger*, and so foorth; and, if you intreate him faire in a frostie morning, he will affoord you whole *Hamlets*." Here, ten years before Shakespeare's *Hamlet*, Nashe identifies a play called *Hamlet* as a blood revenge in the tradition of Seneca; nearby he appears to target Kyd specifically: these writers "leave the trade of Noverint" (Kyd's father's occupation); they "imitate the Kidd in Aesop" (playing on the name of Kyd); and they "intermeddle with Italian translations" (possibly referring to Kyd's *Householder's Philosophy*, his 1588 translation of Tasso's pamphlet). Boas and Erne both note that Nashe uses the phrase "by candle light" to needle Kyd for his poor translation of Tasso's "*ad lumina*," "till dawn" (Boas 455; Erne 150). The second thread is from *Henslowe's Diary*, which lists a performance of *Hamlet* on 9 June 1594, by the Lord Admiral's Men and Lord Chamberlain's Men (which had merged at this time), taking in the small sum of 8 shillings (21). The third is from Thomas Lodge's *Wit's Misery*, a prose pamphlet of social invective published in 1596. In the course of describing various ills as "devils incarnate," he summons up a theatrical allusion to describe the demon "Hate-Vertue" who "walks for the most part in black under colour of gravity, & looks as pale as the Visard of ye ghost which cried so miserally at ye Theator like an oister wife, Hamlet, revenge: he is full of infamy & slander" (56). All three of these threads point to a lost blood revenge called *Hamlet*, and Nashe's comments connect this play to Kyd.

The first quarto of *Hamlet* (Q1, 1603) creates another connection to Kyd, although one shrouded in mystery. This first printed version of *Hamlet* is about half the length of the more familiar second quarto (Q2) and First Folio (F) versions. Its language in places is faithful to the familiar text, especially when Marcellus is on stage; in other places it differs greatly, as in "To be, or not to be; ay, there's the point. / To die, to sleep: is that all? Ay, all" (Irace 58). A number of passages in Q1 echo the language of *The Spanish Tragedy* but do not appear in Q2 or F. Duthie has identified ten such passages, for example:

> (LAERTES:) Reuenge it is must yeeld this heart releefe,
> For woe begets woe, and griefe hangs on griefe. (Duthie 182)

Cf. *The Spanish Tragedy*:

> ISABELLA: O where's the author of this endless woe?
> HIERONIMO: To know the author were some ease of grief,
> For in revenge my heart would find relief. (2.5.39–41)

These similarities provide insight to scholars of *Hamlet*, in part suggesting that Q1 is not the work of Shakespeare but, as Irace suggests, one or more actors reconstructing the text by memory for adaptation by a traveling troupe, perhaps simplified for a less urbane audience (19). If these actors strained to remember *Hamlet* and came up with lines from *The Spanish Tragedy*, this, at least, shows how closely Kyd's play was associated with the revenge tragedy in general and *Hamlet* specifically.

Perhaps the most important connection between Kyd and Shakespeare is through the verse form that Kyd helped develop and Shakespeare brought to new heights. *Hamlet* without blank verse would be like *Citizen Kane* without film; it is impossible to imagine these great works apart from the media used to create them. By 1600 when Shakespeare wrote *Hamlet*, blank verse, the unrhymed iambic pentameter that Ben Jonson named "Marlowe's Mighty Line," had become the standard verse form for the stage. Its early master was, indeed, Marlowe, whose *Tamburlaine the Great* burst onto the stage in the late 1580s, around the same time as *The Spanish Tragedy*, audaciously leaving behind older verse forms, which Marlowe tossed aside as "jigging veins of rhyming mother wits / And such conceits as clownage keeps in pay" (Prologue 1–2).[1] The genius of the mighty line lies in its flexibility. Unlike end-rhymed lines, such as the clumsy fourteen-syllable iambic verse that Jasper Heywood (1535–98) used to

---

1 See Baker 68–81 for a discussion of the roots of blank verse and its migration to the stage.

translate Seneca (see Appendix C2), blank verse can capture the natural cadence of speech with its five beats per line, moving along without stylistic embellishment. When some embellishment is added, the "foundational regularity of the unrhymed line amplifies other forms of reiteration, including consonance and assonance, morphemic repetition, and other acoustic patterns" (McDonald 64). In skillful hands, just the right word in the right place can capture every nuance of grief, joy, love, anger, laughter, and, of course, revenge.

Though Thomas Sackville (1536–1608) and Thomas Norton (1532–84) had used blank verse in *Gorboduc* 25 years earlier, Kyd's play was one of the first in this medium on the Elizabethan stage, and almost certainly the first revenge tragedy. His contribution to the development of blank verse is one of his most important legacies. A few lines from the opening of *The Spanish Tragedy* show him using many of the tools available in blank verse. Here, the ghost describes his descent to the underworld, unable to cross the river Acheron:

> But churlish Charon, only boatman there,
> Said that, my rites of burial not performed,
> I might not side amongst his passengers.
> Ere Sol had slept three nights in Thetis' lap,
> And slaked his smoking chariot in her flood,
> By Don Horatio, our Knight Marshal's son,
> My funerals and obsequies were done. (1.1.20–26)

The first three lines deliver information with little adornment, except the oblique repetition of sound between *churlish* and *Charon*. They move along in regular iambic pentameter, the first balanced exactly in two parts, the second breaking after the second word, the third with no break at all. The fourth sentence begins a flurry of poetic devices, *Sol* echoed in *slept* and *slaked*, *three* in *Thetis*, building up to the name *Don Horatio*, whose murder will be the central act of the play. A rhyming couplet brings the unit of thought to a definite close.

Later, Kyd uses the form to capture intense action. Whereas the murders in *Gorboduc* happen offstage and get reported, Kyd puts the action right in front of the audience:

> HORATIO: What, will you murder me?
> LORENZO: Ay, thus, and thus! These are the fruits of love.
> (2.4.54–55)

Horatio's line breaks off at six syllables. Lorenzo answers in iambic pentameter, except for the substitution of a trochee, *These are*. At the center of the line is the word *These*, whose *th* sound is echoed by the grammatical antecedent *thus and thus*, the stabs themselves a kind of visual antecedent. One might imagine an actor pausing and gesturing toward the slain Horatio as the falling action of the rest of the line allows the audience to absorb the full implication of this murder. Kyd adds a further echo in Act 4 when Hieronimo stabs Lorenzo with emphasis on the word *thus*: "thou shouldst be thus employed" (4.4.56).

Cultural Crossroads

Violence and Entertainment in Elizabethan England

The first crossroads is a literal one, in present-day London, near Marble Arch, where Edgeware Road meets Bayswater Road. On this spot a stone marker memorializes the notorious three-beam gallows, the Triple Tree at Tyburn, where thousands of victims were hanged in front of raucous crowds during the Elizabethan era (see Appendix D5). As Molly Smith argues, public hangings and theatrical performances were bound together in the Elizabethan culture of spectacle, and nowhere more so than in *The Spanish Tragedy*. Smith notes that the Triple Tree was erected in 1571, the same decade as the first public theaters (218), and writes, "the spectacular success of Kyd's play might be attributed in part to the author's ingenious transference of the spectacle of public execution with all its ambiguities from the socio-political to the cultural worlds" (229). Kyd's play manipulates "the distance and framing" (221) that separate the audience from the spectacle of execution, especially in Hieronimo's play where we watch the onstage audience at first entertained and then horrified by the murders of Balthazar and Lorenzo, just as an audience at Tyburn would be entertained and horrified by the hanging of a felon. Smith argues that Horatio's murder in Act 2 is staged in a strikingly similar way to actual hangings at Tyburn, with Pedringano, masked "like a hangman ... conducting the ceremony," while an audience of Balthazar and Bel-imperia look on (224). Similarly, when Pedringano faces the gallows in Act 3, he becomes, for a moment, a carnival king, inverting the social order as the condemned sometimes did in their last moments in front of a crowd (227).

The Spanish Tragedy seems, at first, to create a distinction between justice, as in Pedringano's judicial execution for murdering Serberine, and private revenge, as in Hieronimo and Belimperia's massacre of the royal family. The matter is complicated by our knowledge that Lorenzo and Balthazar face no judicial punishment but rather are killed in an act of "wild justice," as Sir Francis Bacon called acts of revenge (Appendix C7). This same impulse kills the seemingly innocent Castile. In short, neither judicial processes nor private revenge brings a satisfactory conclusion. Callaghan and Kyle argue that actions of the state, whether public executions or torture behind prison walls, were indistinct from private revenge and indeed constituted a form of state retaliation:

> It is in the context of the attempts by the Tudor and Stuart state to gain a monopoly over retaliation for injuries and of the ideological struggle to differentiate the state's frequently bloody operations from those of "wilde justice" that revenge drama becomes one of the most popular genres on the early modern stage. (40)

In the play, judicial actions look extrajudicial, as Lorenzo manages to murder Pedringano by using the state-sanctioned gallows; and extrajudicial murders look official, as Horatio dies in the presence of members of the royal family and a masked hangman.

Another sort of violence, bear-baiting, also had a strong association with the theater, partly because the spaces designated for these activities were similarly designed and located. The most famous venue for this activity was the Bear Garden, in the Paris Garden district on the south side of the Thames, not far from three theaters, Newington Butts (built before 1580), the Swan (built 1595), and the Globe (built 1599). Bear-baiting featured amphitheater seating surrounding a pit where an animal, usually a bear or bull, was tied to a stake and attacked by large dogs loosed by their handlers. The audience took delight in the spectacle, many laying bets on the outcome. The bears and bulls, being expensive, were spared death, but dogs were sometimes killed in the fight. Queen Elizabeth is reported to have enjoyed the spectacle, and in fact bears feature as a central part of an entertainment arranged especially for Elizabeth (see Appendix D1). Yet the events at Paris Garden attracted citizens from all levels of society, who might attend to place a bet or see their favorite bear (the most famous named Sackerson) defend itself against the dogs. Critics of bear-baiting overlapped with critics of theater. For example, the moralist Philip Stubbes (1555–1610) calls it a "filthy, stinking, and loathsome game" and makes a direct connection to plays and playhouses. He describes the "marvelous" collapse of bleachers at a bear-baiting arena in 1584, where men, women, and children "of each sort" had gathered, many of whom were injured and seven killed in the collapse, evidence of divine judgment. Drawing a direct parallel to the theater, he writes, "The like judgment in effect did the Lord show unto them a little before, being assembled at their theaters, to see their bawdy interludes and other fooleries practiced. For, he caused the earth mightily to shake and quaver," which led to the injuries of spectators (Appendix D3). The popularity of violent entertainment, whether in the form of bear-baiting or public executions, without doubt contributed to the success of *The Spanish Tragedy*, which linked violent actions to a satisfying story of blood revenge.

Women and Agency

English culture was full of conflicting currents on the general topic of the role of women, and Kyd's Bel-imperia may be seen as one part of the greater conversation. As a woman who projects a strong sense of agency, she was unusual, but not alone. On the stage, *Gorboduc*'s Queen Videna and *The White Devil*'s Vittoria offer examples of powerful, autonomous, and dignified characters, even if they come to grief. We might also include Salome of *The Tragedy of Mariam* (1613) in this list, except that Elizabeth Cary (1585–1639), having no entry to the male domain of professional playwriting, wrote this as a closet drama (see Appendix E5). In comparison to expectations created for privileged women in some popular reading, Bel-imperia's actions stand out. By having love affairs with Don Andrea and Don Horatio, she violates the standards of Juan Luis Vives (1493–1540), who suggests in his *Instruction of Christian Women* (1529) that such a person is in league with the devil (Appendix E2). Bel-imperia would also fall short of the paradigm of the "excellent woman" offered in Castiglione's *The Book of the Courtier* (1528): she must be a model of "sober and quiet manners" while yet having a "ready liveliness of wit," always steering "wide from all dullness" (Appendix E1). All of this must be accomplished with seeming effortlessness, what Castiglione called *sprezzatura*, an essential skill for courtiers male and female. Bel-imperia is anything but the witty and light court lady described by his Lord Gasper. She pursues her agenda single-mindedly, first pursuing a love affair with Horatio, and then revenging his death. She has a model perhaps in Queen Elizabeth I. In her Tilbury speech of 1588, Elizabeth famously said, "I know I have the body but of a weak and feeble woman, but I have the heart and stomach of a king, and of a king of England too," simultaneously embracing the culturally imposed boundaries of her gender, and blowing these boundaries to pieces: "I myself will be your general, judge, and rewarder of your virtue in the field" (Appendix E3). The bold tone of this speech was typical of Elizabeth's carefully crafted image.

Outside the theatrical genre, the story of Violenta and Didaco, the 42nd novella of William Painter's *Palace of Pleasure* (1566), offers in prose a character that in agency and in dignity holds a kinship with Bel-imperia. Kyd almost certainly knew *Palace of Pleasure* since it supplied the plots of a large number of plays, including *Romeo and Juliet* and *All's Well That Ends Well*; and, as Freeman notes, Kyd's colleague Thomas Achelley published the Violenta story in verse in 1576 (*Thomas Kyd* 16). Translated from the Italian writer Matteo Bandello (1485–1561) and set in Spain, the novella tells the story of Didaco, a wealthy aristocrat, who secretly marries the humble Violenta before he loses interest and publicly takes an aristocratic bride. In retaliation, Violenta lures Didaco into her bedroom and kills him in a brutal revenge, restraining him with a rope, stabbing him to death, plucking out his eyes and tongue, and throwing his carcass out the window. There are several similarities between this story and Kyd's play. Violenta, like Bel-imperia, is justified in her anger, though Bel-imperia's situation is more complex since she's exacting revenge against her own brother for her own loss and on behalf of Horatio. Like Lorenzo and Balthazar, Didaco is shielded from justice by his social station, and the story offers Violenta no judicial path to bring Didaco to account. Violenta, like Bel-imperia, takes matters in hand and uses a knife to exact her revenge. Indeed, the murder itself shares some elements with the murder of Horatio in Kyd's play: in both cases a rope is used to restrain the victim and a knife wielded to kill him. The most striking similarity is that Bel-imperia and Violenta control their final narratives. Bel-imperia kills herself even though Hieronimo, the playwright, "did otherwise determine of her end" (4.4.147); Violenta, "without any rage or passion" tells her story to the judges and an assemblage of people, who are moved to tears, "imputing the fault uppon the dead knight" (Painter 127). Ironically, Violenta dies an aristocrat's death, beheaded in the presence of the Viceroy.

Spain and Portugal

No evidence exists that Kyd traveled to Spain or Portugal, nor does the play strongly evoke its setting, aside from simply stating it as the courts of Spain and Portugal. Many lines are delivered in Italian and Latin, but none in Iberian languages, except for one familiar phrase, *pocas palabras* ("few words") in Act 3. Yet one reason for the success of Kyd's tragedy in the 1580s was that it played on the rising fear that Spain threatened to conquer England. As Hillgarth points out, anti-Spanish sentiment had its roots in the reign of Queen Mary I (r. 1553–58) who, by taking as her husband and consort Philip II of Spain (1527–98), created the fear that England would be dissolved into the Spanish Empire. The earliest anti-Spanish pamphlets appeared in 1555 (Hillgarth 353). In Elizabeth's reign, which started in 1558, anti-Spanish sentiment was fanned by John Foxe's *Acts and Monuments* (1563), which recounts in graphic detail Mary's persecutions of Protestants during her (and Philip's) effort to reintroduce Catholicism to England. In one place Foxe quotes a letter from Philip to Pope Julius III (r. 1550–55) in which he seems to deliver England to the Roman church: "it hath chaunced in the time of your holynes, to place as it were in the lappe of the holy Catholicke churche, such a kingdome as this is" (10.1478). Anxiety over the Spanish threat crossed a significant threshold in 1585, when Elizabeth signed the Treaty of Nonesuch, in which she agreed to support Dutch Protestants against their Spanish Catholic enemies. It served as a *de facto* declaration of war and led to Elizabeth's execution of her cousin Mary Queen of Scots (b. 1542) in 1587 for plotting to return Catholicism to England through a Spanish invasion. The English victory over the invading ships of the Spanish Armada in 1588 was the culminating event of the decade, but tensions between Spain and England continued throughout Elizabeth's reign.

While *The Spanish Tragedy* does not recount any specific history,[1] it does echo recent events in Iberia in a way that would have

---

1   Frank Ardolino argues that the play does in fact show a specific historical awareness framed in an apocalyptic language and structure: Hieronimo, "representative of Protestant England, accomplishes the fall of Babylon-Spain by means of his revenge playlet" (113).

engaged the anxieties of the audience of the 1580s. The second scene of the play opens with a description of a battle between Spain and Portugal, prompted by the Portuguese Viceroy's resistance to paying tribute money to the more powerful Spanish king. The Spanish win the battle, and the two countries put themselves on course to unite through the dynastic marriage of Bel-imperia and Balthazar. In fact, a Portuguese succession crisis did occur just before the appearance of the play. When Portugal's kings Sebastian I and Henry I both died without heirs in, respectively, 1578 and 1580, Spain's Philip II claimed the throne through his mother's line. He vanquished his rival, António, Prior of Crato (1531–95), at the Battle of Terceira in 1582, having already appointed a viceroy. Elizabeth had supported António against Philip, and when Philip appropriated the Portuguese crown, one of England's oldest allies (going back to the Anglo-Portuguese Treaty of 1373) was absorbed into the Spanish Empire, just as England itself almost was during the reign of Mary I, and just as it was threatened to be in the 1580s.

The Spanish Tragedy is one of many works that trade on the anxiety provoked by these and other events involving Spain in the 1580s. Like the pamphlet *A Fig for the Spaniard* (1591), Kyd's play imagines Iberia as a tinderbox, ready to burst into violence at the slightest provocation (Appendix F2). Unlike the pamphlet, which endorses England's ally Portugal over dominant Spain, the play adds conflict that cuts across both countries and falls between aristocrats and commoners. Another indication of this anxiety is Richard Hakluyt's work *A Discourse on Western Planting* (1584), which frames England's approach to the New World as a competition between England and Spain. If successful, Hakluyt imagines England using its riches from the New World to fight the Spanish threat (Appendix F1).

The three crossroads discussed here represent a sampling of the complex ways in which Kyd's tragedy interacted with its broader culture, transferring common spectacles of violence into a theatrical narrative, undermining a common set of expectations for aristocratic women, and playing on anxieties caused by England's rising conflict with Spain. Kyd had a genius for absorbing the currents of his time and channeling them back to the audience. He also had impeccable instincts for creating theater. The play is framed by a ghostly dialogue, which elevates the events on stage and also ties the play back to the familiar literary device of *The Mirror for Magistrates* in which the dead tell their own stories. Kyd then places within this cosmic frame the most ordinary of human experiences—love, jealousy, ambition, fear, rage, and resignation—which the audience sees in noble and common characters alike. That a royal such as Bel-imperia, a civil servant such as Hieronimo, and a common servant such as Pedringano could be seen on the same stage in the grip of comparable emotions is remarkable in itself. Finally, the play's sense of humor, however macabre, was surely an essential ingredient in its success, especially in the way Kyd makes it part of the fabric of the play. Pedringano is no jester but a frightening character whose execution nonetheless provides an occasion for carnivalesque banter with the hangman. Hieronimo, too, for all his grief, adopts a comic tone as he tricks Lorenzo and Balthazar into his trap. All of this contributes to the play's broad emotional range. *The Spanish Tragedy* gave its original audience plenty of reasons to spend an afternoon at the theater. It is no surprise that the play still fascinates readers and audiences more than 400 years later.

Thomas Kyd: A Brief Chronology

1553	Queen Mary I takes the English throne and marries Philip II of Spain a year later.
1558	Thomas Kyd is baptized on 6 November. Queen Mary dies in November, succeeded by Queen Elizabeth I.
1559	*The Mirror for Magistrates*, a popular verse collection in which ghosts tell stories of their falls from power, is published in the first of many editions.
1561	The earliest tragedy in English, *Gorboduc*, by Thomas Norton and Thomas Sackville, is first performed. Richard Mulcaster becomes the first headmaster of the Merchant Taylors' School.
1564	William Shakespeare and Christopher Marlowe are born.
1565	Francis Kyd enrolls his son Thomas in the Merchant Taylors' School.
1571	The infamous gallows referred to as the "Triple Tree" is erected at Tyburn.
1576	Actor James Burbage builds The Theatre, the first successful purpose-built playhouse in London.
1582	Spain vanquishes Portugal at the Battle of Terceira.
c. 1584	Kyd (possibly) wrote for the Queen's Men.
1585	The Treaty of Nonesuch is signed by Queen Elizabeth, essentially declaring war on Spain by committing support to the Protestant Dutch in their fight against the Spanish.
c. 1587	Christopher Marlowe's *Tamburlaine the Great* is first performed and popularizes blank verse as the dominant medium on the English stage.
c. 1585–87	Kyd's *Spanish Tragedy* is first performed.
1588	The Spanish Armada, an invasion force sent by Spain to remove Queen Elizabeth I from the throne, is defeated. Kyd's *The Householder's Philosophy*, a translation from Tasso, is published.
1591	Kyd and Marlowe share a chamber for the purpose of writing, as Kyd recalled in his letter to Sir John Puckering in 1593.

1591–93	Henslowe notes performances of plays that may be related to Kyd's works, including the *Spanish Comedy, Don Horatio, Jeronimo*, and the *Comedy of Jeronimo*, though these plays' titles are almost certainly overlapping.
c. 1592	Shakespeare's first revenge tragedy, *Titus Andronicus*, is performed.
1592	The first edition of *The Spanish Tragedy* appears. Kyd's *Soliman and Perseda* is published.
1593	London playhouses are closed and England's economy distressed due to bubonic plague.
1593	In May, the Dutch Church Libel, one of a series of signs posted to intimidate Flemish immigrants, causes the Queen's Privy Council, fearing a riot, to round up suspects. Kyd is suspected of involvement, arrested, tortured, and released.
1594	Kyd dies in August at the age of 35. A performance of *Hamlet* (presumably Kyd's) is noted in *Henslowe's Diary*. Kyd's final work, a translation of Robert Garnier's *Cornelia*, is published with Kyd's dedication to the Countess of Sussex.
c. 1600	Shakespeare's *Hamlet* is first performed.
1602	A new quarto of *The Spanish Tragedy* appears with five additional passages. The title page announces it to be "Newly corrected, amended, and enlarged with new additions of the Painters part, and others, as it hath of late been divers times acted."
1605	*The First Part of Hieronimo* is printed; connection to Kyd's work unclear.
1633	The last early modern edition of *The Spanish Tragedy* is printed.

A Note on the Text

The Spanish Tragedy might seem, in the broadest sense, to have a straightforward textual history. Ten quarto editions exist from the original era, the first produced in 1592 (Q1) and extant in a single copy in the British Library, shelfmark C.34.d.7. All subsequent editions, including modern editions, are based on that 1592 quarto. An exception involves the 1602 quarto (Q4), whose title page promises it to be "newly corrected, amended, and enlarged with new additions of the Painters part, and others, as it hath of late been divers times acted." This quarto includes a total of five additional passages, which were carried over into the six subsequent quartos printed from 1603 to 1633 (Q5 to Q10). In short, aside from a number of minor textual variants, the play exists in two versions: 1592 (Q1) and 1602 (Q4).

At a greater level of detail, the textual history becomes, in fact, quite complex, and fuller treatments of this complexity can be found in Edwards (xxvii–xlviii), Erne (59–67), and Calvo and Tronch (85–112). However, unlike other textual issues of the era, such as those in Marlowe's plays, *The Spanish Tragedy*'s problems do not prevent a coherent modern edition of the play—as long as readers keep in mind that certain problems cannot be solved perfectly. For example, the play's four-act arrangement and long Act 3 (twice as long as the others) would suggest that the play was originally written in five acts. Some editors have indeed split Act 3 into two (starting "Act 4" at 3.8 and changing Act 4 to "Act 5"), but the results are unsatisfactory, in part because no ghost scene exists to close an editorially created Act 3. Consequently, a modern version must either follow the original four-act arrangement, unbalanced as it is, or create five acts in an editorially intrusive way.

This Broadview Edition is based on the 1592 quarto as reprinted in the Scolar Press Facsimile of 1966, with additions based on the 1602 quarto reproduced in Early English Books Online. The spelling and punctuation have been newly updated for readability in the playtext and in several Appendices. The playtext has been silently and infrequently emended in certain situations, such as where 1602 (or, rarely, another quarto) yields an obviously better reading, or where lines can be broken differently to produce a regular meter. To avoid unnecessary intrusions in the text, accented syllables have been left unmarked and no further emendations have been made to make irregular lines scan. Footnotes will alert readers to other textual changes. All good editors show deference to the wise decisions of those who edited the play earlier: I owe a debt of gratitude to editors Frederick Boas (1901, rev. 1955), Philip Edwards (1959), Andrew Cairncross (1967), and Clara Calvo and Jesus Tronch (2013), whose editions of *The Spanish Tragedy* I have consulted extensively.

The five additional passages of 1602 can be found in Appendix A. A footnote in the playtext marks where each addition appeared and provides a reference to the appropriate passage in the appendix. Some lines from 1592 were replaced in 1602 and some were recycled into the new passages, most extensively in the fifth addition. This replacement and recycling is indicated by setting the replaced lines in a distinct font and the recycled lines, which appear in both 1592 and 1602, in bold.

While many modern editions include the 1602 additions in the body of the play, typically set off in a distinct font, a strong case can be made for keeping them in an appendix. First, and most obviously, they are unlikely to have been written by Thomas Kyd, who died in 1594.[1] Second, the original play that captured the interest of early theatergoers and started the blood revenge genre was the version first printed in 1592, and putting the later additions in an appendix preserves the integrity of the original play. Third, the additions do not fit very well in the play. The remarkable fourth addition, for example, presents a Hieronimo turned inward, driven insane by grief, asking the Painter to recreate the scene of Horatio's death and the excruciating moment when he discovers his son and cries out "like old Priam of Troy" (Appendix A, p. 184). This scene is placed immediately before Hieronimo's *"Vindicta mihi!"* soliloquy (3.13.1ff.), creating an abrupt shift to the revengeful and calculating Hieronimo, here starting to plan how to get even. Perhaps the 1602 scene reflects changing tastes of audiences, at this time showing more interest in the emotional state of the revenger and less in the plotting that leads to the revenge itself. In any case, the play and its additions can most profitably be studied separately.

The question of who wrote the 1602 additions has preoccupied scholars of *The Spanish Tragedy* for nearly 200 years. The only ev-

---

1 Cairncross raises the possibility that the passages were Kyd's, cut from the original play and restored later (xxii–xxiii). However, the drastically different style and uneven fit suggest otherwise.

idence outside the text itself is that in 1601 Philip Henslowe advanced Edward Alleyn 40 shillings for Ben Jonson to write "additions in Jeronimo" (Henslowe 182); almost a year later he paid Jonson 10 pounds for "new additions for Jeronimo" and another work (Henslowe 203). However, even if Jonson wrote some additions, it does not follow necessarily that what he wrote is what appeared in the 1602 quarto. Jonson's case is undermined by the additions' un-Jonsonian style and by the fact that the Painter scene was parodied in 1599 by John Marston in *Antonio and Mellinda*, two years before Henslowe's first payment, as Edwards, among others, points out (lxii). Erne notes that several other writers have been suggested, including John Webster, Thomas Dekker, and Kyd himself (122–23). It should come as no surprise that Shakespeare has been suggested as the author, given his close association with Kyd. In 1968, Warren Stevenson presented a persuasive, if inconclusive, case for Shakespeare based on similarities in diction and style, and he noted that arguments for the Bard's authorship stretch back to Samuel Taylor Coleridge in the early nineteenth century. In 2012, Brian Vickers offered a strong endorsement of Stevenson's thesis by using modern database technology and plagiarism software. Vickers found that the additions share with Shakespeare's works a far higher density of matching trigrams (three-word phrasings) than they share with any of the more than 400 other plays and masques analyzed in the study. He concludes that the results "provide overwhelming evidence for [Shakespeare's] having written these five enlarged scenes in *The Spanish Tragedy*" (29). The argument has merit but has not been widely accepted so far. The larger issue is a reminder that theater was, and continues to be, a radically collaborative enterprise and that it is impossible to identify all the people and social forces that shaped the drama of the era.

Date of Composition

While it is impossible to date *The Spanish Tragedy* precisely, it had to be composed between 1582 and 1592, when Kyd was between 24 and 34 years old. The earlier date is established by the first few lines of Act 2, which Kyd based on Sonnet 47 of Thomas Watson's *Hekatompathia or Passionate Century of Love*, published in 1582. On the later end, Philip Henslowe records a performance of the play in March 1592, and the first quarto was entered in the Stationers' Register later that year. Lukas Erne points out that Thomas Nashe seems to make an allusion to the empty box at Pedringano's hanging (3.6) in his *Anatomie of Absurdities* from September 1588, just two months after the defeat of the Spanish Armada (Erne 57). If Erne is correct, the window narrows to 1582–88. Since there is nothing in the play to suggest Kyd knew of the Armada, it is safe to assume the play was written in the mid-1580s but before 1588.

THE SPANISH TRAGEDY

[Characters in the Play

GHOST of Andrea
REVENGE

KING of Spain
Cyprian, Duke of CASTILE, *the king's brother*
LORENZO, *Castile's son*
BEL-IMPERIA, *Castile's daughter*
Spanish GENERAL

HIERONIMO, *Knight Marshal of Spain*
ISABELLA, *Hieronimo's wife*
HORATIO, *Hieronimo's son*

VICEROY of Portugal
DON PEDRO, *the Viceroy's brother*
BALTHAZAR, *the Viceroy's son*
ALEXANDRO, *Portuguese noble*
VILLUPPO, *Portuguese noble*
Portuguese AMBASSADOR to Spain
Two Portuguese NOBLES

PEDRINGANO, *Bel-imperia's servant*
SERBERINE, *Balthazar's servant*
CHRISTOPHIL, *Lorenzo's servant*
MESSENGER
DEPUTY
Three men of the WATCH
MAID to Isabella
PAGE (Boy), *servant of Lorenzo's household*
HANGMAN
Two PORTINGALES
Old Man (SENEX), *named Bazulto*
SERVANT
Three CITIZENS

Spanish army, trumpeters, drummer, knights and kings in a dumb show,
officers, nuptial torch bearers, Hymen.

In Hieronimo's play:
Soliman, *Turkish Emperor, played by Balthazar*
Erastus, *Knight of Rhodes, played by Lorenzo*
Perseda, *an Italian lady, played by Bel-imperia*
Soliman's bashaw, *played by Hieronimo*

Characters appearing for the first time in the 1602 quarto:
JAQUES, *servant in Hieronimo's household*
PEDRO, *servant in Hieronimo's household*
A PAINTER named Bazardo]

ACT 1, SCENE 1

Enter the GHOST *of Andrea, and with him* REVENGE.

GHOST
When this eternal substance of my soul
Did live imprisoned in my wanton flesh,
Each° in their function serving other's need,   *soul and flesh*
I was a courtier in the Spanish court.
5 My name was Don Andrea, my descent,
Though not ignoble, yet inferior far
To gracious fortunes of my tender youth:[1]
For there in prime and pride° of all   *most flourishing condition*
    my years,
By duteous service and deserving love,
10 In secret I possessed[2] a worthy dame,°   *lady of rank*
Which hight° sweet Bel-imperia by name.   *who was called*
But in the harvest of my summer joys,
Death's winter nipped the blossoms of my bliss,
Forcing divorce° betwixt my love   *separation (by his death)*
    and me.
15 For in the late conflict with Portingale,°   *Portugal*
My valor drew me into danger's mouth,
Till life to death made passage through my wounds.
When I was slain, my soul descended[3] straight
To pass the flowing stream of Acheron,[4]
20 But churlish Charon,[5] only boatman there,
Said that, my rites of burial not performed,
I might not sit amongst his passengers.
Ere Sol had slept three nights in Thetis' lap

---

1 His family status was far lower than that of his beloved, Bel-imperia, as he
   explains below.
2 Had a sexual relationship with (*OED* 5b, citing this example).
3 Andrea's journey to the underworld was modeled in content on Book 6 of Virgil's
   Aeneid (first century BCE), but in form and tone it is very similar to monologues
   by ghosts in *The Mirror for Magistrates*, a collection of poems first published in
   1559. Its "Complaint of the Duke of Buckingham" by Thomas Sackville
   (1536–1608) is a good example of the form. See Baker 110 ff.
4 A river of the classical underworld. In the *Aeneid*, Charon ferries the dead across
   the River Styx, but here, as in Dante's *Inferno* (early fourteenth century), it is
   named the Acheron.
5 The ferryman. His boat can carry only souls whose bodies have received a proper
   burial, as in the *Aeneid*.

And slaked his smoking chariot in her flood,[1]
25 By Don Horatio, our knight marshal's son,
My funerals and obsequies were done.
Then was the ferryman of hell content
To pass me over to the slimy strond°   *shore*
That leads to fell Avernus' ugly waves.[2]
30 There, pleasing Cerberus[3] with honeyed speech,
I passed the perils of the foremost porch.
Not far from hence amidst ten thousand souls,
Sat Minos, Aeacus, and Rhadamanth,[4]
To whom no sooner gan° I make approach,   *began*
35 To crave a passport for my wandering Ghost,
But Minos, in graven leaves of lottery,[5]
Drew forth the manner of my life and death.
This knight, quoth he, both lived and died in love,
And for his love tried fortune of the wars,
40 And by war's fortune lost both love and life.
Why then, said Aeacus, convey him hence,
To walk with lovers in our fields of love,
And spend the course of everlasting time
Under green myrtle trees and cypress shades.
45 No, no, said Rhadamanth, it were not well,
With loving souls to place a martialist;°   *soldier*
He died in war and must to martial fields,
Where wounded Hector[6] lives in lasting pain
And Achilles' Myrmidons[7] do scour the plain.
50 Then Minos, mildest censor° of the three,   *judge*
Made this device to end the difference:
Send him, quoth he, to our infernal king

---

1 Before three days passed. Sol is the Roman sun god, here driving a flaming
   chariot across the sky and extinguishing it in the sea at night; Thetis is a sea
   nymph.
2 A lake in the gorge of the entrance to the underworld. The *Aeneid* describes the air
   above the gorge as deadly (*fell*).
3 The three-headed dog that guards the entrance to the underworld.
4 In Greek myth, Minos, Rhadamanthus, and Aeacus were three wise kings, all sons
   of Zeus, who became the three judges of the underworld after their deaths.
5 A difficult passage; Edwards suggests the image of Minos drawing from an urn
   lottery slips, which are engraved with information about Andrea's life, his "lot"
   (1.1.36 fn).
6 The greatest warrior on Troy's side in the Trojan War.
7 One of the Greek armies, led by the Greeks' greatest warrior, Achilles, in the
   Trojan War.

To doom° him as best seems his majesty.   *to pass sentence on*
To this effect my passport straight was drawn.
55 In keeping on my way to Pluto's court,
Through dreadful shades of ever glooming night,
I saw more sights than thousand tongues can tell,
Or pens can write, or mortal hearts can think.
Three ways there were: that on the right hand side
60 Was ready way unto the foresaid fields,
Where lovers live, and bloody martialists,
But either sort contained within his bounds.
The left hand path declining fearfully,
Was ready downfall to the deepest hell,
65 Where bloody furies shakes their whips of steel,
And poor Ixion[1] turns an endless wheel;
Where usurers are choked with melting gold,
And wantons° are embraced with ugly snakes,   *lascivious women*
And murderers groan with never killing wounds,
70 And perjured wights° scalded in boiling lead,   *persons*
And all foul sins with torments overwhelmed.
'Twixt these two ways, I trod the middle path,[2]
Which brought me to the fair Elysian green,[3]
In midst whereof there stands a stately tower,
75 The walls of brass, the gates of adamant.[4]
Here finding Pluto with his Proserpina,[5]
I showed my passport humbled on my knee,
Whereat fair Proserpina began to smile,
And begged that only she might give my doom.
80 Pluto was pleased and sealed it with a kiss.
Forthwith, Revenge, she rounded thee in th'ear,
And bade thee lead me through the gates of horn,[6]
Where dreams have passage in the silent night.
No sooner had she spoke but we were here,
85 I wot° not how, in twinkling of an eye.   *know*

---

1 For his attempted rape of Hera, Zeus had Ixion bound to a burning wheel forever.
2 The underworld of the *Aeneid* has two paths; the middle path here appears to be
  Kyd's invention.
3 A part of the classical underworld where heroes and those favored by the gods
  reside pleasantly after death.
4 A mythical mineral of great strength.
5 The king (Pluto) and queen (Proserpina) of the underworld in Roman myth.
6 One of the two gates to the underworld mentioned in the *Aeneid*, the other being
  of ivory.

REVENGE
Then know, Andrea, that thou art arrived
Where thou shalt see the author of thy death,
Don Balthazar, the Prince of Portingale,
Deprived of life by Bel-imperia.
90 Here sit we down to see the mystery
And serve for chorus in this tragedy.[1]

ACT 1, SCENE 2

Enter Spanish KING, GENERAL, CASTILE, HIERONIMO.

KING
Now say, Lord General, how fares our camp?

GENERAL
All well, my sovereign liege, except some few
That are deceased by fortune of the war.

KING
But what portends thy cheerful countenance,
5 And posting° to our presence thus in haste?   *hurrying*
Speak man! Hath fortune given us victory?

GENERAL
Victory, my liege, and that with little loss.

KING
Our Portingales will pay us tribute[2] then.

GENERAL
Tribute and wonted° homage therewithal.   *customary*

KING
10 Then blest be heaven, and guider of the heavens,
From whose fair influence such justice flows.

---

1 Ghost and Revenge do not exit but remain on stage for the entire play.
2 Money to acknowledge Portugal's submission to Spain.

CASTILE

O multum dilecte Deo, tibi militat aether,
Et coniuratae curvato poplite gentes
Succumbunt: recti soror est victoria iuris.[1]

KING

15 Thanks to my loving brother of Castile.
    But General, unfold in brief discourse
    Your form of battle and your war's success,
    That, adding all the pleasure of thy news
    Unto the height of former happiness,
20 With deeper wage and greater dignity,
    We may reward thy blissful chivalry.

GENERAL

    Where Spain and Portingale do jointly knit
    Their frontiers, leaning on each other's bound,
    There met our armies in their proud array,
25 Both furnished well, both full of hope and fear,
    Both menacing alike with daring shows,
    Both vaunting sundry colors of device,[2]
    Both cheerly sounding trumpets, drums and fifes,
    Both raising dreadful clamors to the sky,
30 That valleys, hills, and rivers made rebound,
    And heaven itself was frighted with the sound.
    Our battles both were pitched in squadron form,
    Each corner strongly fenced with wings of shot.[3]
    But ere we joined and came to push of pike,[4]
35 I brought a squadron of our readiest shot
    From out our rearward to begin the fight;
    They brought another wing to encounter us.
    Meanwhile, our ordnance° played on either side,   *war implements*
    And captains strove to have their valors tried.
40 Don Pedro, their chief horsemen's colonel,
    Did with his cornet° bravely make attempt   *cavalry wing*
    To break the order of our battle ranks.
    But Don Rogero, worthy man of war,

---

1 O well-loved of God, heaven fights for you and the nations join to submit on bent
   knee: victory is the sister of right justice (trans. Peter Parisi).
2 Proudly and aggressively displaying their flags and heraldic bearings.
3 Fortified with lines of soldiers with firearms.
4 Before we came to close combat and the use of pikes (spear-like weapons).

Marched forth against him with our
  musketeers°   *soldiers with muskets*
45 And stopped the malice of his fell° approach.   *deadly*
While they maintain hot skirmish to and fro,
Both battles join and fall to handy blows.°   *hand-to-hand fighting*
Their violent shot resembling th'ocean's rage,
When roaring loud and with a swelling tide,
50 It beats upon the rampiers[1] of huge rocks,
And gapes to swallow neighbor bounding lands.
Now, while Bellona° rageth here and there,   *Roman goddess of war*
Thick storms of bullets rain[2] like winter's hail,
And shivered lances dark the troubled air.
55 *Pede pes et cuspide cuspis,*
Arma sonant armis, vir petiturque viro.[3]
On every side drop captains to the ground,
And soldiers, some ill maimed, some slain outright;
Here falls a body scindered° from his head,   *separated*
60 There legs and arms lie bleeding on the grass,
Mingled with weapons and unboweled steeds
That, scattering, overspread the purple plain.
In all this turmoil, three long hours and more,
The victory to neither part inclined,
65 Till Don Andrea with his brave lancers
In their main battle made so great a breach
That, half dismayed, the multitude retired.
But Balthazar, the Portingales' young prince,
Brought rescue and encouraged them to stay;
70 Here-hence[4] the fight was eagerly renewed,
And in that conflict was Andrea slain,
Brave man at arms, but weak to Balthazar.
Yet while the prince, insulting over him,
Breathed out proud vaunts,° sounding to our reproach,   *boasts*
75 Friendship and hardy valor joined in one
Pricked forth Horatio, our Knight Marshal's son,
To challenge forth that prince in single fight.
Not long between these twain the fight endured,

---

1 A rampire or fortification, but here describing metaphorically a natural feature.
2 Modern editors typically replace the quartos' *ran* with *rain*, in keeping with the
    metaphor of natural precipitation and the present tense of the rest of the sentence.
3 Foot resounds with foot, spear with spear, arms with arms, and man is attacked by
    man (trans. Peter Parisi).
4 As a result (of Balthazar's encouragements).

But straight the prince was beaten from his horse
80 And forced to yield him° prisoner to his foe.   *himself*
When he was taken, all the rest they fled,
And our carbines° pursued them to the death,   *troops with firearms*
Till, Phoebus waning to the western deep,[1]
Our trumpeters were charged to sound retreat.

KING
85 Thanks good Lord General for these good news,
And, for some argument° of more to come,   *token*
Take this and wear it for thy sovereign's sake,

Gives him his chain.

But tell me now, hast thou confirmed a peace?

GENERAL
No peace, my liege, but peace conditional,
90 That if with homage tribute be well paid,
The fury of your forces will be stayed.
And to this peace their Viceroy hath subscribed.

Gives the King a paper.

And made a solemn vow that during life
His tribute shall be truly paid to Spain.

KING
95 These words, these deeds, become thy person well.
But now, Knight Marshal, frolic with thy king,
For 'tis thy son that wins this battle's prize.

HIERONIMO
Long may he live to serve my sovereign liege,
And soon decay unless he serve my liege.

A tucket° far off.   *trumpet flourish*

KING
100 Nor thou nor he shall die without reward.
What means this warning of this trumpet's sound?

---

1 Until the sun (Phoebus Apollo) set.

GENERAL
This tells me that your grace's men of war,
Such as war's fortune hath reserved from death,
Come marching on towards your royal seat
105 To show themselves before your majesty,
For so I gave in charge at my depart,
Whereby, by demonstration, shall appear
That all, except three hundred or few more,
Are safe returned and by their foes enriched.

The army enters, BALTHAZAR *between* LORENZO *and* HORATIO
captive.

KING
110 A gladsome sight! I long to see them here.

They enter and pass by.

Was that the warlike Prince of Portingale
That by our nephew was in triumph led?

GENERAL
It was, my liege, the Prince of Portingale.

KING
But what was he that on the other side
115 Held him by th'arm as partner of the prize?

HIERONIMO
That was my son, my gracious sovereign,
Of whom, though from his tender infancy,
My loving thoughts did never hope but well.
He never pleased his father's eyes till now,
120 Nor filled my heart with over-cloying° joys.   *over-satiating*

KING
Go, let them march once more about these walls,
That staying them we may confer and talk
With our brave prisoner and his double guard.
Hieronimo, it greatly pleaseth us
125 That in our victory thou have a share
By virtue of thy worthy son's exploit.

[*Army*] *Enters again.*

Bring hither the young prince of Portingale.
The rest march on, but, ere° they be dismissed,   *before*
We will bestow on every soldier
130 Two ducats,° and on every leader, ten,   *gold coins*
That they may know our largesse welcomes them.

Exeunt all [*Army*] *but* BALTHAZAR, LORENZO, HORATIO.

Welcome, Don Balthazar; welcome, nephew;
And thou, Horatio, thou art welcome too.
Young prince, although thy father's hard misdeeds,
135 In keeping back the tribute that he owes,
Deserve but evil measure at our hands,
Yet shalt thou know that Spain is honorable.

BALTHAZAR
The trespass that my father made in peace
Is now controlled by fortune of the wars,
140 And cards once dealt, it boots° not ask why so.   *helps*
His men are slain, a weakening to his realm;
His colors seized, a blot unto his name;
His son distressed, a corsive° to his heart.   *corrosive*
These punishments may clear his late offence.

KING
145 Ay, Balthazar, if he observe this truce,
Our peace will grow the stronger for these wars.
Meanwhile, live thou, though not in liberty,
Yet free from bearing any servile yoke,
For in our hearing thy deserts° were great,   *merits*
150 And in our sight thyself art gracious.

BALTHAZAR
And I shall study to deserve this grace.

KING
But tell me, for their holding makes me doubt,
To which of these twain art thou prisoner.

LORENZO
To me, my liege.

HORATIO
       To me, my sovereign.

LORENZO
155 This hand first took his courser° by the reins.   *battle horse*

HORATIO
But first my lance did put him from his horse.

LORENZO
I seized his weapon and enjoyed it first.

HORATIO
But first I forced him lay his weapons down.

KING
Let go his arm, upon our privilege.

[*They*] *let him go.*

160 Say worthy prince, to whether° didst thou yield?   *which of the two*

BALTHAZAR
To him in courtesy, to this perforce:[1]
He spake me fair, this other gave me strokes;
He promised life, this other threatened death;
He won my love, this other conquered me;
165 And truth to say, I yield myself to both.

HIERONIMO
But that I know your grace for just and wise,
And might seem partial in this difference,
Enforced by nature and by law of arms,
My tongue should plead for young Horatio's right.
170 He hunted well that was a lion's death,

---

1 Balthazar refers to Lorenzo first then Horatio in lines 161–64.

Not he that in a garment wore his skin:
So hares may pull dead lions by the beard.[1]

KING
Content thee marshal. Thou shalt have no wrong,
And for thy sake thy son shall want° no right.   *lack*
175 Will both abide the censure of my doom?°   *judgment*

LORENZO
I crave no better than your grace awards.

HORATIO
Nor I, although I sit beside° my right.   *set aside, i.e., waive*

KING
Then by my judgment thus, your strife shall end.
You both deserve and both shall have reward.
180 Nephew, thou tookst his weapon and his horse;
His weapons and his horse are thy reward.
Horatio, thou didst force him first to yield;
His ransom therefore is thy valor's fee.
Appoint the sum as you shall both agree.
185 But nephew, thou shalt have the prince in guard,
For thine estate best fitteth such a guest.
Horatio's house were small for all his train,°   *Balthazar's attendants*
Yet in regard thy substance° passeth his,   *wealth*
And that just guerdon° may befall desert,[2]   *reward*
190 To him we yield the armor of the prince.
How likes Don Balthazar of this device?

BALTHAZAR
Right well, my liege, if this proviso were
That Don Horatio bear us company,
Whom I admire and love for chivalry.

KING
195 Horatio, leave him not that loves thee so.

---

1   The one who kills a lion is a good hunter, unlike one who just wears the lion's
    skin. Even a hare can be brave in front of a lion that's already dead.
2   Befit (Horatio's) merit.

Now let us hence to see our soldiers paid,
And feast our prisoner as our friendly guest.

Exeunt.

ACT 1, SCENE 3[1]

Enter VICEROY, ALEXANDRO, VILLUPPO.

VICEROY
Is our ambassador dispatched for Spain?

ALEXANDRO
Two days, my liege, are past since his depart.

VICEROY
And tribute payment gone along with him?

ALEXANDRO
Ay, my good lord.

VICEROY
5 Then rest we here awhile in our unrest,
And feed our sorrows with some inward sighs,
For deepest cares break never into tears.
But wherefore° sit I in a regal throne?   *why*
This better fits a wretch's endless moan.[2]
10 Yet this is higher than my fortune's reach,
And therefore better than my state deserves.

Falls to the ground.

Ay, ay, this earth, image of melancholy,
Seeks him whom fates adjudge to misery.
Here let me lie; now am I the lowest.
15 *Qui iacet in terra non habet unde cadat,*
In me consumpsit vires fortuna nocendo,

---

1   The location now moves to the court of the Portuguese Viceroy.
2   The Viceroy progressively moves toward the ground in the next six lines. Some
    editors place the stage direction two lines earlier, following the 1623 quarto.

Nil superest ut iam possit obesse magis.[1]
Yes, Fortune[2] may bereave me of my crown.
Here, take it now; let Fortune do her worst.
20 She will not rob me of this sable weed.°   *black (mourning) garment*
Oh no, she envies none but pleasant things;
Such is the folly of despiteful chance.
Fortune is blind and sees not my deserts;
So is she deaf and hears not my laments.
25 And, could she hear, yet she is willful mad,
And therefore will not pity my distress.
Suppose that she could pity me? What then?
What help can be expected at her hands,
Whose foot is[3] standing on a rolling stone,
30 And mind more mutable than fickle winds?
Why wail I then where's hope of no redress?
Oh yes, complaining makes my grief seem less.
My late ambition hath distained my faith;[4]
My breach of faith occasioned bloody wars;
35 Those bloody wars have spent my treasure,
And with my treasure my people's blood,
And with their blood, my joy and best belov'd,
My best belov'd, my sweet and only son.
Oh wherefore° went I not to war myself?   *why*
40 The cause was mine; I might have died for both.
My years were mellow, his but young and green;
My death were natural, but his was forced.

ALEXANDRO
No doubt, my liege, but still the prince survives.

VICEROY
Survives, ay, where?

---

1 The man lying on the ground has no further to fall; Fortune has exhausted her
   strength in harming me; nothing remains that can harm me more (trans. Peter
   Parisi).
2 Fortuna, the Roman goddess of fortune and personification of luck. She was often
   depicted standing precariously on an orb in the wind (see lines 29–30 below).
3 Most editors add *is* here to fill out the pentameter, though it does not appear in
   the quartos.
4 My recent ambition to breach my agreement with Spain has dishonored me,
   undermined my trustworthiness.

ALEXANDRO

45 In Spain, a prisoner by mischance of war.

VICEROY

Then they have slain him for his father's fault.

ALEXANDRO

That were a breach to common law of arms.

VICEROY

They reck no laws that meditate revenge.[1]

ALEXANDRO

His ransom's worth will stay from° foul revenge.   *prevent*

VICEROY

50 No, if he lived, the news would soon be here.

ALEXANDRO

Nay, evil news fly faster still than good.

VICEROY

Tell me no more of news, for he is dead.

VILLUPPO

My sovereign, pardon the author of ill news,
And I'll bewray° the fortune of thy son.   *reveal*

VICEROY

55 Speak on, I'll guerdon° thee whate'er it be.   *reward*
Mine ear is ready to receive ill news,
My heart grown hard 'gainst mischief's battery.
Stand up, I say, and tell thy tale at large.[2]

VILLUPPO

Then hear that truth which these mine eyes have seen.
60 When both the armies were in battle joined,
Don Balthazar, amidst the thickest troops,
To win renown, did wondrous feats of arms:

---

1   Those who consider revenge have no regard for laws against it. The revengers
    Hieronimo and Bel-imperia prove this point later in the play.
2   Freely, without fear; fully.

Amongst the rest I saw him hand to hand
In single fight with their lord general,
65 Till Alexandro, that here counterfeits
Under the color of a duteous friend,
Discharged his pistol at the prince's back,
As though he would have slain their general.
But therewithal Don Balthazar fell down,
70 And when he fell, then we began to fly,
But had he lived, the day had sure been ours.

ALEXANDRO
Oh wicked forgery! Oh traitorous miscreant!

VICEROY
Hold thou thy peace; but now, Villuppo, say,
Where then became the carcass of my son?

VILLUPPO
75 I saw them drag it to the Spanish tents.

VICEROY
Ay, ay, my nightly dreams have told me this.
Thou false, unkind,° unthankful, traitorous beast,   *unnatural*
Wherein had Balthazar offended thee,
That thou shouldst thus betray him to our foes?
80 Wast Spanish gold that bleared so thine eyes,
That thou couldst see no part of our deserts?
Perchance because thou art Terceira's[1] lord,
Thou hadst some hope to wear this diadem,°   *crown*
If first my son and then myself were slain.
85 But thy ambitious thought shall break thy neck.
Ay, this was it that made thee spill his blood,

Takes the crown and puts it on again.

But I'll now wear it till thy blood be spilt.

ALEXANDRO
Vouchsafe,° dread sovereign, to hear me speak.   *grant*

---

1   An island in the Portuguese Azores where, in 1582, Philip II of Spain (r. 1556–98)
    defeated António, Prior of Crato (1531–95) for control of Portugal. England's
    support for António was to no avail.

VICEROY
Away with him; his sight is second hell.
90 Keep him till we determine of his death.[1]
If Balthazar be dead, he shall not live.
Villuppo, follow us for thy reward.

Exit VICEROY.

VILLUPPO
Thus have I with an envious forged tale,
Deceived the king, betrayed mine enemy,
95 And hope for guerdon° of my villainy.   *reward*

Exit.

ACT 1, SCENE 4

Enter HORATIO *and* BEL-IMPERIA.

BEL-IMPERIA
Signior Horatio, this is the place and the hour
Wherein I must entreat thee to relate
The circumstance of Don Andrea's death,
Who living was my garland's sweetest flower,
5 And in his death hath buried my delights.

HORATIO
For love of him and service to yourself,
I nill° refuse this heavy doleful charge.   *will not*
Yet tears and sighs, I fear, will hinder me.
When both our armies were enjoined in fight,
10 Your worthy chevalier amidst the thick'st,
For glorious cause still aiming at the fairest,°   *most honorable action*
Was at the last by young Don Balthazar,
Encountered hand to hand. Their fight was long;
Their hearts were great, their clamors menacing,
15 Their strength alike, their strokes both dangerous.
But wrathful Nemesis,[2] that wicked power,

---

1 Presumably Alexandro and others exit here, then the Viceroy two lines later,
  leaving Villuppo alone on stage.
2 Greek goddess of retribution or vengeance, here seeming to object to Andrea's
  honorable character.

Envying at Andrea's praise and worth,
Cut short his life to end his praise and worth.
She,° she herself, disguised in armor's mask,   *Nemesis*
20 As Pallas was before proud Pergamus,[1]
Brought in a fresh supply of halberdiers,[2]
Which paunched° his horse and dinged°   *stabbed in the belly/knocked*
   him to the ground.
Then young Don Balthazar, with ruthless rage,
Taking advantage of his foe's distress,
25 Did finish what his halberdiers begun,
And left not till Andrea's life was done.
Then, though too late, incensed with just remorse,
I with my band set forth against the prince,
And brought him prisoner from his halberdiers.

BEL-IMPERIA
30 Would thou hadst slain him that so slew my love.
But then was Don Andrea's carcass lost?

HORATIO
No, that was it for which I chiefly strove,
Nor stepped I back till I recovered him.
I took him up and wound him in mine arms,
35 And, wielding him unto my private tent,
There laid him down and dewed him with my tears,
And sighed and sorrowed as became a friend.
But neither friendly sorrow, sighs, nor tears,
Could win pale death from his usurped right.
40 Yet this I did, and less I could not do:
I saw him honored with due funeral.
This scarf I plucked from off his liveless° arm,   *lifeless*
And wear it in remembrance of my friend.

BEL-IMPERIA
I know the scarf; would he had kept it still,
45 For had he lived he would have kept it still,

---

1 A reference to the death of the Trojan hero Hector in Homer's *Iliad*. Pallas
   Athena, disguised as Hector's brother, rearms Achilles with his spear, which allows
   him a second and deadly throw at Hector. This all occurs in front of Pergamus,
   another name for Troy.
2 Soldiers armed with halberds (weapons resembling a spear combined with a
   battle-axe).

And worn it for his Bel-imperia's sake,
For 'twas my favor[1] at his last depart.
But now wear thou it both for him and me,
For after him thou hast deserved it best.
50 But for thy kindness in his life and death,
Be sure, while Bel-imperia's life endures,
She will be Don Horatio's thankful friend.

HORATIO
And, madam, Don Horatio will not slack
Humbly to serve fair Bel-imperia.
55 But now, if your good liking stand thereto,
I'll crave your pardon to go seek the prince,
For so the duke your father gave me charge.

Exit.

BEL-IMPERIA
Ay, go, Horatio—leave me here alone,
For solitude best fits my cheerless mood.
60 Yet what avails to wail Andrea's death
From whence Horatio proves my second love?
Had he not loved Andrea as he did,
He could not sit in Bel-imperia's thoughts.
But how can love find harbor in my breast
65 Till I revenge the death of my belov'd?
Yes, second love shall further my revenge.
I'll love Horatio, my Andrea's friend,
The more to spite the prince that wrought his end,
And where Don Balthazar, that slew my love,
70 Himself now pleads for favor at my hands,
He shall, in rigor of my just disdain,
Reap long repentance for his murderous deed.
For what was't else but murderous cowardice,
So many to oppress one valiant knight,
75 Without respect of honor in the fight?
And here he comes that murdered my delight.

Enter LORENZO *and* BALTHAZAR.

---

1 Token or object of favor, in the sense of *OED* 7a.

LORENZO
Sister, what means this melancholy walk?

BEL-IMPERIA
That for a while I wish no company.

LORENZO
But here the prince is come to visit you.

BEL-IMPERIA
80 That argues that he lives in liberty.

BALTHAZAR
No, madam, but in pleasing servitude.

BEL-IMPERIA
Your prison then belike is your conceit.[1]

BALTHAZAR
Ay, by conceit my freedom is enthralled.

BEL-IMPERIA
Then with conceit enlarge° yourself again.   *free*

BALTHAZAR
85 What if conceit have laid my heart to gage?[2]

BEL-IMPERIA
Pay that you borrowed and recover it.

BALTHAZAR
I die[3] if it return from whence it lies.

BEL-IMPERIA
A heartless man and live? A miracle.

BALTHAZAR
Ay, Lady, love can work such miracles.

---

1 Your prison then is likely to be the product of your imagination.
2 Committed my heart as a deposit.
3 Playing on the word *die* as slang for orgasm.

LORENZO
90 Tush, tush, my lord; let go these ambages,°   *indirect statements*
And in plain terms acquaint her with your love.

BEL-IMPERIA
What boots° complaint, when there's no remedy?   *is the benefit of*

BALTHAZAR
Yes, to your gracious self must I complain,
In whose fair answer lies my remedy,
95 On whose perfection all my thoughts attend,
On whose aspect mine eyes find beauty's bower,
In whose translucent breast my heart is lodged.

BEL-IMPERIA
Alas, my lord, these are but words of course,[1]
And but devised[2] to drive me from this place.

She in going in lets fall her glove, which HORATIO *coming out takes up.*

HORATIO
100 Madam, your glove.

BEL-IMPERIA
Thanks, good Horatio, take it for thy pains.

BALTHAZAR
Signior Horatio stooped in happy time.

HORATIO
I reaped more grace than I deserved or hoped.

LORENZO
My lord, be not dismayed for what is past;
105 You know that women oft are humorous.°   *moody*
These clouds will overblow with little wind.
Let me alone, I'll scatter them myself.
Meanwhile, let us devise to spend the time
In some delightful sports and reveling.

---

1 Just as one would expect; ordinary.
2 Q3 and later replaced 1592's *devise* with *devised.*

HORATIO
110 The king, my lords, is coming hither straight
To feast the Portingale ambassador.
Things were in readiness before I came.

BALTHAZAR
Then here it fits us to attend the king,
To welcome hither our ambassador,
115 And learn my father and my country's health.

Enter the banquet, trumpets, the KING *and* AMBASSADOR.

KING
See, Lord Ambassador, how Spain entreats°   *treats*
Their prisoner Balthazar, the Viceroy's son.
We pleasure more in kindness than in wars.

AMBASSADOR
Sad is our king, and Portingale laments,
120 Supposing that Don Balthazar is slain.

BALTHAZAR
So am I slain by beauty's tyranny.
You see, my lord, how Balthazar is slain:
I frolic with the Duke of Castile's son,
Wrapped every hour in pleasures of the court,
125 And graced with favors of his majesty.

KING
Put off your greetings till our feast be done;
Now come and sit with us and taste our cheer.

Sit to the banquet.

Sit down, young prince; you are our second guest.
Brother, sit down; and, nephew, take your place.
130 Signior Horatio, wait thou upon our cup,
For well thou hast deserved to be honored.
Now, lordings, fall to. Spain is Portugal
And Portugal is Spain. We both are friends,
Tribute is paid, and we enjoy our right.
135 But where is old Hieronimo, our marshal?
He promised us in honor of our guest

To grace our banquet with some pompous[1] jest.

Enter HIERONIMO with a drum,[2] three knights, each his scutcheon;[3]
then he fetches three kings; they take their crowns and them captive.[4]

Hieronimo, this masque contents mine eye,
Although I sound not well° the mystery.   *do not understand*

HIERONIMO
140 The first armed knight that hung his scutcheon up,[5]

He takes the scutcheon and gives it to the king.

Was English Robert, Earl of Gloucester,[6]
Who, when king Stephen[7] bore sway in Albion,°   *England*
Arrived with five and twenty thousand men
In Portingale, and, by success of war,
145 Enforced the king, then but a Saracen,[8]
To bear the yoke of the English monarchy.

KING
My lord of Portingale, by this you see
That which may comfort both your king and you,
And make your late discomfort seem the less.
150 But say, Hieronimo, what was the next?

HIERONIMO
The second knight that hung his scutcheon up,

He doth as he did before.

Was Edmund, Earl of Kent,[9] in Albion

---

1 Stately, in the sense of *OED* A2.
2 Drummer.
3 Shield displaying a coat of arms.
4 The knights capture the kings, as in Hieronimo's three examples that follow.
5 The episodes of English history that Hieronimo describes in the following passages do not correspond neatly to any historical record that Kyd is likely to have known.
6 King Henry I's illegitimate son (d. 1147).
7 King Stephen of England (r. 1135–54).
8 A non-Christian, usually a Muslim.
9 Edmund Langley (1327–77), a son of King Edward III.

When English Richard[1] wore the diadem.
He came likewise and razed Lisbon walls,
155 And took the king of Portingale in fight,
For which, and other suchlike service done,
He after was created Duke of York.

KING
This is another special argument,
That Portingale may deign to bear our yoke,
160 When it by little England hath been yoked.
But now, Hieronimo, what were the last?

HIERONIMO
The third and last, not least in our account,

Doing as before.

Was, as the rest, a valiant Englishman,
Brave John of Gaunt, the Duke of Lancaster,[2]
165 As by his scutcheon plainly may appear.
He with a puissant army came to Spain
And took our King of Castile prisoner.

AMBASSADOR
This is an argument for our Viceroy,
That Spain may not insult for her success,
170 Since English warriors likewise conquered Spain
And made them bow their knees to Albion.

KING
Hieronimo, I drink to thee for this device,
Which hath pleased both the ambassador and me.
Pledge° me, Hieronimo, if thou love the king.   *drink a toast to*

[HIERONIMO] *Takes the cup of Horatio.*

175 My lord, I fear we sit but overlong,
Unless our dainties were more delicate.[3]

---

1 King Richard II of England (r. 1377–99).
2 John of Gaunt (1340–99), a son of King Edward III.
3 Unless our foods were more delightful (in polite modesty).

But welcome are you to the best we have.
Now let us in, that you may be dispatched;[1]
I think our council is already set.

Exeunt omnes.

ACT 1, SCENE 5

GHOST[2]
Come we for this, from depth of underground,
To see him feast that gave me my death's wound?
These pleasant sights are sorrow to my soul,
Nothing but league and love and banqueting?

REVENGE
5 Be still, Andrea; ere we go from hence,°   *before we leave*
I'll turn their friendship into fell despite,°   *deadly spite*
Their love to mortal hate, their day to night,
Their hope into despair, their peace to war,
Their joys to pain, their bliss to misery.

---

1 Let us leave the banquet room and go into the council chamber where we can
   officially send you back to your king with our message.
2 Ghost and Revenge are already on stage.

ACT 2, SCENE 1

Enter LORENZO *and* BALTHAZAR.[1]

LORENZO
My lord, though Bel-imperia seem thus coy,
Let reason hold you in your wonted joy,
In time, the savage bull sustains the yoke;
In time, all haggard hawks will stoop to lure;[2]
5 In time, small wedges cleave the hardest oak;
In time, the flint is pierced with softest shower;
And she, in time, will fall from her disdain
And rue the suff'rance of your friendly pain.

BALTHAZAR
No, she is wilder and more hard withal°   *in addition*
10 Than beast or bird or tree or stony wall.[3]
But wherefore blot I° Bel-imperia's name?   *but why do I tarnish*
It is my fault, not she, that merits blame.
My feature is not to content her sight;
My words are rude and work her no delight.
15 The lines I send her are but harsh and ill,
Such as do drop from Pan and Marsyas' quill.[4]
My presents are not of sufficient cost,
And, being worthless, all my labors lost.
Yet might she love me for my valiancy;
20 Ay, but that's slandered by captivity.
Yet might she love me to content her sire;
Ay, but her reason masters his desire.
Yet might she love me as her brother's friend;
Ay, but her hopes aim at some other end.
25 Yet might she love me to uprear[5] her state;
Ay, but perhaps she hopes some nobler mate.

---

1 Ghost and Revenge remain on stage.
2 A device made of feathers that falconers use to recall their hawks.
3 Lines 1–10 are adapted from Thomas Watson's *Hekatompathia*, sonnet 47, published in 1582.
4 The nature god (Pan) and a satyr (Marsyas), known for rustic music and aggressive sexuality. At least three senses of the word *quill* could be at work here, as a writing instrument, as a musical pipe (*OED* 3c), or as a plectrum for a stringed musical instrument (*OED* 1c).
5 Elevate her, or Spain's, political standing.

Yet might she love me as her beauty's[1] thrall;
Ay, but I fear she cannot love at all.

LORENZO
My lord, for my sake, leave these ecstasies,
30 And doubt not but we'll find some remedy,
Some cause there is that lets you not be loved.
First, that must needs be known and then removed.
What if my sister love some other knight?

BALTHAZAR
My summer's day will turn to winter's night.

LORENZO
35 I have already found a stratagem,
To sound the bottom of this doubtful theme.
My lord, for once you shall be ruled by me;
Hinder me not whate'er you hear or see.
By force or fair means will I cast about
40 To find the truth of all this question out.
Ho, Pedringano!

PEDRINGANO
Signior.

LORENZO
Vien qui presto![2]

Enter PEDRINGANO.

PEDRINGANO
Hath your lordship any service to command me?

LORENZO
45 Ay, Pedringano, service of import,
And not to spend the time in trifling words.
Thus stands the case: it is not long, thou knowst,
Since I did shield thee from my father's wrath
For thy conveyance° in Andrea's love,   *underhanded dealings*

---

1 *Beauteous* of the quartos is typically emended to *beauty's* by modern editors.
2 Come here quickly (Italian).

50 For which thou wert adjudged to punishment.
I stood betwixt thee and thy punishment,
And since, thou knowest how I have favored thee.
Now to these favors will I add reward,
Not with fair words, but store of golden coin,
55 And lands and livings joined with dignities,
If thou but satisfy my just demand.
Tell truth and have me for thy lasting friend.

PEDRINGANO
Whate'er it be your lordship shall demand,
My bounden duty bids me tell the truth,
60 If case it lie in me to tell the truth.[1]

LORENZO
Then, Pedringano, this is my demand:
Whom loves my sister Bel-imperia?
For she reposeth° all her trust in thee.   places
Speak, man, and gain both friendship and reward.
65 I mean, whom loves she in Andrea's place?

PEDRINGANO
Alas, my lord, since Don Andrea's death,
I have no credit with her as before,
And therefore know not if she love or no.

LORENZO
Nay, if thou dally then I am thy foe,

Draws his sword.[2]

70 And fear shall force what friendship cannot win.
Thy death shall bury what thy life conceals.
Thou diest for more esteeming her than me.

PEDRINGANO
Oh stay,° my lord.   stop

---

1 If it happens to be in my capacity to tell the truth (probably spoken as an aside).
2 Stage direction from 1602 quarto.

LORENZO
Yet speak the truth, and I will guerdon° thee,   *reward*
75 And shield thee from whatever can ensue,
And will conceal whate'er proceeds from thee.
But if thou dally once again, thou diest.

PEDRINGANO
If Madam Bel-imperia be in love—

LORENZO
What, villain, ifs and ans?[1]

Offers to kill him.[2]

PEDRINGANO
80 Oh stay, my lord! She loves Horatio.

BALTHAZAR *starts back.*

LORENZO
What? Don Horatio, our Knight Marshal's son?

PEDRINGANO
Even him, my lord.

LORENZO
Now say but how know'st thou he is her love?
And thou shalt find me kind and liberal.
85 Stand up, I say, and fearless tell the truth.

PEDRINGANO
She sent him letters, which myself perused,
Full fraught with lines and arguments of love,
Preferring him before Prince Balthazar.

---

1 A traditional phrase to mock a conditional statement; *an* means *if* in this context.
   A version of the saying is "If ifs and ans were pots and pans, where would be the
   tinker?" (*Brewer's Dictionary of Phrase and Fable* 584).
2 Stage direction from 1602 quarto.

LORENZO
Swear on this cross[1] that what thou say'st is true,
90 And that thou wilt conceal what thou has told.

PEDRINGANO
I swear to both by him that made us all.

LORENZO
In hope thine oath is true, here's thy reward,
But if I prove thee perjured and unjust,
This very sword whereon thou took'st thine oath,
95 Shall be the worker of thy tragedy.

PEDRINGANO
What I have said is true, and shall, for me,
Be still[2] concealed from Bel-imperia.
Besides, your honor's liberality
Deserves my duteous service, even till death.

LORENZO
100 Let this be all that thou shalt do for me.
Be watchful when and where these lovers meet,
And give me notice in some secret sort.

PEDRINGANO
I will, my lord.

LORENZO
Then shalt thou find that I am liberal.
105 Thou know'st that I can more advance thy state
Than she; be therefore wise and fail me not.
Go and attend her, as thy custom is,
Lest absence make her think thou dost amiss.

Exit PEDRINGANO.

Why so: *tam armis quam ingenio.*[3]
110 Where words prevail not, violence prevails.

---

1 The hilt of the sword that Lorenzo is holding, as he makes clear at line 94.
2 Forever, or at least in a continuing way.
3 As much with arms as with wisdom (trans. Peter Parisi).

But gold doth more than either of them both.
How likes Prince Balthazar this stratagem?

BALTHAZAR
Both well and ill; it makes me glad and sad:
Glad, that I know the hinderer of my love;
115 Sad, that I fear she hates me whom I love.
Glad, that I know on whom to be revenged;
Sad, that she'll fly me if I take revenge.
Yet must I take revenge or die myself,
For love resisted grows impatient.
120 I think Horatio be my destined plague:
First, in his hand he brandished a sword,
And with that sword he fiercely waged war,
And in that war he gave me dangerous wounds,
And by those wounds he forced me to yield,
125 And by my yielding I became his slave.
Now, in his mouth he carries pleasing words,
Which pleasing words do harbor sweet conceits,°   *notions*
Which sweet conceits are limed[1] with sly deceits,
Which sly deceits smooth Bel-imperia's ears,
130 And through her ears dive down into her heart,
And in her heart set him where I should stand.
Thus hath he tane° my body by his force,   *taken*
And now by sleight would captivate my soul.
But in his fall I'll tempt the Destinies,[2]
135 And either lose my life or win my love.

LORENZO
Let's go, my lord; your staying stays° revenge.   *delays*
Do you but follow me and gain your love.
Her favor must be won by his remove.

Exeunt.

---

1   Set to trap with. A reference to spreading sticky birdlime on twigs to catch birds.
2   The Fates, in classical mythology three goddesses that determine a life's course.

ACT 2, SCENE 2

Enter HORATIO *and* BEL-IMPERIA.

HORATIO
Now, madam, since, by favor of your love,
Our hidden smoke is turned to open flame,
And that with looks and words we feed our thoughts,
Two chief contents,° where more cannot be had,   *satisfactions*
5 Thus in the midst of love's fair blandishments,
Why show you sign of inward languishments?

PEDRINGANO *showeth all to the prince* [BALTHAZAR] *and*
LORENZO, *placing them in secret* [*above*].¹

BEL-IMPERIA
My heart, sweet friend, is like a ship at sea:
She wisheth port, where, riding all at ease,
She may repair what stormy times have worn,
10 And leaning on the shore may sing with joy
That pleasure follows pain, and bliss annoy.°   *and bliss follows trouble*
Possession of thy love is th'only port
Wherein my heart, with fears and hopes long tossed,
Each hour doth wish and long to make resort,
15 There to repair the joys that it hath lost,
And sitting safe to sing in Cupid's choir,
That sweetest bliss is crown of love's desire.

BALTHAZAR
Oh sleep, mine eyes; see not my love profaned.
Be deaf, my ears; hear not my discontent.
20 Die heart; another joys° what thou deserves.   *enjoys*

LORENZO
Watch still, mine eyes, to see this love disjoined.
Hear still, mine ears, to hear them both lament.
Live, heart, to joy at fond° Horatio's fall.   *foolish*

---

1   The 1592 quarto places the stage direction *Balthazar above* after line 17. Follow-
    ing Edwards, this edition transfers *above* to this stage direction to indicate how the
    conspirators position themselves in secret to watch and comment on Horatio and
    Bel-imperia. The Ghost and Revenge continue to be onstage and presumably
    eavesdrop on the entire scene.

BEL-IMPERIA
Why stands Horatio speechless all this while?

HORATIO
25 The less I speak, the more I meditate.

BEL-IMPERIA
But whereon dost thou chiefly meditate?

HORATIO
On dangers past, and pleasures to ensue.

BALTHAZAR
On pleasures past, and dangers to ensue.

BEL-IMPERIA
What dangers and what pleasures dost thou mean?

HORATIO
30 Dangers of war, and pleasures of our love.

LORENZO
Dangers of death, but pleasures none at all.

BEL-IMPERIA
Let dangers go; thy war shall be with me,
But such a war[1] as breaks no bond of peace.
Speak thou fair words; I'll cross them with fair words.
35 Send thou sweet looks; I'll meet them with sweet looks.
Write loving lines; I'll answer loving lines.
Give me a kiss; I'll countercheck[2] thy kiss.
Be this our warring peace, or peaceful war.

HORATIO
But gracious madam, then appoint the field
40 Where trial of this war shall first be made.

BALTHAZAR
Ambitious villain, how his boldness grows.

---

1   *Warring*, in the quartos, is typically emended to *war* in modern editions to pre-
    serve the pentameter and the repetition from the previous line.
2   Match, in playful opposition.

BEL-IMPERIA
Then be thy father's pleasant bower the field,
Where first we vowed a mutual amity.
The court were dangerous; that place is safe.
45 Our hour shall be when Vesper° 'gins to rise,   *the evening star*
That summons home distressful travelers.
There, none shall hear us but the harmless birds.
Happily,° the gentle nightingale   *perhaps*
Shall carol us asleep ere we be ware,[1]
50 And, singing with the prickle at her breast,[2]
Tell our delight and mirthful dalliance.
Till then, each hour will seem a year and more.

HORATIO
But, honey sweet and honorable love,
Return we now into your father's sight;
55 Dangerous suspicion waits on our delight.

LORENZO
Ay, danger mixed with jealous despite
Shall send thy soul into eternal night.

Exeunt.

ACT 2, SCENE 3

Enter KING *of Spain, Portingale* AMBASSADOR, *Don Cyprian*
[Duke of CASTILE], *etc.*

KING
Brother Castile, to the prince's love,
What says your daughter Bel-imperia?

CASTILE
Although she coy it° as becomes her kind,   *acts coy*
And yet dissemble that she loves the prince,
5 I doubt not, I, but she will stoop in time.
And were she froward,° which she will not be,   *contrary*

---

1 Aware, in the sense of "before we know it."
2 The nightingale traditionally held a thorn against its breast to stay awake for
   singing. Shakespeare and John Fletcher (1579–1625) allude to this same tradition
   in *Two Noble Kinsmen* (c. 1613) 3.4.25–26.

Yet herein shall she follow my advice,
Which is to love him or forgo my love.

KING
Then, Lord Ambassador of Portingale,
10 Advise thy king to make this marriage up
For strengthening of our late confirmed league.
I know no better means to make us friends.
Her dowry shall be large and liberal;
Besides that, she is daughter and half heir
15 Unto our brother here Don Cyprian,
And shall enjoy the moiety° of his land.   *half*
I'll grace her marriage with an uncle's gift,
And this it is: in case the match go forward,
The tribute which you pay shall be released,
20 And if by Balthazar she have a son,
He shall enjoy the kingdom after us.

AMBASSADOR
I'll make the motion to my sovereign liege,
And work it, if my counsel may prevail.

KING
Do so, my lord, and if he give consent,
25 I hope his presence here will honor us
In celebration of the nuptial day.
And let himself determine of the time.

AMBASSADOR
Wilt please your grace command me aught° beside?   *anything*

KING
Commend me to the king,° and so farewell.   *Viceroy*
30 But where's Prince Balthazar to take his leave?

AMBASSADOR
That is performed already, my good lord.

KING
Amongst the rest of what you have in charge,
The prince's ransom must not be forgot.
That's none of mine, but his that took him prisoner,

35 And well for his forwardness deserves reward.
It was Horatio, our Knight Marshal's son.

AMBASSADOR
Between us there's a price already pitched
And shall be sent with all convenient speed.

KING
Then once again farewell, my lord.

AMBASSADOR
40 Farewell, my lord of Castile and the rest.

Exit.

KING
Now, brother, you must take some little pains
To win fair Bel-imperia from her will;
Young virgins must be ruled by their friends.
The prince is amiable and loves her well.
45 If she neglect him and forgo his love,
She both will wrong her own estate and ours.
Therefore, whiles I do entertain the prince
With greatest pleasure that our court affords,
Endeavor you to win your daughter's thought.
50 If she give back,[1] all this will come to naught.

Exeunt.

ACT 2, SCENE 4

Enter HORATIO, BEL-IMPERIA, *and* PEDRINGANO.

HORATIO
Now that the night begins with sable wings
To overcloud the brightness of the sun,
And that in darkness pleasures may be done,
Come, Bel-imperia, let us to the bower,
5 And there in safety pass a pleasant hour.

---

1 Turn away from the marriage proposal.

BEL-IMPERIA
I follow thee, my love, and will not back,°   *retreat*
Although my fainting heart controls my soul.

HORATIO
Why, make you doubt of Pedringano's faith?°   *trustworthiness*

BEL-IMPERIA
No, he is as trusty as my second self.
10 Go, Pedringano, watch without° the gate,   *outside*
And let us know if any make approach.

PEDRINGANO
[*Aside*] Instead of watching, I'll deserve more gold
By fetching Don Lorenzo to this match.

Exit PEDRINGANO.

HORATIO
What means my love?

BEL-IMPERIA
                            I know not what myself,
15 And yet my heart foretells me some mischance.

HORATIO
Sweet, say not so; fair Fortune is our friend,
And heavens have shut up day to pleasure us.
The stars thou seest hold back their twinkling shine,
And Luna° hides herself to pleasure us.   *the moon*

BEL-IMPERIA
20 Thou has prevailed; I'll conquer my misdoubt,
And in thy love and counsel drown my fear.
I fear no more; love now is all my thoughts.
Why sit we not? For pleasure asketh ease.

HORATIO
The more thou sitst within these leafy bowers,
25 The more Flora° deck it with her flowers.   *Roman goddess of flowers*

BEL-IMPERIA
Ay, but if Flora spy Horatio here,
Her jealous eye will think I sit too near.

HORATIO
Hark, madam, how the birds record° by night   *sing*
For joy that Bel-imperia sits in sight.

BEL-IMPERIA
30 No, Cupid° counterfeits the nightingale,   *Roman god of love*
To frame sweet music to Horatio's tale.

HORATIO
If Cupid sing, then Venus[1] is not far;
Ay, thou art Venus or some fairer star.

BEL-IMPERIA
If I be Venus, thou must needs be Mars,°   *Roman god of war*
35 And where Mars reigneth, there must needs be wars.[2]

HORATIO
Then thus begin our wars: put forth thy hand,
That it may combat with my ruder[3] hand.

BEL-IMPERIA
Set forth thy foot to try the push of mine.

HORATIO
But first, my looks shall combat against thine.

BEL-IMPERIA
40 Then ward° thyself; I dart this kiss at thee.   *protect*

HORATIO
Thus I retort the dart thou threw'st at me.

---

1 Roman goddess of sensual love, Cupid's mother.
2 Typically emended from *war* to *wars* in modern editions to preserve the end
   rhyme with Mars.
3 Less gentle, more violent, in the spirit of the mock war that follows.

BEL-IMPERIA
Nay then, to gain the glory of the field,
My twining arms shall yoke[1] and make thee yield.

HORATIO
Nay then, my arms are large and strong withal;
45 Thus elms by vines are compassed till they fall.

BEL-IMPERIA
Oh, let me go, for in my troubled eyes,
Now may'st thou read that life in passion dies.[2]

HORATIO
Oh, stay a while, and I will die with thee;
So shalt thou yield, and yet have conquered me.

BEL-IMPERIA
50 Who's there? Pedringano? We are betrayed!

Enter LORENZO, BALTHAZAR, SERBERINE, PEDRINGANO,
disguised.

LORENZO
My lord, away with her—take her aside.
Oh sir, forbear; your valor is already tried.
Quickly dispatch, my masters.

They hang him in the arbor.[3]

HORATIO
What, will you murder me?

LORENZO
55 Ay, thus, and thus! These are the fruits of love.

They stab him.

---

1 Join battle (*OED*, verb 9).
2 As a double entendre, to die in mock battle and to die as slang for orgasm. The
   murderers add the literal sense a few lines later.
3 A shady place formed by pruned trees.

BEL-IMPERIA
Oh, save his life and let me die for him!
Oh, save him, brother! Save him, Balthazar!¹
I loved Horatio, but he loved not me.

BALTHAZAR
But Balthazar loves Bel-imperia.

LORENZO
60 Although his life were still° ambitious proud,   *perpetually*
Yet is he at the highest now he is dead.

BEL-IMPERIA
Murder! Murder! Help, Hieronimo, help!

LORENZO
Come, stop her mouth. Away with her.

Exeunt.

ACT 2, SCENE 5

Enter HIERONIMO *in his shirt,° etc.*   *nightshirt*

HIERONIMO
What outcries pluck me from my naked bed
And chill my throbbing heart with trembling fear,
Which never danger yet could daunt before?
Who calls Hieronimo? Speak, here I am.
5 I did not slumber, therefore 'twas no dream.
No, no, it was some woman cried for help,
And here within this garden did she cry,
And in this garden must I rescue her.
But stay, what murderous spectacle is this?
10 A man hanged up and all the murderers gone,
And in my bower to lay the guilt on me.
This place was made for pleasure, not for death.

He cuts him down.

---

1 That Bel-imperia recognizes Lorenzo and Balthazar seems to contradict the earlier
stage direction that has them entering disguised. Perhaps only Pedringano is
disguised.

Those garments that he wears I oft have seen.
Alas, it is Horatio, my sweet son!
15 Oh, no, but he that whilom° was my son;   *in the past*
Oh, was it thou that call'dst me from my bed?
Oh, speak if any spark of life remain.
I am thy father; who hath slain my son?
What savage monster, not of humankind,
20 Hath here been glutted with thy harmless blood?
And left thy bloody corpse dishonored here
For me, amidst this° dark and deathful shades,   *these*
To drown thee with an ocean of my tears?
O heavens, why made you night to cover sin?
25 By day this deed of darkness had not been.
O earth, why didst thou not in time devour
The vile profaner of this sacred bower?
O poor Horatio, what had'st thou misdone?
To leese° thy life ere life was new begun.   *lose*
30 O wicked butcher, whatsoe'er thou wert,
How couldst thou strangle virtue and desert?
Ay me, most wretched that have lost my joy,
In leesing my Horatio, my sweet boy.

Enter ISABELLA.

ISABELLA
My husband's absence makes my heart throb.
35 Hieronimo!

HIERONIMO
Here, Isabella, help me lament,
For sighs are stopped, and all my tears are spent.

ISABELLA
What world of grief—my son Horatio!
Oh, where's the author of this endless woe?

HIERONIMO
40 To know the author were some ease of grief,
For in revenge my heart would find relief.

ISABELLA
Then, is he gone? And is my son gone too?
Oh, gush out tears, fountains and floods of tears!

Blow sighs and raise an everlasting storm,
45 For outrage fits our cursed wretchedness.[1]

HIERONIMO
Sweet lovely rose, ill plucked before thy time.
Fair worthy son, not conquered but betrayed.
I'll kiss thee now, for words with tears are stayed.[2]

ISABELLA
And I'll close up the glasses of his sight,
50 For once these eyes were only my delight.

HIERONIMO
Seest thou this handkercher° besmeared with blood?   *handkerchief*
It shall not from me till I take revenge.
Seest thou those wounds that yet are bleeding fresh?
I'll not entomb them till I have revenged.
55 Then will I joy amidst my discontent.
Till then, my sorrow never shall be spent.

ISABELLA
The heavens are just; murder cannot be hid.
Time is the author both of truth and right,
And time will bring this treachery to light.

HIERONIMO
60 Meanwhile, good Isabella, cease thy plaints,
Or at the least dissemble them awhile;
So shall we sooner find the practice out,
And learn by whom all this was brought about.
Come, Isabel, now let us take him up

They take him up.

65 And bear him in from out this cursed place.
I'll say his dirge; singing fits not this case.
O aliquis mihi quas pulchrum ver educat herbas

Hieronimo sets his breast unto his sword.

---

1 The first of five additional passages that appeared in the 1602 quarto was inserted
   after this line; see Appendix A.
2 Stopped. The 1602 quarto's *stayed* seems more suitable than 1592's *stained*.

Misceat, et nostor detur medicina dolori;
Aut, si qui faciunt animis oblivia, succos
70 *Praebeat; ipse metam magnum quaecunque per orbem*
Gramina Sol pulchras effert in luminis oras;
Ipse bibam quicquid meditatur saga veneni,
Quicquid et herbarum vi caeca nenia nectit:
Omnia perpetiar, lethum quoque, dum semel omnis
75 *Noster in extincto moriatur pectore sensus.*
Ergo tuos oculos nunquam, mea vita, videbo,
Et tua perpetuus sepelivit lumina somnus?
Emoriar tecum, sic, sic juvat ire sub umbras.
At tamen absistam properato cedere letho,
80 *Ne mortem vindicta tuam tum nulla sequatur.*[1]

Here he throws it from him and bears the body away.

ACT 2, SCENE 6

GHOST[2]
Brought'st thou me hither to increase my pain?
I looked that Balthazar should have been slain,
But 'tis my friend Horatio that is slain,
And they abuse fair Bel-imperia,
5 On whom I doted more than all the world,
Because she loved me more than all the world.

---

1 O that someone might mix such herbs for me as sweet spring bears forth, and may
  medicine be given for our pain; or, if someone makes oblivion for minds, let him
  furnish juices; I myself shall gather whatever grasses the sun brings forth throughout the great world into the lovely shores of light; I myself shall drink whatever
  poison the witch conjures and whatever herbs the funeral goddess binds with
  secret power; I shall endure all things, even death, until at once all sense dies in
  my dead heart. Shall I never, my life, see your face? Has a perpetual sleep
  entombed your eyes? Let me die with you, thus; thus it is sweet to pass into
  shadow. But nevertheless I shall refuse a hastened end lest then no vengeance
  should pursue your death (trans. Peter Parisi).
2 Ghost and Revenge are already onstage.

REVENGE
Thou talkest of harvest when the corn° is green;   *grain*
The end is crown of every work well done;[1]
The sickle comes not till the corn be ripe.
10 Be still, and ere I lead thee from this place,
I'll show thee Balthazar in heavy case.

---

1 The final product will show the value. "The end crowns the work," from the Latin *finis coronat opus*, was a traditional saying. Note Shakespeare's use of the phrase: "The end crowns all" (*Troilus and Cressida* 4.7.107).

ACT 3, SCENE 1

Enter VICEROY *of Portingale*, NOBLES, VILLUPPO.

VICEROY
Infortunate° condition of kings,   *unfortunate*
Seated amidst so many helpless doubts!
First, we are placed upon extremest height,
And oft supplanted with exceeding heat,[1]
5 But ever subject to the wheel of chance:°   *Fortune's wheel*
And at our highest, never joy we so,
As we both doubt° and dread our overthrow.   *fear, suspect*
So striveth not the waves with sundry winds,
As Fortune toileth in the affairs of kings,
10 That would be° feared, yet fear to be beloved,   *who wish to be*
Sith° fear or love to kings is flattery.[2]   *since*
For instance, lordings, look upon your king,
By hate deprived of his dearest son,
The only hope of our successive line.

FIRST NOBLE
15 I had not thought that Alexandro's heart
Had been envenomed with such extreme hate,
But now I see that words have several works,
And there's no credit in the countenance.[3]

VILLUPPO
No, for, my lord, had you beheld the train°   *deceit*
20 That feigned love had colored in his looks
When he in camp consorted° Balthazar,   *accompanied*
Far more inconstant had you thought the sun,
That hourly coasts the center of the earth,[4]
Than Alexandro's purpose to the prince.

---

1 Later quartos changed *heat* to *hate*.
2 The first 11 lines of the Viceroy's speech are adapted from the Chorus's medita-
tion on kings and Fortune in Seneca's *Agamemnon* (lines 57–76).
3 No authenticity in his trustworthy appearance.
4 That sails around the earth keeping the same distance from the center (in a geo-
centric universe).

VICEROY

25 No more, Villuppo, thou hast said enough,
And with thy words thou slayest our wounded thoughts,
Nor shall I longer dally with the world,
Procrastinating Alexandro's death.
Go some of you and fetch the traitor forth,
30 That, as he is condemned, he may die.

Enter ALEXANDRO *with a* NOBLEMAN *and* Halberts.[1]

SECOND NOBLE

In such extremes will naught but patience serve.

ALEXANDRO

But in extremes, what patience shall I use?
Nor discontents it me to leave the world,
With whom° there nothing can prevail but wrong.   *which*

SECOND NOBLE

Yet hope the best.

ALEXANDRO

35   'Tis heaven is my hope.
As for the earth, it is too much infect
To yield me hope of any of her mold.°   *any human being*

VICEROY

Why linger ye? Bring forth that daring fiend,
And let him die for his accursed deed.

ALEXANDRO

40 Not that I fear the extremity of death,
For nobles cannot stoop to servile fear,
Do I, O king, thus discontented live.
But this, oh, this torments my laboring soul,
That thus I die suspected of a sin,
45 Whereof, as heavens have known my secret thoughts,
So am I free from this suggestion.

---

1 Attendants armed with halberds (see p. 63, note 2).

VICEROY
No more, I say. To the tortures! When?[1]
Bind him, and burn his body in those flames[2]

They bind him to the stake.

That shall prefigure those unquenched fires
50 Of Phlegethon[3] prepared for his soul.

ALEXANDRO
My guiltless death will be avenged on thee,
On thee, Villuppo, that hath maliced thus
Or for thy meed° hast falsely me accused.   *reward*

VILLUPPO
Nay, Alexandro, if thou menace me,
55 I'll lend a hand to send thee to the lake
Where those thy words shall perish with thy works,
Injurious traitor, monstrous homicide!

Enter AMBASSADOR.

AMBASSADOR
Stay! Hold awhile!
And here, with pardon of his majesty,
Lay hands upon Villuppo.

VICEROY
60   Ambassador,
What news hath urged this sudden entrance?

AMBASSADOR
Know, sovereign Lord, that Balthazar doth live.

VICEROY
What sayest thou? Liveth Balthazar, our son?

AMBASSADOR
Your highness' son, Lord Balthazar, doth live,

---

1 An expression of impatience.
2 In England, burning at the stake was a punishment for heresy, not for treason.
3 A river of fire in the classical underworld.

65 And, well entreated in the court of Spain,
Humbly commends him to your majesty.
These eyes beheld, and these my followers,
With these, the letters of the king's commends,° *greetings*

Gives him letters.

Are happy witnesses of his highness' health.

The king looks on the letters, and proceeds.

VICEROY[1]
70 "Thy son doth live, your tribute is received,
Thy peace is made, and we are satisfied.
The rest resolve upon as things proposed
For both our honors and thy benefit."

AMBASSADOR
These are his highness' farther articles.

He gives him more letters.

VICEROY
75 Accursed wretch to intimate these ills
Against the life and reputation
Of noble Alexandro! Come, my lord, unbind him.
Let him unbind thee that is bound to death,
To make quittal[2] for thy discontent.

They unbind him.

ALEXANDRO
80 Dread lord, in kindness[3] you could do no less
Upon report of such a damned fact,
But thus we see our innocence hath saved
The hopeless life which thou, Villuppo, sought
By thy suggestions to have massacred.

---

1 The Viceroy reads aloud.
2 To requite, repay. The king suggests that Villuppo, perhaps assisted by attendants
(as the stage direction suggests), should unbind Alexandro as a requital for his
suffering, now that Villuppo himself is headed for death for his treachery.
3 In keeping with your nature as a monarch.

VICEROY

85 Say, false Villuppo, wherefore° didst thou thus   *why*
Falsely betray Lord Alexandro's life?
Him, whom thou knowest that no unkindness else,
But even the slaughter of our dearest son,
Could once have moved us to have misconceived.[1]

ALEXANDRO

90 Say, treacherous Villuppo. Tell the king.
Or wherein hath Alexandro used thee ill?

VILLUPPO

Rent with remembrance of so foul a deed,
My guilty soul submits me to thy doom,°   *sentence*
For, not for Alexandro's injuries,
95 But for reward and hope to be preferred,°   *advanced*
Thus have I shamelessly hazarded his life.

VICEROY

Which, villain, shall be ransomed with thy death,
And not so mean a torment as we here
Devised for him, who thou saidst slew our son,
100 But with the bitterest torments and extremes
That may be yet invented for thine end.

ALEXANDRO *seems to entreat.*

Entreat me not. Go, take the traitor hence.

Exit VILLUPPO.

And, Alexandro, let us honor thee
With public notice of thy loyalty.
105 To end° those things articulated here   *bring to fruition*
By our great lord, the mighty king of Spain,
We with our council will deliberate.
Come, Alexandro, keep us company.

Exeunt.

---

1 Him (Alexandro) whom you know I would never have suspected of any wrongdoing except in something as extreme as the murder of my son.

ACT 3, SCENE 2

HIERONIMO

 O eyes, no eyes, but fountains fraught with tears;

 O life, no life, but lively° form of death;   *living*

 O world, no world, but mass of public wrongs,

 Confused and filled with murder and misdeeds.

5 O sacred heavens, if this unhallowed deed,

 If this inhuman and barbarous attempt,

 If this incomparable murder thus

 Of mine°—but now no more—my son,   *my*

 Shall unrevealed and unrevenged pass,

10 How should we term your dealings to be just,

 If you unjustly deal with those that in your justice trust?

 The night, sad secretary[1] to my moans,

 With direful visions wake my vexed soul,

 And with the wounds of my distressful son

15 Solicit me for notice of his death.

 The ugly fiends do sally forth of hell,

 And frame° my steps to unfrequented paths,   *direct*

 And fear° my heart with fierce inflamed thoughts. *frighten*

 The cloudy day my discontents records,

20 Early begins to register my dreams,

 And drive me forth to seek the murtherer.[2]

 Eyes, life, world, heavens, hell, night and day,

 See, search, show, send some man, some mean, that may—

A letter falleth.

 What's here? A letter, tush, it is not so,

25 A letter written to Hieronimo.[3]

Red ink.[4]

---

1 Confidant, in the root sense of one who is trusted with a secret. With dreams and
 images of Horatio's wounds, the night fills Hieronimo with anguish.

2 Following the sense of the night as Hieronimo's secretary (line 12), a dark
 (cloudy) day brings to mind (records) his anguish and writes a formal notice (register) of his dreams even before night comes, so driving him to seek Horatio's
 murderer.

3 Hieronimo reads the letter aloud in the next six lines.

4 Presumably to emphasize that the ink is blood.

"For want of ink, receive this bloody writ.
Me hath my hapless brother hid from thee.
Revenge thyself on Balthazar and him,
For these were they that murdered thy son.
30 Hieronimo, revenge Horatio's death,
And better fare than Bel-imperia doth."
What means this unexpected miracle?
My son slain by Lorenzo and the prince?
What cause had they Horatio to malign?
35 Or what might move thee, Bel-imperia,
To accuse thy brother, had he been the mean?[1]
Hieronimo, beware. Thou art betrayed,
And to entrap thy life, this train° is layed.   *trick, bait*
Advise thee, therefore, be not credulous.
40 This is devised to endanger thee,
That thou, by this, Lorenzo[2] shouldst accuse,
And he, for thy dishonor done, should draw
Thy life in question and thy name in hate.
Dear was the life of my beloved son,
45 And of his death behooves me be revenged;
Then hazard not thine own, Hieronimo,
But live t'effect thy resolution.
I, therefore, will by circumstances try
What I can gather to confirm this writ,
50 And, hearkening° near the Duke of Castile's house,   *listening*
Close,° if I can, with Bel-imperia,   *approach*
To listen more, but nothing to bewray.°   *divulge*

Enter PEDRINGANO.

HIERONIMO
Now, Pedringano.

PEDRINGANO
          Now, Hieronimo.

---

1   What would make Bel-imperia accuse her brother even if he were the instrument
    (mean) of the murder?
2   That you (addressing himself) should accuse Lorenzo.

HIERONIMO
Where's thy lady?

PEDRINGANO
            I know not; here's my lord.

Enter LORENZO.

LORENZO
How now, who's this? Hieronimo?

HIERONIMO
55   My lord.

PEDRINGANO
He asketh for my lady Bel-imperia.

LORENZO
What to do, Hieronimo? The duke, my father, hath
Upon some disgrace awhile removed her hence,
But if it be aught° I may inform her of,   *anything*
60 Tell me, Hieronimo, and I'll let her know it.

HIERONIMO
Nay, nay, my lord, I thank you. It shall not need.
I had a suit[1] unto her, but too late,
And her disgrace makes me unfortunate.

LORENZO
Why so, Hieronimo? Use me.

HIERONIMO[2]
65 Oh, no, my lord, I dare not; it must not be.
I humbly thank your lordship.

LORENZO
Why then, farewell.

---

1 Legal matter or simple request (Hieronimo seems deliberately vague).
2 The second of five additional passages that appeared in the 1602 quarto replaced
   the following two lines (in distinct font); see Appendix A and the Note on the Text
   (p. 40).

HIERONIMO
My grief no heart, my thoughts no tongue can tell.

Exit.

LORENZO
Come hither, Pedringano. Seest thou this?

PEDRINGANO
70 My lord, I see it and suspect it, too.

LORENZO
This is that damned villain Serberine
That hath, I fear, revealed Horatio's death.

PEDRINGANO
My lord, he could not; 'twas so lately° done,   *recently*
And since he hath not left my company.

LORENZO
75 Admit he have not, his condition's such[1]
As fear or flattering words may make him false.
I know his humor,° and therewith repent   *temperament*
That e'er I used him in this enterprise.
But, Pedringano, to prevent the worst,
80 And 'cause I know thee secret as my soul,
Here, for thy further satisfaction, take thou this,

Gives him more gold.

And hearken to me. Thus it is devised:
This night thou must, and prithee so resolve,
Meet Serberine at Saint Luigi's Park—
85 Thou knowest 'tis here, hard by,° behind the house—   *very near*
There take thy stand, and see thou strike him sure,
For die he must, if we do mean to live.

PEDRINGANO
But how shall Serberine be there, my lord?

---

1 Even conceding that he hasn't, his nature is such.

LORENZO
Let me alone; I'll send to him to meet
90 The prince and me, where thou must do this deed.

PEDRINGANO
It shall be done, my lord, it shall be done,
And I'll go arm myself to meet him there.

LORENZO
When things shall alter, as I hope they will,
Then shalt thou mount¹ for this. Thou knowest my mind.

Exit PEDRINGANO.

*Che le Ieron.*²

Enter PAGE.

PAGE
                    My lord.

LORENZO
95   Go, sirrah,³
To Serberine, and bid him forthwith meet
The prince and me at S[aint] Luigi's Park,
Behind the house. This evening, boy!

PAGE
I go, my lord.

LORENZO
100 But, sirrah, let the hour be eight o'clock.
Bid him not fail.

---

1 Get advancement; climb the gallows to be hanged.
2 The meaning of this line is unclear, though various suggestions have been made.
   Boas speculates it might be a corruption of the page's name (403); Freeman suggests the Italian phrase *Chi la Ieron* (*Some there, Jeron*) as an "apprehensive reaction
   to hearing a noise," the name possibly a shortened form of Hieronimo (Jeronimo)
   (*Thomas Kyd* 68); Calvo and Tronch emend to *Chi l'è? Jeron!* (*Who's there, Jeron?*)
   and provide a substantial explanatory footnote (199). Regardless of specific
   meaning, the situation suggests Lorenzo summoning the Page.
3 A term of address to a social inferior.

PAGE

       I fly, my lord.

Exit.

LORENZO
Now, to confirm the complot thou hast cast[1]
Of all these practices, I'll spread the watch,
Upon precise commandment from the king,
105 Strongly to guard the place where Pedringano
This night shall murder hapless Serberine.
Thus must we work that will avoid distrust;
Thus must we practice to prevent mishap;
And thus one ill, another must expulse.[2]
110 This sly inquiry of Hieronimo
For Bel-imperia breeds suspicion,
And this suspicion bodes a further ill.
As for myself, I know my secret fault,
And so do they, but I have dealt for° them.   *considered*
115 They that for coin their souls endangered
To save my life, for coin shall venture theirs,
And better 'tis that base companions die,
Than by their life to hazard our good haps.[3]
Nor shall they live for me to fear their faith.[4]
120 I'll trust myself; myself shall be my friend,
For die they shall: slaves are ordained to no other end.

Exit.

ACT 3, SCENE 3

Enter PEDRINGANO with a pistol.

PEDRINGANO
Now, Pedringano, bid thy pistol hold,°   *hold true (be reliable)*
And hold on, Fortune; once more favor me:

---

1 The conspiracy I have devised.
2 Thus, to avoid suspicion, one wicked act must drive another out.
3 Those that can be paid to endanger their souls to keep me free of danger can be
    paid to risk their lives; it is better for these unimportant people to die than for
    them to continue living and present a risk to me.
4 Nor shall they stay alive if I have to fear they might betray me.

Give but success to mine attempting spirit,
And let me shift for taking of mine aim.[1]
5 Here is the gold; this is the gold proposed.
It is no dream that I adventure for,
But Pedringano is possessed thereof.
And he that would not strain his conscience
For him that thus his liberal purse hath stretched,
10 Unworthy such a favor, may he fail,
And, wishing, want, when such as I prevail.[2]
As for the fear of apprehension,
I know, if need should be, my noble lord
Will stand between me and ensuing harms.
15 Besides, this place is free from all suspect;
Here, therefore, will I stay and take my stand.

Enter the watch.

FIRST WATCHMAN
I wonder much to what intent it is
That we are thus expressly charged to watch.

SECOND WATCHMAN
'Tis by commandment in the king's own name.

THIRD WATCHMAN
20 But we were never wont to watch and ward
So near the duke his brother's house before.

SECOND WATCHMAN
Content yourself; stand close; there's somewhat in't.°   *something to it*

Enter SERBERINE.

SERBERINE
Here, Serberine, attend and stay thy pace,°   *stop*
For here did Don Lorenzo's page appoint
25 That thou by his command shouldst meet with him.

---

1 Fortune, give me one more success; let me succeed in my aim (literal aim with the
pistol and figurative aim in gaining the riches Lorenzo promised).
2 The person who refuses to commit a wicked act for a bribe deserves to fail; I hope
he regrets his choice and comes up lacking, while somebody like me prospers.

How fit a place, if one were so disposed,
Methinks this corner is to close[1] with one.

PEDRINGANO
Here comes the bird that I must seize upon.
Now, Pedringano, or never play the man!

SERBERINE
30 I wonder that his lordship stays so long,
Or wherefore° should he send for me so late?   *why*

PEDRINGANO
For this, Serberine, and thou shalt ha't.°   *have it*

Shoots the dag.°   *pistol*

So, there he lies; my promise is performed.

[*Enter*] *The Watch.*

FIRST WATCHMAN
Hark, gentlemen, this is a pistol shot.

SECOND WATCHMAN
35 And here's one slain. Stay the murderer!

PEDRINGANO
Now, by the sorrows of the souls in hell,

He strives with the watch.

Who first lays hand on me, I'll be his priest.[2]

THIRD WATCHMAN
Sirrah, confess, and therein play the priest.
Why hast thou thus unkindly° killed the man?   *unnaturally, cruelly*

PEDRINGANO
40 Why, because he walked abroad so late.

---

1 Approach for some nefarious purpose, as in a back alley.
2 I'll kill him and (ironically) play his priest.

THIRD WATCHMAN
Come, sir, you had been better kept your bed
Than have committed this misdeed so late.

SECOND WATCHMAN
Come, to the Marshal's with the murderer.

FIRST WATCHMAN
On to Hieronimo's. Help me here
45 To bring the murdered body with us, too.

PEDRINGANO
Hieronimo! Carry me before whom you will;
Whate'er he be, I'll answer him and you—
And do your worst, for I defy you all.

Exeunt.

ACT 3, SCENE 4

Enter LORENZO *and* BALTHAZAR.

BALTHAZAR
How now, my lord, what makes you rise so soon?

LORENZO
Fear of preventing our mishaps too late.

BALTHAZAR
What mischief is it that we not mistrust?[1]

LORENZO
Our greatest ills we least mistrust, my lord,
5 And inexpected harms do hurt us most.

BALTHAZAR
Why, tell me, Don Lorenzo, tell me, man,
If aught concerns our honor and your own.

---

1 That we fail to suspect.

LORENZO
Nor you, nor me, my lord, but both in one,
For I suspect, and the presumption's great,
10 That by those base[1] confederates in our fault,
Touching the death of Don Horatio,
We are betrayed to old Hieronimo.

BALTHAZAR
Betrayed, Lorenzo? Tush, it cannot be.

LORENZO
A guilty conscience urged with the thought
15 Of former evils easily cannot err.
I am persuaded, and dissuade me not,
That all's revealed to Hieronimo.
And, therefore, know that I have cast° it thus—   *contrived*
But here's the page. How now, what news with thee?

PAGE
20 My lord, Serberine is slain.

BALTHAZAR
Who? Serberine, my man?

PAGE
Your highness' man, my lord.

LORENZO
Speak, page, who murdered him?

PAGE
He that is apprehended for the fact.

LORENZO
Who?

PAGE
25   Pedringano.

---

1 Lower-class, i.e., Pedringano and Serberine.

BALTHAZAR
Is Serberine slain that loved his lord so well?
Injurious villain! Murderer of his friend!

LORENZO
Hath Pedringano murdered Serberine?
My lord, let me entreat you to take the pains
30 To exasperate° and hasten his revenge   *make more fierce*
With your complaints unto my lord the king.
This their dissension breeds a greater doubt.

BALTHAZAR
Assure thee, Don Lorenzo, he shall die,
Or else his highness hardly shall deny.[1]
35 Meanwhile, I'll haste° the marshal's sessions,   *hurry*
For die he shall for this his damned deed.

Exit BALTHAZAR.

LORENZO
Why so this fits our former policy,°   *scheme*
And thus experience bids the wise to deal.°   *take action*
I lay the plot; he prosecutes the point.
40 I set the trap; he breaks the worthless twigs
And sees not that wherewith the bird was limed.
Thus hopeful men that mean to hold their own
Must look like fowlers° to their dearest friends.   *bird hunters*
He runs to kill whom I have holp° to catch,   *helped*
45 And no man knows it was my reaching fatch.°   *far-sighted scheme*
'Tis hard to trust unto a multitude,
Or anyone, in mine opinion,
When men themselves their secrets will reveal.

Enter a messenger with a letter.

LORENZO
Boy.

PAGE
   My lord.

---

1 Would deny a death sentence for Pedringano only with great difficulty.

LORENZO

What's he?

MESSENGER
50 I have a letter to your lordship.

LORENZO
From whence?

MESSENGER
From Pedringano that's imprisoned.

LORENZO
So, he is in prison then?

MESSENGER
Aye, my good lord.

LORENZO
55 What would he with us? He writes us here:
To stand good lord and help him in distress.[1]
Tell him I have his letters, know his mind,
And what we may, let him assure him of.
Fellow, be gone; my boy shall follow thee.

Exit MESSENGER.

60 This works like wax,[2] yet once more try thy wits.
Boy, go convey this purse to Pedringano.
Thou knowest the prison; closely give it him,
And be advised that none be there about.
Bid him be merry still, but secret,
65 And, though the marshal sessions be today,
Bid him not doubt of his delivery.
Tell him his pardon is already signed,
And thereon bid him boldly be resolved,
For were he ready to be turned off,

---

1 Lorenzo is partly reading and paraphrasing the letter at hand. *To stand good lord* was an expression meaning to be a steady protector (*OED stand* 15c).
2 Wax is easily shaped and molded.

70 As 'tis my will the uttermost be tried,[1]
Thou with this pardon shalt attend him still.
Show him this box; tell him his pardon's in't,
But open't not, an if thou lovest thy life,
But let him wisely keep his hopes unknown.
75 He shall not want while Don Lorenzo lives.
Away!

PAGE
      I go, my lord, I run.

LORENZO
But sirrah, see that this be cleanly done.

Exit PAGE.

Now stands our fortune on a tickle point,
And now or never ends Lorenzo's doubts.
80 One only thing is uneffected yet,
And that's to see the executioner.
But to what end? I list° not trust the air   *prefer*
With utterance of our pretense° therein,   *purpose*
For fear the privy whispering of the wind
85 Convey our words amongst unfriendly ears
That lie too open to advantages.
E quel che voglio io, nessun lo sa;
Intendo io, quel mi basterà.[2]

Exit.

ACT 3, SCENE 5

Enter PAGE *with the box.*

PAGE
My master hath forbidden me to look in this box, and, by my troth,
'tis likely, if he had not warned me, I should not have had so much

---

1 Lorenzo is disingenuously saying that he will make every effort to save
  Pedringano.
2 And what I want, no one knows; I know, which will be enough for me
  (Italian).

idle time, for we men's-kind in our minority are like women in
their uncertainty: that[1] they are most forbidden, they will soonest
5 attempt—so I now. By my bare honesty here's nothing but the bare
empty box! Were it not sin against secrecy, I would say it were a
piece of gentlemanlike knavery. I must go to Pedringano and tell
him his pardon is in this box; nay, I would have sworn it, had I not
seen the contrary. I cannot choose but smile to think how the villain
10 will flout the gallows, scorn the audience, and descant[2] on the
hangman, and all presuming of his pardon from hence. Wilt not be
an odd jest for me to stand and grace every jest he makes, pointing
my finger at this box,[3] as who would say, "Mock on, here's thy
warrant"? Is't not a scurvy jest, that a man should jest himself to
15 death? Alas, poor Pedringano, I am in a sort sorry for thee, but if I
should be hanged with thee, I cannot weep.

Exit.

ACT 3, SCENE 6

Enter HIERONIMO *and the* DEPUTY.

HIERONIMO
Thus must we toil in other men's extremes,
That know not how to remedy our own,
And do them justice, when unjustly we,
For all our wrongs, can compass no redress.[4]
5 But shall I never live to see the day
That I may come, by justice of the heavens,
To know the cause that may my cares allay?
This toils my body; this consumeth age,
That only I to all men just must be,
10 And neither gods nor men be just to me.

---

1 What.
2 Make comments.
3 Scholars have long noticed that Lorenzo's treatment of Pedringano parallels the
treatment by Sir Robert Dudley, Earl of Leicester (1532–88), of a servant named
Gates, whose story circulated in London in the early 1580s. Much later, a poem
called "Leicester's Ghost" appeared, which recounts the incident in a way obviously influenced by this scene in the play. It includes the memorable line, "For his
reprieval, like a crafty fox, / I sent no pardon, but an empty box."
4 Attain no justice for the injuries we have suffered.

DEPUTY
Worthy Hieronimo, your office asks
A care° to punish such as do transgress.   *grave attention*

HIERONIMO
So is't my duty to regard his death,
Who, when he lived, deserved my dearest blood.
15 But come, for that we came for, let's begin,
For here lies that which bids me to be gone.

Enter OFFICERS, Boy [PAGE], *and* PEDRINGANO, *with a letter
in his hand, bound.*

DEPUTY
Bring forth the prisoner, for the court is set.

PEDRINGANO
Gramercy,° boy, but it was time to come,   *thanks*
For I had written to my lord anew,
20 A nearer° matter that concerneth him,   *more private*
For fear his lordship had forgotten me,
But sith° he hath remembered me so well—   *since*
Come, come, come on, when shall we to this gear?°   *hangman's rope*

HIERONIMO
Stand forth, thou monster, murderer of men,
25 And here, for satisfaction of the world,
Confess thy folly and repent thy fault,
For there's thy place of execution.

PEDRINGANO
This is short work. Well, to your marshalship,
First, I confess, nor fear I death therefore,
30 I am the man; 'twas I slew Serberine.
But sir, then you think this shall be the place
Where we shall satisfy you for this gear?

DEPUTY
Ay, Pedringano.

PEDRINGANO
                Now I think not so.

HIERONIMO
Peace, impudent! For thou shalt find it so.
35 For blood with blood shall, while I sit as judge,
Be satisfied, and the law discharged.
And though myself cannot receive the like,
Yet will I see that others have their right.
Dispatch! The fault's approved and confessed,
40 And by our law he is condemned to die.[1]

HANGMAN
Come, on sir. Are you ready?

PEDRINGANO
To do what, my fine officious knave?

HANGMAN
To go to this gear.

PEDRINGANO
Oh sir, you are too forward. Thou wouldst fain[2] furnish me with a
45 halter[3] to disfurnish me of my habit.[4] So I should go out of this
gear, my raiment, into that gear, the rope. But, hangman, now I spy
your knavery, I'll not change without boot,[5] that's flat.

HANGMAN
Come, sir.

PEDRINGANO
So then I must up?

HANGMAN
50 No remedy.

PEDRINGANO
Yes, but there shall be for my coming down.

---

1   The hangman enters here in the 1615 quarto. However, as Edwards points out,
    the hangman could be one of the officers who enter at the beginning of the scene
    (64).
2   Gladly.
3   Noose.
4   Hangmen traditionally received the clothing of those they executed.
5   Something valuable in return.

HANGMAN
Indeed, here's a remedy for that.

PEDRINGANO
How? Be turned off?[1]

HANGMAN
Ay, truly. Come, you are ready? I pray, sir, dispatch; the day goes
55 away.

PEDRINGANO
What, do you hang by the hour? If you do, I may chance to break
your old custom.

HANGMAN
Faith,[2] you have reason, for I am like to break your young neck.

PEDRINGANO
Dost thou mock me, hangman? Pray God I be not preserved to
60 break your knave's pate for this.

HANGMAN
Alas sir, you are a foot too low to reach it, and I hope you will never
grow so high while I am in the office.

PEDRINGANO
Sirrah, dost see yonder boy with the box in his hand?

HANGMAN
What, he that points to it with his finger?

PEDRINGANO
65 Ay, that companion.

HANGMAN
I know him not, but what of him?

---

1 Hanging at this time was simple strangulation at the end of a rope. To "turn off
   the ladder" was the expression used when the victim was separated from the
   ladder (or other support) to hang from the noose.
2 In faith (a mild oath).

PEDRINGANO
Dost thou think to live till his old doublet will make thee a new
truss?[1]

HANGMAN
Ay, and many a fair year after, to truss up many an honester man
70 than either thou or he.

PEDRINGANO
What hath he in his box, as thou thinkst?

HANGMAN
Faith, I cannot tell, nor I care not greatly. Methinks you should
rather hearken to your soul's health.

PEDRINGANO
Why, sirrah hangman? I take it that that is good for the body is like-
75 wise good for the soul, and, it may be, in that box is balm for both.

HANGMAN
Well, thou art even the merriest piece of man's flesh that e're
groaned at my office door.

PEDRINGANO
Is your roguery become an office with a knave's name?

HANGMAN
Ay, and that shall all they witness that see you seal it with a thief's
80 name.

PEDRINGANO
I prithee request this good company to pray with me.

HANGMAN
Ay, marry, sir, this is a good motion. My masters, you see, here's a
good fellow.

PEDRINGANO
Nay, nay, now I remember me. Let them alone till some other time,
85 for now I have no great need.

---

1 Until he gets the boy's clothes, when he grows up to be executed. Both *doublet* and
  truss are items of clothing. To *truss up* in the next line means to hang.

HIERONIMO

I have not seen a wretch so impudent.
Oh monstrous times where murder's set so light,
And where the soul that should be shrined in heaven
Solely delights in interdicted things,
90 Still wandering in the thorny passages,
That intercepts itself of happiness.
Murder, Oh bloody monster, God forbid
A fault so foul should scape unpunished.
Dispatch and see this execution done.
95 This makes me to remember thee, my son.

Exit HIERONIMO.

PEDRINGANO

Nay, soft, no haste.

DEPUTY

Why, wherefore stay you?° Have you hope of life?   *why delay?*

PEDRINGANO

Why, ay.

HANGMAN

As how?

PEDRINGANO

100 Why, rascal, by my pardon from the king.

HANGMAN

Stand you on that, then you shall off with this.

He turns him off.

DEPUTY

So, executioner, convey him hence,
But let his body be unburied.
Let not the earth be choked or infect
105 With that which heaven contemns and men neglect.

Exeunt.

ACT 3, SCENE 7

Enter HIERONIMO.

HIERONIMO
Where shall I run to breathe abroad my woes,
My woes whose weight hath wearied the earth?
Or mine exclaims, that have surcharged the air
With ceaseless plaints for my deceased son?
5 The blustering winds, conspiring with my words,
At my lament, have moved the leafless trees,
Disrobed the meadows of their flowered green,
Made mountains marsh with spring tides of my tears,
And broken through the brazen gates of hell.
10 Yet still tormented is my tortured soul,
With broken sighs and restless passions,
That, winged, mount and, hovering in the air,
Beat at the windows of the brightest heavens,
Soliciting for justice and revenge.
15 But they are placed in those empyreal[1] heights,
Where, countermured° with walls of   *fortified with walls*
    diamond,
I find the place impregnable, and they
Resist my woes and give my words no way.

Enter HANGMAN *with a letter.*

HANGMAN
Oh Lord, sir, God bless you, sir, the man, sir, Petergade,[2] sir, he
20 that was so full of merry conceits—

HIERONIMO
Well, what of him?

HANGMAN
Oh Lord, sir, he went the wrong way; the fellow had a fair commission to the contrary. Sir, here is his passport.[3] I pray you, sir, we
have done him wrong.

---

1   In two senses: empyreal (heavenly), imperial (royal).
2   The hangman's garbled version of the name "Pedringano."
3   The illiterate hangman mistakes this letter for the royal commutation Pedringano
    claimed to have. Thus, being hanged was the "wrong way."

HIERONIMO
25 I warrant thee, give it me.

HANGMAN
You will stand between the gallows and me?[1]

HIERONIMO
Ay, ay.

HANGMAN
I thank your lord worship.

Exit HANGMAN.

HIERONIMO
And yet, though somewhat nearer me concerns,
30 I will, to ease the grief that I sustain,
Take truce with sorrow while I read on this:
"My lord, I write as mine extremes require,[2]
That you would labor my delivery.[3]
If you neglect, my life is desperate,
35 And in my death I shall reveal the troth.°   truth
You know, my lord, I slew him for your sake
And was confederate with the prince and you.
Won by rewards and hopeful promises,
I holp° to murder Don Horatio, too."   helped
40 Holp he to murder mine Horatio?
And actors in th'accursed tragedy
Wast thou, Lorenzo, Balthazar, and thou,
Of whom my son, my son, deserved so well?
What have I heard, what have mine eyes beheld?
45 O sacred heavens, may it come to pass
That such a monstrous and detested deed,
So closely smothered and so long concealed
Shall thus by this be venged[4] or revealed?

---

1 He is concerned that he could be hanged for the mistake.
2 Hieronimo reads aloud from the letter. Many editors change *write* to *writ* (past
   tense) to agree with 1592's *required*. This edition reproduces the line as in the 1623
   quarto (Q9) with the verbs in present tense, which is more idiomatic for a letter.
3 You would prevent me from being hanged, with a play on being born.
4 Avenged. At this point the word refers to just punishment (royal, divine) rather
   than the private revenge he is ultimately driven to.

Now see I what I durst not then suspect,
50 That Bel-imperia's letter was not feigned,°   *forged*
Nor feigned she, though falsely they have wronged
Both her, myself, Horatio, and themselves.
Now may I make compare 'twixt hers and this
Of every accident;° I ne'er could find   *event*
55 Till now, and now I feelingly perceive,
They did what heaven unpunished would not leave.
Oh false Lorenzo, are these thy flattering looks?
Is this the honor that thou didst my son?
And Balthazar, bane to thy soul and me,
60 Was this the ransom he reserved thee for?
Woe to the cause of these constrained wars;
Woe to thy baseness and captivity;
Woe to thy birth, thy body, and thy soul,
Thy cursed father, and thy conquered self.
65 And banned° with bitter execrations be   *cursed*
The day and place where he did pity thee.
But wherefore° waste I mine unfruitful words,   *why*
When naught but blood will satisfy my woes?
I will go plain me to my lord the king,
70 And cry aloud for justice through the court.
Wearing the flints[1] with these my withered feet,
And either purchase justice by entreats,
Or tire them all with my revenging threats.

Exit.

ACT 3, SCENE 8[2]

Enter ISABELLA *and her* MAID.

ISABELLA
So that you say this herb will purge the eye
And this the head?
Ah, but none of them will purge the heart.
No, there's no medicine left for my disease,

---

1 Being present so much at court that he wears down hard paving stones with his
   feet.
2 Some editors start a new act here in order to produce a five-act play. Erne argues
   that Kyd likely conceived the play in five acts but that the existing evidence is not
   enough justify editing it in this way (67). See the Note on the Text, p. 39.

5 Nor any physic to recure° the dead.   *medicine to bring back*

She runs lunatic.

Horatio! Oh where's Horatio?

MAID
Good madam, affright not thus yourself
With outrage for your son Horatio.
He sleeps in quiet in the Elysian fields.[1]

ISABELLA
10 Why, did I not give you gowns and goodly things,
Bought you a whistle and a whipstalk° too,   *whip handle*
To be revenged on their villainies?

MAID
Madam, these humors° do torment my soul.   *emotional outbursts*

ISABELLA
My soul? Poor soul, thou talks of things
15 Thou know'st not what. My soul hath silver wings
That mounts me up unto the highest heavens.
To heaven, ay, there sits my Horatio,
Backed with a troop of fiery cherubins,°   *an order of angels*
Dancing about his newly healed wounds,
20 Singing sweet hymns and chanting heavenly notes,
Rare harmony to greet his innocence,
That lived[2]—ay, died, a mirror[3] in our days.
But say, where shall I find the men, the murderers,
That slew Horatio? Whither shall I run
25 To find them out that murdered my son?

Exeunt.

---

1 See p. 49, note 3.
2 The 1592 quarto uses *died* here; subsequent quartos use *lived*. Isabella's abrupt
   correction emphasizes her unstable emotional state.
3 A model of excellence (*OED* 1b).

ACT 3, SCENE 9

BEL-IMPERIA *at a window.*

BEL-IMPERIA
What means this outrage that is offered me?
Why am I thus sequestered from the court?
No notice? Shall I not know the cause
Of this my secret and suspicious ills?
5 Accursed brother, unkind° murderer,   *unnatural*
Why bends thou thus thy mind to martyr me?
Hieronimo, why writ I of thy wrongs?
Or why art thou so slack in thy revenge?
Andrea, oh Andrea, that thou sawest[1]
10 Me for thy friend, Horatio handled thus,
And him for me thus causeless murdered.
Well, force perforce,[2] I must constrain myself
To patience and apply me to the time,
Till heaven, as I have hoped, shall set me free.

Enter CHRISTOPHIL.

CHRISTOPHIL
15 Come, madam Bel-imperia, this may not be.

Exeunt.

ACT 3, SCENE 10

Enter LORENZO, BALTHAZAR, *and the* PAGE.

LORENZO
Boy, talk no further; thus far, things go well.
Thou art assured that thou sawest him dead?

PAGE
Or else, my lord, I live not.

---

1   Andrea, I wish you had seen. (Note that the Ghost of Andrea is on stage
    observing.)
2   Out of necessity, being forced.

118   THOMAS KYD

LORENZO

That's enough.
As for his resolution in his end,
5 Leave that to him with whom he sojourns now.
Here, take my ring and give it to Christophil,
And bid him let my sister be enlarged,°   *released*
And bring her hither straight.

Exit PAGE.

This that I did was for a policy°   *scheme*
10 To smooth and keep the murder secret,
Which, as a nine days' wonder,[1] being
    o'erblown,°   *having blown over*
My gentle sister will I now enlarge.

BALTHAZAR
And time, Lorenzo, for my lord the duke,
You heard, enquired for her yester-night.

LORENZO
15 Why, and, my lord, I hope you heard me say
Sufficient reason why she kept away.
But that's all one. My lord, you love her?

BALTHAZAR

Ay.

LORENZO
Then in your love beware, deal cunningly,
Salve all suspicions; only soothe° me up.   *back*
20 And if she hap to stand on terms with us
As for her sweetheart, and concealment so,
Jest with her gently. Under feigned jest
Are things concealed that else would breed unrest.
But here she comes.

Enter BEL-IMPERIA.

LORENZO

Now, sister.

---

1 The proverbial amount of time a novelty attracts attention (*OED nine* A3a).

BEL-IMPERIA

                 Sister? No,[1]

25 Thou art no brother, but an enemy.

Else wouldst thou not have used° thy sister so: *treated*

First, to affright me with thy weapons drawn,

And with extremes abuse my company,

And then to hurry me like whirlwinds' rage

30 Amidst a crew of thy confederates,

And clap me up where none might come at me,

Nor I at any to reveal my wrongs.

What madding° fury did possess thy wits?   *frenzied*

Or wherein is't that I offended thee?

LORENZO

35 Advise you better, Bel-imperia,

For I have done you no disparagement,

Unless, by more discretion than deserved,

I sought to save your honor and mine own.

BEL-IMPERIA

Mine honor? Why, Lorenzo, wherein is't

40 That I neglect my reputation so

As you, or any, need to rescue it?

LORENZO

His highness and my father were resolved

To come confer with old Hieronimo

Concerning certain matters of estate

45 That by the Viceroy was determined.

BEL-IMPERIA

And wherein was mine honor touched in that?

BALTHAZAR

Have patience, Bel-imperia, hear the rest.

LORENZO

Me, next in sight, as messenger they sent

To give him notice that they were so nigh.

---

1 Having just been witness to the murder of her beloved Horatio and falsely imprisoned, Bel-imperia speaks with a justifiably indignant and ironic tone throughout
this scene.

50 Now, when I came consorted° with the prince   *accompanied*
   And, unexpected, in an arbor there,
   Found Bel-imperia with Horatio—

BEL-IMPERIA
How then?

LORENZO
Why then, remembering that old disgrace,
55 Which you for Don Andrea had endured,
   And now were likely longer to sustain
   By being found so meanly accompanied,
   Thought rather, for I knew no readier mean,[1]
   To thrust Horatio forth° my father's way.   *away from*

BALTHAZAR
60 And carry you obscurely somewhere else,
   Lest that his highness should have found you there.

BEL-IMPERIA
Even so, my lord? And you are witness
That this is true which he entreateth of?
You, gentle brother, forged° this for my sake,   *fabricated*
65 And you, my lord, were made his instrument,
   A work of worth, worthy the noting, too.
   But what's the cause that you concealed me since?

LORENZO
Your melancholy, sister, since the news
Of your first favorite, Don Andrea's, death,
70 My father's old wrath hath exasperate.°   *increased*

BALTHAZAR
And better wast for you, being in disgrace,
To absent yourself and give his fury place.

BEL-IMPERIA
But why had I no notice of his ire?

---

1 I knew no better course of action.

LORENZO
That were to add more fuel to your fire,
75 Who burnt like Aetna[1] for Andrea's loss.

BEL-IMPERIA
Hath not my father then inquired for me?

LORENZO
Sister, he hath, and thus excused I thee.

He whispereth in her ear.

But Bel-imperia, see the gentle prince,
Look on thy love, behold young Balthazar,
80 Whose passions by thy presence are increased,
And in whose melancholy thou mayst see,
Thy hate, his love; thy flight, his following thee.

BEL-IMPERIA
Brother, you are become an orator,
I know not, I, by what experience.
85 Too politic for me, past all compare,
Since last I saw you—but content yourself,
The prince is meditating higher things.

BALTHAZAR
'Tis of thy beauty then that conquers kings,
Of those thy tresses, Ariadne's[2] twines,
90 Wherewith my liberty thou hast surprised,
Of that thine ivory front,° my sorrow's map,   *forehead*
Wherein I see no haven to rest my hope.

BEL-IMPERIA
To love and fear, and both at once, my lord,
In my conceit,° are things of more import,   *mind*
95 Than women's wits are to be busied with.

---

1 Mt. Etna, an active volcano in Sicily.
2 The mythical character who fell in love with Theseus, led him out of the labyrinth
   with her thread (twine), and was later abandoned by him. That the analogy is a
   bad fit for the situation at hand shows just how clumsy a suitor Balthazar is.

BALTHAZAR
'Tis I that love.

BEL-IMPERIA
     Whom?

BALTHAZAR
         Bel-imperia.

BEL-IMPERIA
But I that fear.

BALTHAZAR
     Whom?

BEL-IMPERIA
         Bel-imperia.

LORENZO
Fear yourself?

BEL-IMPERIA
       Ay, brother.

LORENZO
          How?

BEL-IMPERIA
             As those
That what they love are loath and fear to lose.

BALTHAZAR
100 Then, fair, let Balthazar your keeper be.

BEL-IMPERIA
No, Balthazar doth fear as well as we.
Et tremulo metui pavidum iunxere timorem,
Et vanum stolidae proditionis opus.[1]

Exit.

---

1 They have joined panicked fear to trembling terror, a vain work of slow betrayal
  (trans. Peter Parisi).

LORENZO
Nay, an° you argue things so cunningly,   *if*
105 We'll go continue this discourse at court.

BALTHAZAR
Led by the lodestar° of her heavenly looks,   *guiding star*
Wends poor oppressed Balthazar,
As o'er the mountains walks the wanderer,
Incertain to effect his pilgrimage.

Exeunt.

ACT 3, SCENE 11

Enter two Portingales, and HIERONIMO *meets them.*

FIRST PORTINGALE
By your leave, sir.[1]

HIERONIMO
Good leave have you; nay, I pray you, go,
For I'll leave you, if you can leave me so.

SECOND PORTINGALE
Pray you, which is the next way to my lord the duke's?

HIERONIMO
The next way from me.

FIRST PORTINGALE
5   To his house, we mean.

HIERONIMO
Oh, hard by, 'tis yon house that you see.

SECOND PORTINGALE
You could not tell us if his son were there?

HIERONIMO
Who, my lord Lorenzo?

---

1 The third of five additional passages that first appeared in the 1602 quarto was
   inserted after this line; see Appendix A.

FIRST PORTINGALE
　　　　　　　　Aye, sir.

He goeth in at one door and comes out at another.

HIERONIMO
　　　　　　　　Oh, forbear,
For other talk for us far fitter were.
10　But if you be importunate to know
The way to him and where to find him out,
Then list to me, and I'll resolve your doubt.
There is a path upon your left hand side[1]
That leadeth from a guilty conscience
15　Unto a forest of distrust and fear.
A darksome place and dangerous to pass,
There shall you meet with melancholy thoughts,
Whose baleful humors, if you but uphold,°　　　　　　*continue*
It will conduct you to despair and death,
20　Whose rocky cliffs, when you have once beheld
Within a hugy° dale of lasting night,　　　　　　*huge*
That, kindled with the world's iniquities,
Doth cast up filthy and detested fumes.
Not far from thence, where murderers have built
25　A habitation for their cursed souls,
There, in a brazen cauldron fixed by Jove[2]
In his fell° wrath upon a sulfur flame,　　　　　　*deadly*
Yourselves shall find Lorenzo bathing him°　　　　　　*himself*
In boiling lead and blood of innocents.

FIRST PORTINGALE
Ha, ha, ha!

HIERONIMO
30　　　　　　Ha, ha, ha, why, ha, ha, ha!
Farewell, good ha, ha, ha.

Exit.

1　Echoing the Ghost of Andrea's description of the "left hand path ... to the deepest
　hell" (1.1.64).
2　A poetic name for Jupiter, the highest Roman diety.

SECOND PORTINGALE
Doubtless this man is passing° lunatic,   *exceedingly*
Or imperfection of his age doth make him dote.[1]
Come, let's away to seek my lord the duke.

Exeunt.

ACT 3, SCENE 12

Enter HIERONIMO *with a poniard in one hand and a rope in the other.*

HIERONIMO
Now, sir, perhaps I come and see the king;
The king sees me and fain° would hear my suit.   *gladly*
Why, is not this a strange and seld-seen° thing,   *seldom seen*
That standers-by with toys° should strike   *frivolous things to say*
   me mute?
5   Go to. I see their shifts° and say no more.   *schemes*
Hieronimo, 'tis time for thee to trudge.
Down by the dale that flows with purple gore
Standeth a fiery tower. There sits a judge
Upon a seat of steel and molten brass,
10   And 'twixt his teeth he holds a firebrand
That leads unto the lake where hell doth stand.
Away, Hieronimo, to him begone.
He'll do thee justice for Horatio's death.
Turn down this[2] path; thou shalt be with him straight,
15   Or this, and then thou need'st not take thy breath.
This way or that way, soft and fair[3]—not so,
For if I hang or kill myself, let's know
Who will revenge Horatio's murther° then?   *murder*
No, no, fie, no! Pardon me. I'll none of that.

He flings away the dagger and halter.

20   This way I'll take, and this way comes the king.

He takes them up again.

---

1   Behave erratically, especially due to senility in old age.
2   Indicating one of the instruments of suicide, then the other in the next line.
3   Gently, easily (in the sense of *OED adv. soft* 7).

And here I'll have a fling at him, that's flat.°   *certain*
And, Balthazar, I'll be with thee to bring,
And thee, Lorenzo—here's the king. Nay, stay,
And here, ay here; there goes the hare[1] away.

Enter KING, AMBASSADOR, CASTILE, *and* LORENZO.

KING
25 Now show, Ambassador, what our Viceroy saith.
Hath he received the articles we sent?

HIERONIMO
Justice! Oh, justice to Hieronimo!

LORENZO
Back! Seest thou not the king is busy?

HIERONIMO
Oh, is he so?

KING
30 Who is he that interrupts our business?

HIERONIMO
Not I. [*aside*] Hieronimo, beware, go by, go by.

AMBASSADOR
Renowned king, he hath received and read
Thy kingly proffers° and thy promised league,   *formal offers*
And, as a man extremely overjoyed
35 To hear his son so princely entertained,
Whose death he had so solemnly bewailed,
This, for thy further satisfaction
And kingly love, he kindly lets thee know:
First, for the marriage of his princely son
40 With Bel-imperia, thy beloved niece,
The news are more delightful to his soul
Than myrrh or incense° to the   *fragrant religious offering*
offended heavens.
In person, therefore, will he come himself
To see the marriage rites solemnized,

---

1 The king, his target, who slips by without stopping.

45 And, in the presence of the court of Spain,
To knit a sure inexplicable¹ band
Of kingly love and everlasting league
Betwixt the crowns of Spain and Portingale.
There will he give his crown to Balthazar
50 And make a queen of Bel-imperia.

KING
Brother, how like you this, our Viceroy's love?

CASTILE
No doubt, my lord, it is an argument
Of honorable care° to keep his friend,   *appropriately serious thought*
And wondrous zeal to Balthazar, his son.
55 Nor am I least indebted to his grace,
That bends his liking to my daughter thus.

AMBASSADOR
Now, last, dread lord, here hath his highness sent,
Although he send not that his son return,
His ransom due to Don Horatio.

HIERONIMO
60 Horatio? Who calls Horatio?

KING
And well remembered; thank his majesty.
Here, see it given to Horatio.

HIERONIMO
Justice! Oh justice, justice, gentle king!

KING
Who is that? Hieronimo?

HIERONIMO
65 Justice, oh justice, oh my son, my son,
My son, whom naught can ransom or redeem!

---

1 As a modifier to *band*, 1602's *inexplicable* (cannot be untwisted, disentangled)
makes more sense than 1592's *inexecrable*.

LORENZO
Hieronimo, you are not well advised.

HIERONIMO
Away, Lorenzo! Hinder me no more,
For thou hast made me bankrupt of my bliss.
70 Give me my son; you shall not ransom him.
Away! I'll rip the bowels of the earth,

He diggeth with his dagger.

And ferry over to th'Elysian plains,
And bring my son to show his deadly wounds.
Stand from about me!
75 I'll make a pickaxe of my poniard,
And here surrender up my marshalship,
For I'll go marshal up the fiends in hell
To be avenged on you all for this.

KING
What means this outrage?
80 Will none of you restrain his fury?

HIERONIMO
Nay, soft and fair,° you shall not need to strive.   *stay calm*
Needs must he go that the devils drive.[1]

Exit.

KING
What accident hath happed° Hieronimo?   *happened by chance to*
I have not seen him to demean him° so.   *himself*

LORENZO
85 My gracious lord, he is with extreme pride
Conceived of young Horatio his son,
And, covetous of having to himself
The ransom of the young Prince Balthazar,
Distract and in a manner lunatic.

---

1 The ones that the avenging spirits are chasing must go.

KING

90 Believe me, nephew, we are sorry for't.
This is the love that fathers bear their sons.
But gentle brother, go give to him this gold,
The prince's ransom. Let him have his due,
For what he hath, Horatio shall not want.°   *lack*
95 Haply, Hieronimo hath need thereof.

LORENZO

But if he be thus helplessly distract,
'Tis requisite° his office be resigned   *required*
And given to one of more discretion.

KING

We shall increase his melancholy so.
100 'Tis best that we see further in it first.
Till when, ourself will [not] exempt the place.[1]
And, brother, now bring in the ambassador,
That he may be a witness of the match
'Twixt Balthazar and Bel-imperia,
105 And that we may prefix a certain time
Wherein the marriage shall be solemnized,
That we may have thy lord, the Viceroy, here.

AMBASSADOR

Therein your highness highly shall content
His majesty, that longs to hear from hence.

KING

110 On then, and hear you, Lord Ambassador.

Exeunt.

---

1 Following Edwards, *not* has been added to make the line logically follow the king's
train of thought, that he is unwilling to remove Hieronimo from his position. This
also completes the line's iambic pentameter.

ACT 3, SCENE 13

Enter HIERONIMO *with a book in his hand.*[1]

HIERONIMO
Vindicta mihi.[2]
Ay, heaven will be revenged of every ill,
Nor will they suffer murder unrepaid.
Then stay, Hieronimo, attend their will,
5 For mortal men may not appoint their time.
Per scelus semper tutum est sceleribus iter.[3]
Strike, and strike home, where wrong is offered thee,
For evils unto ills conductor be,
And death's the worst of resolution.
10 For he that thinks with patience to contend°   *endeavor*
To quiet life, his life shall easily end.
Fata si miseros iuvant, habes salutem;
Fata si vitam negant, habes sepulchrum.[4]
If destiny thy miseries do ease,
15 Then hast thou health, and happy shalt thou be;
If destiny deny thee life, Hieronimo,
Yet shalt thou be assured of a tomb.
If neither, yet let this thy comfort be:
Heaven covereth him that hath no burial.
20 And to conclude, I will revenge his death.
But how? Not as the vulgar wits of men,
With open but inevitable ills,
As by a secret yet a certain mean,
Which under kindship° will be cloaked best.   *kindness*
25 Wise men will take their opportunity,
Closely and safely fitting things to time,
But in extremes advantage hath no time,[5]
And, therefore, all times fit not for revenge.

---

1   The fourth of five additional passages that appeared in the 1602 quarto replaced
    this stage direction (in distinct font) and formed a new scene between 3.12 and
    3.13; see Appendix A.
2   "Vengeance is mine" (Latin), a short phrase from Romans 12:19 that exhorts the
    reader to leave revenge to God; Hieronimo articulates this idea in the next lines.
    See Appendix C1.
3   The path through crime is made safe by crimes (trans. Peter Parisi).
4   Translated in the ensuing four lines (14–17).
5   In an extreme situation, it's not possible to wait for the perfect time.

Thus, therefore, will I rest me in unrest,
30 Dissembling quiet in unquietness,[1]
Not seeming that I know their villainies,
That my simplicity may make them think
That ignorantly I will let all slip.
For ignorance, I wot,° and well they know,   *know*
35 *Remedum malorum iners est.*[2]
Nor aught avails it me° to menace them,   *there is no benefit to me*
Who, as a wintry storm upon a plain,
Will bear me down with their nobility.
No, no, Hieronimo, thou must enjoin
40 Thine eyes to observation and thy tongue
To milder speeches than thy spirit affords,
Thy heart to patience and thy hands to rest,
Thy cap to courtesy and thy knee to bow,
Till to revenge thou know when, where, and how.

A noise within.

45 How now, what noise? What coil° is that you keep?   *commotion*

Enter a servant.

SERVANT
Here are a sort of poor petitioners
That are importunate,° and it shall please you, sir,   *persistent*
That you should plead their cases to the king.

HIERONIMO
That I should plead their several actions?
50 Why, let them enter, and let me see them.

Enter three CITIZENS *and an old man* [SENEX].

FIRST CITIZEN
So I tell you this for learning and for law:
There's not any advocate in Spain
That can prevail or will take half the pain
That he will in pursuit of equity.

---

1 Pretending to be calm while really agitated.
2 [finishing the thought] ... is a dull cure for evils (trans. Peter Parisi).

HIERONIMO

55 Come near, you men that thus importune me.
  [*aside*] Now must I bear a face of gravity,
  For thus I used before my marshalship
  To plead in causes as corregidor.°   *a Spanish magistrate*
  [*aloud*] Come on, sirs; what's the matter?

SECOND CITIZEN

60 Sir, an action.

HIERONIMO
Of battery?

FIRST CITIZEN
Mine of debt.

HIERONIMO
Give place.°   *make room*

SECOND CITIZEN
No sir, mine is an action of the case.°   *a legal action*

THIRD CITIZEN

65 Mine an *eiectione firmae*° by a lease.   *ejection notice*

HIERONIMO
Content you, sirs; are you determined
That I should plead your several actions?

FIRST CITIZEN
Ay, sir, and here's my declaration.

SECOND CITIZEN
And here is my band.°   *legal agreement, bond*

THIRD CITIZEN
              And here is my lease.

They give him papers.

HIERONIMO

70 But wherefore° stands yon silly° man so mute,   *why/pitiful*
  With mournful eyes and hands to the heaven upreared?
  Come hither, father, let me know thy cause.

SENEX

O worthy sir, my cause, but slightly known,
May move the hearts of warlike Myrmidons[1]
75 And melt the Corsic° rocks with ruthful tears.   *Corsican*

HIERONIMO

Say, father, tell me, what's thy suit.

SENEX

No, sir. Could my woes
Give way unto my most distressful words,
Then should I not in paper, as you see,
80 With ink bewray what blood began in me.[2]

HIERONIMO

What's here? [*reads aloud*] "The humble supplication
Of Don Bazulto for his murdered son?"

SENEX

Ay, sir.

HIERONIMO

No, sir, it was my murdered son, oh my son,
85 Oh my son, oh my son, Horatio!
But mine or thine, Bazulto, be content.
Here, take my handkercher and wipe thine eyes,
Whiles wretched, I in thy mishaps may see
The lively° portrait of my dying self.   *living*

He draweth out a bloody napkin.°   *cloth*

90 Oh no, not this! Horatio, this was thine,
And when I dyed it in thy dearest blood,
This was a token 'twixt thy soul and me,
That of thy death revenged I should be.
But here, take this, and this. What, my purse?
95 Ay, this and that and all of them are thine,
For all as one[3] are our extremities.

---

1 Fierce soldiers led by the Greek hero Achilles; see also 1.1.49.
2 If my emotions would allow me to speak it, I would not use ink to reveal my
  tragedy, which began with blood ties.
3 All these things are worthless (compared with murder and revenge).

FIRST CITIZEN
Oh, see the kindness of Hieronimo.

SECOND CITIZEN
This gentleness shows him a gentleman.

HIERONIMO
See, see, oh see thy shame Hieronimo.
100 See here a loving father to his son;
Behold the sorrows and the sad laments
That he delivereth for his son's decease.
If love's effects so strives in lesser things,
If love enforce such moods in meaner[1] wits,
105 If love express such power in poor
    estates,°   *without material advantages*
Hieronimo, whenas a raging sea,
Tossed with the wind and tide, o'erturnest then
The upper billow's course of waves to keep,
Whilst lesser waters labor in the deep,
110 Then shamest thou not Hieronimo to neglect
The sweet revenge of thy Horatio?[2]
Though on this earth justice will not be found,
I'll down to hell and in this passion
Knock at the dismal gates of Pluto's[3] court,
115 Getting by force, as once Alcides[4] did,
A troop of furies and tormenting hags
To torture Don Lorenzo and the rest.
Yet, lest the triple-headed porter[5] should
Deny my passage to the slimy strond,°   *shore*
120 The Thracian poet thou shalt counterfeit.

---

1 Those of a lower social standing.
2 What starts as a lyrical passage in the first three lines quickly gets tangled in clumsy syntax and a difficult metaphor. The basic sense is the if/then statement: if people with lesser means can take action, then why can't I? The metaphor of the sea repeats this basic idea, contrasting the stormy waters at the top with the calm waters far beneath the waves.
3 See p. 49, note 5.
4 Another name for the Greek hero Heracles (in Rome, Hercules), who successfully rescued some underworld figures.
5 Cerberus, the three-headed dog that guards the entrance to the underworld in the *Aeneid*.

Come on, old father, be my Orpheus,[1]
And if thou canst no notes upon the harp,
Then sound the burden of thy sore heart's grief,
Till we do gain that Proserpine may grant,
125 Revenge on them that murdered my son.
Then will I rent° and tear them thus and thus,   *rend*
Shivering their limbs in pieces with my teeth.

Tear the papers.

FIRST CITIZEN
Oh sir, my declaration!

Exit HIERONIMO *and they after.*

SECOND CITIZEN
          Save my bond!

Enter HIERONIMO.

Save my bond!

THIRD CITIZEN
130 Alas, my lease! It cost me ten pound,
And you, my lord, have torn the same.

HIERONIMO
That cannot be; I gave it never a wound.
Show me one drop of blood fall from the same.
How is it possible I should slay it then?
135 Tush, no. Run after, catch me if you can.

Exeunt all but the old man.

Bazulto [SENEX] *remains till* HIERONIMO *enters again, who staring him in the face speaks.*

---

1 Orpheus, the "Thracian poet" of the preceding line, descended to the underworld
to rescue his wife Eurydice. Hieronimo suggests that the old man accompany him
to the underworld to persuade its queen, Proserpina, to grant revenge on
Horatio's murderers. Instead of music, as Orpheus used, the old man would strike
notes of grief to move Proserpina.

HIERONIMO

And art thou come, Horatio, from the depth
To ask for justice in this upper earth?
To tell thy father thou art unrevenged?
To wring more tears from Isabella's eyes,
140 Whose lights are dimmed with overlong laments?
Go back, my son; complain to Aeacus,[1]
For here's no justice. Gentle boy, be gone,
For justice is exiled from the earth.
Hieronimo will bear thee company.
145 Thy mother cries on righteous Rhadamanth
For just revenge against the murderers.

SENEX

Alas, my lord, whence springs this troubled speech?

HIERONIMO

But let me look on my Horatio.
Sweet boy, how art thou changed in death's black shade.
150 Had Proserpine no pity on thy youth,
But suffered thy fair crimson colored spring
With withered winter to be blasted° thus?   *blighted*
Horatio, thou art older than thy father,
Ah, ruthless fate,[2] that favor thus transforms.

SENEX

155 Ah, my good lord, I am not your young son.

HIERONIMO

What, not my son? Thou, then, a fury art,
Sent from the empty kingdom of black night,
To summon me to make appearance
Before grim Minos and just Rhadamanth,
160 To plague Hieronimo that is remiss
And seeks not vengeance for Horatio's death.

---

1 One of the three judges of the underworld in Greek myth, along with Rhadamanthus and Minos.
2 Editors typically change 1592's *father* to *fate*, following Dodsley, the first modern
editor of the play.

SENEX
I am a grieved man and not a ghost,
That came for justice for my murdered son.

HIERONIMO
Ay, now I know thee, now thou namest my son.
165 Thou art the lively° image of my grief;   *living*
Within thy face, my sorrows I may see.
Thy eyes are gummed with tears, thy cheeks are wan,
Thy forehead troubled, and thy muttering lips
Murmur sad words abruptly broken off
170 By force of windy sighs thy spirit breathes.
And all this sorrow riseth for thy son,
And selfsame sorrow feel I for my son.
Come in, old man; thou shalt to Isabell.
Lean on my arm, I thee. Thou me shalt stay,[1]
175 And thou, and I, and she will sing a song,
Three parts in one, but all of discords framed—
Talk not of cords, but let us now be gone,
For with a cord Horatio was slain.

Exeunt.

ACT 3, SCENE 14

Enter KING *of Spain, the Duke* [of CASTILE], LORENZO, BALT-
HAZAR, *and* BEL-IMPERIA [*in one group, and the*] VICEROY *and*
DON PEDRO [*in another*].[2]

KING
Go, brother, it is the Duke of Castile's cause;
Salute the Viceroy in our name.

CASTILE
                              I go.

VICEROY
·   Go forth, Don Pedro, for thy nephew's sake,
And greet the Duke of Castile.

---

1   You will be a support to me.
2   The names in this stage direction have been rearranged to accommodate the
    greetings that take place in the next few lines.

DON PEDRO

It shall be so.

KING

5 And now to meet these Portuguese,
For as we now are, so sometimes were these,
Kings and commanders of the western Indies.
Welcome, brave Viceroy, to the court of Spain,
And welcome all his honorable train.°   *attendants*
10 'Tis not unknown to us for why you come,
Or have so kingly crossed the seas.
Sufficeth it in this we note the troth,°   *pledge*
And more than common love you lend to us.
So is it that mine honorable niece,
15 For it beseems us now that it be known,
Already is betrothed to Balthazar,
And, by appointment and our condescent,°   *consent*
Tomorrow are they to be married.
To this intent we entertain thyself,
20 Thy followers, their pleasure, and our peace.
Speak, men of Portingale. Shall it be so?
If ay, say so; if not, say flatly no.

VICEROY

Renowned king, I come not as thou thinkst,
With doubtful followers, unresolved men,
25 But such as have upon thine articles
Confirmed thy motion and contented me.
Know, sovereign, I come to solemnize
The marriage of thy beloved niece,
Fair Bel-imperia, with my Balthazar—
30 With thee, my son, whom sith° I live to see,   *since*
Here, take my crown; I give it her and thee,
And let me live a solitary life,
In ceaseless prayers,
To think how strangely heaven hath thee preserved.

KING

35 See, brother, see how nature strives in him.
Come, worthy Viceroy, and accompany
Thy friend with thine extremities.°   *highly emotional state*
A place more private fits this princely mood.

VICEROY
Or° here or where your highness thinks it good.   *either*

Exeunt all but CASTILE *and* LORENZO.

CASTILE
40 Nay, stay, Lorenzo. Let me talk with you.
Seest thou this entertainment of these kings?

LORENZO
I do, my lord, and joy to see the same.

CASTILE
And knowest thou why this meeting is?

LORENZO
For her, my lord, whom Balthazar doth love,
45 And to confirm their promised marriage.

CASTILE
She is thy sister.

LORENZO
                    Who, Bel-imperia?
Ay, my gracious lord, and this is the day
That I have longed so happily to see.

CASTILE
Thou wouldst be loath that any fault of thine
50 Should intercept° her in her happiness.   *hinder*

LORENZO
Heavens will not let Lorenzo err so much.

CASTILE
Why then, Lorenzo, listen to my words:
It is suspected, and reported, too,
That thou, Lorenzo, wrongst Hieronimo,
55 And in his suits towards his majesty
Still keepst him back and seeks to cross his suit.

LORENZO
That I, my lord?

CASTILE

I tell thee, son, myself have heard it said,
When, to my sorrow, I have been ashamed
60 To answer for thee, though thou art my son.
Lorenzo, knowest thou not the common love
And kindness that Hieronimo hath won
By his deserts within the court of Spain?
Or seest thou not the King my brother's care
65 In his behalf and to procure his health?
Lorenzo, shouldst thou thwart his passions,
And he exclaim against[1] thee to the king,
What honor wert in this assembly,
Or what a scandal wert among the kings,
70 To hear Hieronimo exclaim on thee?
Tell me, and look thou tell me truly, too,
Whence grows the ground of this report in court?

LORENZO

My lord, it lies not in Lorenzo's power
To stop the vulgar liberal[2] of their tongues.
75 A small advantage makes a water-breach,[3]
And no man lives that long contenteth all.°   *keeps everyone happy*

CASTILE

Myself have seen thee busy to keep back
Him and his supplications from the king.

LORENZO

Yourself, my lord, hath seen his passions,
80 That ill beseemed the presence of a king,
And, for I pitied him in his distress,
I held him thence with kind and courteous words.
As free from malice to Hieronimo
As to my soul, my lord.

---

1   Accuse. *Exclaim on*, line 70, has the same meaning.
2   Common slander. The *OED* does not record the use of *liberal* as a noun in this
    sense, but the adjectival definition at 3a captures the meaning: "Unrestrained by
    prudence or decorum."
3   A small opportunity for water to leak can lead it to burst through violently (as in a
    breached dam). Lorenzo argues that he doesn't have the power to stop every small
    rumor before it causes a bigger problem.

CASTILE

85 Hieronimo, my son, mistakes thee then?

LORENZO

My gracious father, believe me, so he doth,
But what's a silly° man distract in mind   *feeble-minded*
To think upon the murder of his son?
Alas, how easy is it for him to err.
90 But, for his satisfaction and the world's,
'Twere good, my lord, that Hieronimo and I
Were reconciled, if he misconster° me.   *misconstrue*

CASTILE

Lorenzo, thou hast said; it shall be so.
Go, one of you, and call Hieronimo.

Enter BALTHAZAR *and* BEL-IMPERIA.

BALTHAZAR

95 Come, Bel-imperia, Balthazar's content,
My sorrow's ease, and sovereign of my bliss,
Sith° heaven hath ordained thee to be mine,   *since*
Disperse those clouds and melancholy looks
And clear them up with those thy sun-bright eyes,
100 Wherein my hope and heaven's fair beauty lies.

BEL-IMPERIA

My looks, my lord, are fitting for my love,
Which, new begun, can show no brighter yet.

BALTHAZAR

New kindled flames should burn as morning sun.

BEL-IMPERIA

But not too fast, lest heat and all be done.
I see my lord my father.

BALTHAZAR

105   Truce, my love.
I will go salute him.

CASTILE

                    Welcome, Balthazar,

142   THOMAS KYD

Welcome, brave prince, the pledge of Castile's peace,
And welcome, Bel-imperia. How now, girl?
Why comest thou sadly to salute us thus?
110 Content thyself, for I am satisfied.
It is not now as when Andrea lived.
We have forgotten and forgiven that,
And thou art graced with a happier love.
But, Balthazar, here comes Hieronimo.
115 I'll have a word with him.

Enter HIERONIMO *and a* SERVANT.

HIERONIMO
And where's the duke?

SERVANT
              Yonder.

HIERONIMO
                    Even so.
What new device° have they devised, trow?[1]   *scheme*
Pocas palabras,[2] mild as the lamb.
Is't I will be revenged? No, I am not the man.

CASTILE
120 Welcome, Hieronimo.

LORENZO
Welcome, Hieronimo.

BALTHAZAR
Welcome, Hieronimo.

HIERONIMO
My lords, I thank you for Horatio.

CASTILE
Hieronimo, the reason that I sent
To speak with you is this—

---

1 An expletive equivalent to *Do you suppose?*
2 Few words (Spanish).

HIERONIMO
125   What, so short?
Then I'll be gone; I thank you for't.

CASTILE
Nay, stay, Hieronimo! Go call him, son.

LORENZO
Hieronimo, my father craves a word with you.

HIERONIMO
With me, sir? Why, my lord, I thought you had done.

LORENZO
No. [*aside*] Would he had!

CASTILE
130   Hieronimo, I hear
You find yourself aggrieved at my son,
Because you have not access unto the king,
And say 'tis he that intercepts° your suits.   *hinders*

HIERONIMO
Why, is not this a miserable thing, my lord?

CASTILE
135 Hieronimo, I hope you have no cause,
And would be loath that one of your deserts
Should once have reason to suspect my son,
Considering how I think of you myself.

HIERONIMO
You son, Lorenzo? Whom, my noble lord?
140 The hope of Spain, mine honorable friend?
Grant me the combat of them, if they dare.

Draws out his sword.

I'll meet him face to face to tell me so.
These be the scandalous reports of such
As love not me and hate my lord too much.
145 Should I suspect Lorenzo would prevent

Or cross my suit that loved my son so well?
My lord, I am ashamed it should be said.

LORENZO
Hieronimo, I never gave you cause.

HIERONIMO
My good lord, I know you did not.

CASTILE
                                        There then pause,
150 And for the satisfaction of the world,
Hieronimo, frequent my homely° house,   *modest, welcoming*
The Duke of Castile, Cyprian's ancient seat,
And when thou wilt, use me, my son, and it,
But here, before Prince Balthazar and me,
155 Embrace each other and be perfect friends.

HIERONIMO
Ay, marry, my lord, and shall.
Friends, quoth he; see, I'll be friends with you all,
Specially with you,° my lovely lord,   *Lorenzo*
For divers° causes it is fit for us   *many*
160 That we be friends. The world is suspicious,
And men may think what we imagine not.

BALTHAZAR
Why, this is friendly done, Hieronimo.

LORENZO
And thus,[1] I hope, old grudges are forgot.

HIERONIMO
What else,° it were a shame it should not be so.   *no matter what*

CASTILE
165 Come on, Hieronimo, at my request.
Let us entreat your company today.

Exeunt [except HIERONIMO].

---

1 Most editors follow Dodsley and emend the original *that* to *thus*.

HIERONIMO
Your lordship's to command—pha! Keep your way.
Chi mi fa piu carezze che non suole
Tradito mi ha, o tradir mi vuole.[1]

Exit.

ACT 3, SCENE 15

GHOST *and* REVENGE.[2]

GHOST
Awake Erichtho![3] Cerberus, awake!
Solicit Pluto, gentle Proserpine,[4]
To combat Acheron and Erebus.
For ne'er by Stix and Phlegethon in hell,[5]
4.1 [Was I distress'd with outrage sore as this],[6]
5 Nor ferried Charon[7] to the fiery lakes
Such fearful sights as poor Andrea sees.
Revenge, awake!

REVENGE
Awake, for why?

GHOST
Awake, Revenge, for thou art ill advised
10 To sleep away what thou art warned to watch!

---

1   The one who offers me more than ordinary affection has betrayed me, or wants to
    betray me (Italian).
2   The quartos include a stage direction here and in 4.5 that starts with *Enter*,
    though the Ghost and Revenge are already on stage.
3   A sorceress of Greek myth.
4   See 1.1.76.
5   Most editors move *in hell* from the end of line 3 to line 4 to correct the quartos'
    corrupt text. The Acheron, Styx, and Phlegethon are rivers of the underworld; ·
    Erebus is another name for the underworld, especially associated with darkness.
6   To make sense of a textually corrupt passage, Edwards assumes a missing line
    between 4 and 5 and proposes the line included here (numbered 4.1) as "some-
    thing of the order of" the missing line. Other editors, including Cairncross, emend
    Nor ferried in line 5 to *o'er ferried*. Either approach makes more sense than the
    original text.
7   The ferryman of the underworld; see also 1.1.19–20 and notes.

REVENGE
Content thyself and do not trouble me.

GHOST
Awake, Revenge, if love, as love hath had,
Have yet the power or prevalence in hell!
Hieronimo with Lorenzo is joined in league
15 And intercepts our passage to revenge.
Awake, Revenge, or we are woebegone!

REVENGE
Thus worldlings ground° what they have dreamed   *make facts of*
    upon.
Content thyself, Andrea. Though I sleep,
Yet is my mood° soliciting their souls.   *mind*
20 Sufficeth thee that poor Hieronimo
Cannot forget his son Horatio.
Nor dies Revenge, although he sleep awhile,
For in unquiet, quietness is feigned,
And slumbering is a common worldly wile.
25 Behold, Andrea, for an instance, how
Revenge hath slept, and then imagine thou
What 'tis to be subject to destiny.

Enter a dumb show.[1]

GHOST
Awake, Revenge, reveal this mystery.

REVENGE
The two first the nuptial torches bore,
30 As brightly burning as the midday's sun,
But after them doth Hymen[2] hie as fast,
Clothed in sable and a saffron robe,
And blows them out and quencheth them with blood,
As discontent that things continue so.

GHOST
35 Sufficeth me, thy meaning's understood,
And thanks to thee and those infernal powers

---

1 A play with no speaking.
2 God of marriage in classical mythology.

That will not tolerate a lover's woe.
Rest thee, for I will sit to see the rest.

REVENGE
Then argue not, for thou hast thy request.[1]

---

1 The quartos' stage direction, *Exeunt*, has been omitted here since Ghost and
Revenge remain on stage.

ACT 4, SCENE 1

Enter BEL-IMPERIA *and* HIERONIMO.

BEL-IMPERIA
Is this the love thou bear'st Horatio?
Is this the kindness that thou counterfeits?
Are these the fruits of thine incessant tears?
Hieronimo, are these thy passions,
5 Thy protestations, and thy deep laments,
That thou wert wont to weary men withal?
O unkind[1] father, O deceitful world,
With what excuses canst thou show thyself?
With what dishonor, and the hate of men,[2]
10 From this dishonor and the hate of men,
Thus to neglect the life and loss of him
Whom both my letters, and thine own belief,
Assures thee to be causeless slaughtered?
Hieronimo, for shame, Hieronimo!
15 Be not a history to aftertimes
Of such ingratitude unto thy son.[3]
Unhappy mothers of such children then—
But monstrous fathers, to forget so soon
The death of those whom they with care and cost
20 Have tendered so, thus careless should be lost.
Myself, a stranger in respect of thee,
So loved his life, as still I wish their° deaths.   *his murderers'*
Nor shall his death be unrevenged by me,
Although I bear it out for fashion's° sake.   *appearance's*
25 For here I swear in sight of heaven and earth,
Shouldst thou neglect the love thou shouldst retain
And give it over and devise no more,[4]
Myself should send their hateful souls to hell
That wrought his downfall with extremest death.

---

1 Unnatural or undutiful (in the broad sense of *OED* 3b).
2 The awkward repetition of these phrases suggests a compositor's error. See Edwards.
3 Don't become known in the future as a parent who failed to avenge his son's death.
4 Give up and stop plotting against the murderers.

HIERONIMO

30 But may it be that Bel-imperia
Vows such revenge as she has deigned to say?
Why then, I see that heaven applies our drift,[1]
And all the saints do sit soliciting
For vengeance on those cursed murtherers.
35 Madam, 'tis true, and now I find it so.
I found a letter, written in your name,
And in that letter, how Horatio died.
Pardon, oh pardon, Bel-imperia,
My fear and care° in not believing it,   *caution*
40 Nor think I thoughtless think upon a mean
To let his death be unrevenged at full,[2]
And here I vow, so you but give consent,
And will conceal my resolution,
I will ere long determine of their deaths,
45 That causeless thus have murdered my son.

BEL-IMPERIA

Hieronimo, I will consent, conceal,
And, aught° that may effect for thine avail,   *do anything*
Join with thee to revenge Horatio's death.

HIERONIMO

On then! Whatsoever I devise,
50 Let me entreat you grace my practices,
For why,° the plot's already in mine head.   *because*
Here they are.

Enter BALTHAZAR *and* LORENZO.

BALTHAZAR

How now, Hieronimo.
What, courting Bel-imperia?

HIERONIMO

Ay, my lord, such courting as, I promise you,
55 She hath my heart, but you, my lord, have hers.

---

1 That heaven drives the impulse we have in common.
2 Thoughtlessly considered a way to allow his death to go unrevenged.

LORENZO
But now, Hieronimo, or never,
We are to entreat your help.

HIERONIMO
                My help?
Why, my good lords, assure yourselves of me,
For you have given me cause—
Ay, by my faith, have you.

BALTHAZAR
60   It pleased you,
At the entertainment of the ambassador,
To grace the king so much as with a show.
Now, were your study so well furnished,
As for the passing of the first night's sport,[1]
65 To entertain my father with the like,
Or any such-like pleasing motion,
Assure yourself it would content them well.

HIERONIMO
Is this all?

BALTHAZAR
Ay, this is all.

HIERONIMO
70 Why then, I'll fit you—say no more.
When I was young, I gave my mind
And plied myself to fruitless poetry,
Which, though it profit the professor[2] naught,
Yet is it passing° pleasing to the world.   *exceedingly*

LORENZO
And how for that?

HIERONIMO
75   Marry,[3] my good lord, thus—
And yet methinks you are too quick with us—

---

1 Entertainment on the first night of the wedding festivities.
2 The one professing himself a poet, i.e., Hieronimo.
3 By the Virgin Mary, an oath.

When in Toledo, there I studied,
It was my chance to write a tragedy.
See here, my lords,

He shows them a book.

80 Which, long forgot, I found this other day.
Now, would your lordships favor me so much
As but to grace me with your acting it?
I mean each one of you to play a part.
Assure you it will prove most passing strange
85 And wondrous plausible to that assembly.

BALTHAZAR
What, would you have us play a tragedy?[1]

HIERONIMO
Why, Nero[2] thought it no disparagement,
And kings and emperors have tane° delight,   *taken*
To make experience of their wits in plays!

LORENZO
90 Nay, be not angry, good Hieronimo.
The prince but asked a question.

BALTHAZAR
                              In faith,
Hieronimo, and° you be in earnest,   *if*
I'll make one.

LORENZO
                    And I another.

---

1 Balthazar may be surprised that he, a nobleman, is being asked to act in a play,
   something usually left to commoners; he may also be surprised that the wedding
   entertainment consists of a tragedy rather than a comedy.
2 The Roman emperor Nero Claudius Caesar (37–68 CE) was said to have used
   condemned prisoners on stage to take on roles in which they were actually killed
   (Freeman, *Thomas Kyd* 63). The allusion escapes Lorenzo and Balthazar.

HIERONIMO

Now, my good lord, could you entreat
95 Your sister Bel-imperia to make one?
For what's a play without a woman in it?[1]

BEL-IMPERIA

Little entreaty shall serve me, Hieronimo,
For I must needs be employed in your play.

HIERONIMO

Why, this is well. I tell you, lordings,
100 It was determined to have been acted
By gentlemen and scholars, too,
Such as could tell what to speak.

BALTHAZAR

And now it shall be played by princes and
Courtiers, such as can tell how to speak,
105 If, as it is our country manner,[2]
You will but let us know the argument.°   *subject matter*

HIERONIMO

That shall I roundly.° The Chronicles   *plainly and immediately*
of Spain[3]
Record this written of a knight of Rhodes:[4]
He was betrothed and wedded at the length
110 To one Perseda, an Italian dame,
Whose beauty ravished all that her beheld,
Especially the soul of Soliman,
Who at the marriage was the chiefest guest.
By sundry means sought Soliman to win
115 Perseda's love and could not gain the same.
Then gan° he break his passions to a friend,   *began*

---

1   Women were not allowed to act in public plays in Elizabethan England, but they
did participate in masques at court.
2   As the practice is in our country.
3   The story of Soliman and Perseda appears in Henry Wotton's *A Courtlie Controver-
sie of Cupids Cautels* (1578), which was published by the bookseller Francis
Coldocke, a Kyd family friend.
4   A Greek island in the Aegean Sea near the coast of Turkey. It was conquered by
the Ottoman Empire in 1522 led by Suleiman the Magnificent (1494–1566).

One of his bashaws[1] whom he held full dear.
Her had this bashaw long solicited,
And saw she was not otherwise to be won
120 But by her husband's death, this knight of Rhodes,
Whom presently by treachery he slew.
She, stirred with an exceeding hate therefore,°   *for that reason*
As cause of this, slew Soliman,
And to escape the bashaw's tyranny
125 Did stab herself, and this the tragedy.

LORENZO
Oh, excellent!

BEL-IMPERIA
            But say, Hieronimo,
What then became of him that was the bashaw?

HIERONIMO
Marry, thus: moved with remorse of his misdeeds,
Ran to a mountain top and hung himself.

BALTHAZAR
130 But which of us is to perform that part?

HIERONIMO
Oh, that will I, my lords; make no doubt of it.
I'll play the murderer, I warrant you,
For I already have conceited° that.   *conceived of*

BALTHAZAR
And what shall I?

HIERONIMO
135 Great Soliman, the Turkish emperor.

LORENZO
And I?

HIERONIMO
      Erastus, the Knight of Rhodes.

---

1 Pasha, Turkish title of high rank.

BEL-IMPERIA
And I?

HIERONIMO
Perseda, chaste and resolute.
And here, my lords, are several abstracts[1] drawn
For each of you to note your parts
140 And act it as occasion's offered you.
You must provide a Turkish cap,
A black mustachio, and a falchion.°   *curved sword*

Gives a paper to BALTHAZAR.

You, with a cross, like to a knight of Rhodes.

Gives another to LORENZO.

And madam, you must attire yourself

He giveth BEL-IMPERIA *another.*

145 Like Phoebe, Flora, or the huntress,[2]
Which to your discretion shall seem best.
And as for me, my lords, I'll look to one,
And with the ransom that the Viceroy sent,
So furnish[3] and perform this tragedy
150 As all the world shall say Hieronimo
Was liberal in gracing of it so.

BALTHAZAR
Hieronimo, methinks a comedy
Were better.[4]

HIERONIMO
A comedy?
Fie, comedies are fit for common wits!

---

1 Summaries, as opposed to lines written out (*OED* B2a).
2 Like a moon goddess (Phoebe), the goddess of flowers (Flora), or a female hunter
   (huntress, also a reference to Diana, patroness of hunting), perhaps with menacing
   emphasis on *huntress* given their plan to murder Lorenzo and Balthazar.
3 Supply costuming and materials to stage the play.
4 More appropriate entertainment for a wedding.

155 But to present a kingly troop° withal,   *royal group*
    Give me a stately written tragedy,
    Tragedia cothurnata,[1] fitting kings,
    Containing matter and not common things.
    My lords, all this must be performed
160 As fitting for the first night's reveling.
    The Italian tragedians were so sharp of wit,
    That in one hour's meditation,
    They would perform anything in action.[2]

LORENZO
And well it may, for I have seen the like
165 In Paris, 'mongst the French tragedians.

HIERONIMO
In Paris? Mass,° and well remembered.   *By the Mass, an oath*
There's one thing more that rests for us to do.

BALTHAZAR
What's that, Hieronimo?
Forget not anything.

HIERONIMO
                              Each one of us
170 Must act his part in unknown languages,
    That it may breed the more variety,
    As you, my lord, in Latin, I in Greek,
    You in Italian, and, for because I know
    That Bel-imperia hath practiced the French,
175 In courtly French shall all her phrases be.

BEL-IMPERIA
You mean to try my cunning, then, Hieronimo.

BALTHAZAR
But this will be a mere confusion,
And hardly shall we all be understood.

---

1 Tragedy in elevated style.
2 Chambers notes that several Italian companies visited England in the 1570s and
  surmises that they mostly performed commedia dell'arte, its improvised comedy
  best suited to traveling companies in foreign cultures (2: 261–65). Hieronimo may
  be loosely associating Italian players with improvisation.

HIERONIMO
It must be so, for the conclusion
180 Shall prove the invention and all was good.[1]
And I myself, in an oration,
And with a strange and wondrous show besides,
That I will have there behind a curtain,
Assure yourself, shall make the matter known.
185 And all shall be concluded in one scene,
For there's no pleasure tane in tediousness.

BALTHAZAR
How like you this?

LORENZO
                              Why thus, my lord,
We must resolve to sooth his humors up.

BALTHAZAR
On then, Hieronimo; farewell till soon.

HIERONIMO
You'll ply this gear?[2]

LORENZO
                              I warrant you.[3]

Exeunt all but HIERONIMO.

HIERONIMO

190   Why, so,
       Now shall I see the fall of Babylon,[4]

---

1   The result will demonstrate that the idea was a good one.
2   Apply yourself to your part in the play (perhaps referring to the summary Hieron-
    imo just handed him).
3   I assure you (a common colloquial phrase).
4   An ancient city, mentioned in the Old and New Testaments, synonymous with luxury
    and vice, here representing Lorenzo, Balthazar, and the power of their families.
    English Protestants also derisively referred to Rome and the Papacy as Babylon.
    Ardolino argues that the inset play is meant to represent the fall of England's Catholic
    enemies in a cosmic struggle between Protestantism and Catholicism. Neill points
    out that the Geneva Bible called the city Babel; in the Genesis story, the Tower of
    Babel was abandoned after God imposed a confusion of languages on its builders.

Wrought by the heavens in this confusion.
And if the world like not this tragedy,
Hard is the hap° of old Hieronimo.   *fortune*

Exit.

ACT 4, SCENE 2

Enter ISABELLA *with a weapon.*

ISABELLA
Tell me no more! Oh monstrous homicides!
Since neither piety nor pity moves
The king to justice or compassion,
I will revenge myself upon this place
5 Where thus they murdered my beloved son.

She cuts down the arbor.

Down with these branches and these loathsome bows
Of this unfortunate and fatal pine.
Down with them, Isabella. Rent them up
And burn the roots from whence the rest is sprung.
10 I will not leave a root, a stalk, a tree,
A bow, a branch, a blossom, nor a leaf,
No, not an herb within this garden plot.
Accursèd complot[1] of my misery,
Fruitless forever may this garden be.
15 Barren, the earth, and blissless, whosoever
Imagines not to keep it unmanured.
An eastern wind co-mixt with noisome° airs   *noxious*
Shall blast° the plants and the young saplings.   *wither*
The earth with serpents shall be pestered,
20 And passengers° for fear to be infect,   *passers-by*
Shall stand aloof and, looking at it, tell,
There, murdered, died the son of Isabel.
Ay, here he died, and here I him embrace.
See where his ghost solicits with his wounds
25 Revenge on her that should revenge his death.
Hieronimo, make haste to see thy son,

---

1 Conspiracy, playing on the word *plot* in the previous line.

For sorrow and despair hath cited[1] me
To hear Horatio plead with Rhadamanth.[2]
Make haste, Hieronimo, to hold excused
30 Thy negligence in pursuit of their deaths,
Whose hateful wrath bereaved him of his breath.
Ah, nay, thou dost delay their deaths,
Forgivest[3] the murderers of thy noble son,
And none but I bestir me to no end,
35 And as I curse this tree from further fruit,
So shall my womb be cursed for his sake,
And with this weapon will I wound the breast,

She stabs herself.[4]

The hapless breast that gave Horatio suck.

ACT 4, SCENE 3

Enter HIERONIMO, *he knocks up° the curtain.*   *fastens up*

Enter the Duke of CASTILE.

CASTILE
How now, Hieronimo, where's your fellows
That you take all this pain?

HIERONIMO
Oh, sir, it is for the author's credit
To look that all things may go well.
5 But, good my lord, let me entreat your grace
To give the king the copy of the play.
This is the argument° of what we show.   *subject matter*

CASTILE
I will, Hieronimo.

---

1 Summoned, as if to appear in court.
2 Rhadamanthus, a judge in the underworld in Greek mythology, associated with
   severity. See also 1.1.33, 3.13.145.
3 Emended from *forgives*. See Calvo and Tronch 4.2.33n.
4 The 1602 quarto places this stage direction after the next line.

HIERONIMO
One thing more, my good lord.

CASTILE
10 What's that?

HIERONIMO
Let me entreat your grace,
That when the train° are passed into the gallery,[1]   *procession*
You would vouchsafe to throw me down the key.

CASTILE
I will, Hieronimo.

Exit CASTILE.

HIERONIMO
15 What, are you ready, Balthazar?
Bring a chair and a cushion for the king.

Enter BALTHAZAR *with a chair.*

Well done, Balthazar, hang up the title.[2]
Our scene is Rhodes. What, is your beard on?

BALTHAZAR
Half on; the other is in my hand.

HIERONIMO
20 Dispatch,° for shame, are you so long?   *hurry*

Exit BALTHAZAR.

Bethink thyself,° Hieronimo.   *collect your thoughts*
Recall thy wits; recompt° thy former wrongs   *recount*
Thou hast received by murder of thy son.

---

1 The area where the king and others will sit to watch the play must be arranged in
   such a way to accommodate the coming events: the doors are locked, the key is
   thrown down, the body of Horatio is first hidden then revealed to the royal party,
   and the doors are broken open for the party to get out.
2 A title board, perhaps to indicate the setting (*OED* 1a uses this line as an
   example).

And, lastly, not least, how Isabel,
25 Once his mother and thy dearest wife,
All woe begone for him, hath slain herself.
Behooves thee then, Hieronimo, to be
Revenged; the plot is laid of dire revenge.
On then, Hieronimo. Pursue revenge,
30 For nothing wants° but acting of revenge.   *is lacking*

Exit HIERONIMO.

ACT 4, SCENE 4

Enter Spanish KING, VICEROY, *Duke of* CASTILE, *and their train.*

KING
Now, Viceroy, shall we see the tragedy
Of Soliman the Turkish emperor,
Performed of pleasure by your son the prince,
My nephew Don Lorenzo, and my niece.

VICEROY
5 Who, Bel-imperia?

KING
Ay, and Hieronimo, our marshal,
At whose request they deign to do't themselves.
These be our pastimes in the court of Spain.
Here, brother, you shall be the book-keeper.[1]
10 This is the argument° of that they show.   *subject matter*

He giveth him a book.

> *Gentlemen, this play of Hieronimo, in sundry languages,*
> *was thought good to be set down in English, more*
> *largely, for the easier understanding to*
> *every public reader.*[2]

---

1   In Elizabethan theater, the book-keeper held the "book" or the complete script of
    the play and also managed the stage during the production, keeping actors on
    their cues (see Gurr, *Shakespearean Stage* 138).
2   Whether Hieronimo's play was originally performed in Latin, Greek, Italian, and
    French as he describes in 4.1 is not certain, but if so the chaotic effect *(continued)*

Enter BALTHAZAR, BEL-IMPERIA, *and* HIERONIMO.

BALTHAZAR (*as Soliman*)
15 *Bashaw, that Rhodes is ours, yield heavens the honor,*
And holy Mahomet,[1] *our sacred prophet,*
And be thou graced with every excellence
That Soliman can give or thou desire.
But thy desert in conquering Rhodes is less
20 *Than in reserving this fair Christian nymph,*
Perseda, blissful lamp of excellence,
Whose eyes compel like powerful adamant°   magnets
The warlike heart of Soliman to wait.[2]

KING
See, Viceroy, that is Balthazar, your son
25 That represents the emperor Soliman.
How well he acts his amorous passion!

VICEROY
Ay, Bel-imperia hath taught him that.

CASTILE
That's because his mind runs all on Bel-imperia.

HIERONIMO (*as the bashaw*)
Whatever joy earth yields betide your majesty.

BALTHAZAR (*as Soliman*)
30 *Earth yields no joy without Perseda's love.*

HIERONIMO (*as the bashaw*)
Let then Perseda on your grace attend.

BALTHAZAR (*as Soliman*)
She shall not wait on me, but I on her,

---

would have been striking. We know that Kyd had a working knowledge of Latin,
Italian, and French, and he may have studied Greek at the Merchant Taylors'
School. This note tells readers that for the benefit of their understanding these
passages are published in English, as opposed to performed in foreign languages.
"More largely" probably means "at greater length."
1 The prophet Mohammad of Islam.
2 Attend upon her, court her favor.

Drawn by the influence of her lights,[1] *I yield.*
But let my friend the Rhodian knight come forth,
35 *Erasto, dearer than my life to me,*
That he may see Perseda my beloved.

Enter [LORENZO as] Erasto.

KING
Here comes Lorenzo. Look upon the plot
And tell me, brother, what part plays he?

BEL-IMPERIA (*as Perseda*)
Ah, my Erasto, welcome to Perseda.

LORENZO (*as Erasto*)
40 *Thrice happy is Erasto that thou livest.*
Rhode's loss is nothing to° Erasto's joy.   *compared to*
Sith° his Perseda lives, his life survives.   *since*

BALTHAZAR (*as Soliman*)
Ah, bashaw, here is love between Erasto [2]
And fair Perseda, sovereign of my soul.

HIERONIMO (*as the bashaw*)
45 *Remove Erasto, mighty Soliman,*
And then Perseda will be quickly won.

BALTHAZAR (*as Soliman*)
Erasto is my friend, and while he lives,
Perseda never will remove her love.

HIERONIMO (*as the bashaw*)
Let not Erasto live to grieve great Soliman.

BALTHAZAR (*as Soliman*)
50 *Dear is Erasto in our princely eye.*

HIERONIMO (*as the bashaw*)
But if he be your rival, let him die.

---

1 Eyes, following the lamp metaphor started in Soliman's speech at line 21.
2 The exchange in lines 43–53 comprises asides between Soliman and the bashaw.

BALTHAZAR (*as Soliman*)
Why, let him die, so love commandeth me.
Yet grieve I that Erasto should so die.

HIERONIMO (*as the bashaw*)
Erasto, Soliman saluteth thee
55 *And lets thee wit° by me his highness' will,*   know
Which is, thou shouldst be thus employed.

(Stabs him.)

BEL-IMPERIA (*as Perseda*)
                                                    Ay me,
Erasto! See, Soliman, Erasto's slain.

BALTHAZAR (*as Soliman*)
Yet liveth Soliman to comfort thee.
Fair queen of beauty, let not favor die,
60 *But with a gracious eye behold his grief,*
That with Perseda's beauty is increased,
If by Perseda's grief be not released.[1]

BEL-IMPERIA (*as Perseda*)
Tyrant, desist soliciting vain suits.
Relentless are mine ears to thy laments,
65 *As thy butcher is pitiless and base,*
Which seized on my Erasto, harmless knight.
Yet by thy power thou thinkest to command
And to thy power Perseda doth obey,
But were she able, thus she would revenge
70 *Thy treacheries on thee, ignoble prince,*

(Stabs him.)

And on herself, she would be thus revenged.

(Stabs herself.)

KING
Well said, old marshal; this was bravely done.

---

1 Don't let your affections die but rather look kindly on my (Soliman's) grief, which
   increases with the thought of not attracting your (Perseda's) attentions, which is
   what would happen if your grief prevents you from releasing me from mine.

HIERONIMO
But Bel-imperia plays Perseda well.

VICEROY
Were this in earnest, Bel-imperia,
75 You would be better to my son than so.

KING
But now what follows for Hieronimo?

HIERONIMO
Marry, this follows for Hieronimo:
Here we break off our sundry languages,
And thus conclude I in our vulgar tongue.°   *ordinary language*
80 Haply° you think, but bootless° are your thoughts,   *perhaps/useless*
That this is fabulously counterfeit,°   *imaginatively fictional*
And that we do as all tragedians do:
To die today for, fashioning our scene,
The death of Ajax[1] or some Roman peer,
85 And in a minute starting up again,
Revive to please tomorrow's audience.
No, princes, know I am Hieronimo,
The hopeless father of a hapless son,
Whose tongue is tuned to tell his latest tale,
90 Not to excuse gross errors in the play.
I see your looks urge instance° of these words;   *illustration*
Behold the reason urging me to this.

Shows his dead son.

See here my show; look on this spectacle.
Here lay my hope, and here my hope hath end.
95 Here lay my heart, and here my heart was slain.
Here lay my treasure, here my treasure lost.
Here lay my bliss, and here my bliss bereft.
But hope, heart, treasure, joy, and bliss,
All fled, failed, died, yea, all decayed with this.
100 From forth these wounds came breath that gave me life.
They murdered me that made these fatal marks.
The cause was love, whence° grew this mortal hate.   *from which*
The hate, Lorenzo and young Balthazar,

---

1 In Trojan War legend, Ajax committed suicide.

The love, my son to Bel-imperia.
105 But night, the coverer of accursed crimes,
With pitchy silence hushed these traitors' harms,
And lent them leave, for they had sorted
    leisure°   *selected an opportunity*
To take advantage in my garden plot
Upon my son, my dear Horatio.
110 There, merciless, they butchered up my boy,
In black dark night, to pale dim cruel death.
He shrieks! I heard, and yet methinks I hear
His dismal outcry echo in the air.
With soonest speed I hasted to the noise,
115 Where, hanging on a tree, I found my son,
Through girt° with wounds and slaughtered as   *wholly covered*
    you see.
And grieved I, think you, at this spectacle?
Speak, Portuguese,° whose loss resembles mine.   *Viceroy*
If thou canst weep upon thy Balthazar,
120 'Tis like I wailed for my Horatio.
And you, my lord, whose reconciled son
Marched in a net[1] and thought himself unseen,
And rated° me for brainsick lunacy   *berated*
With "God amend that mad Hieronimo,"
125 How can you brook° our play's catastrophe?   *tolerate*
And here behold this bloody handkercher,
Which at Horatio's death, I, weeping, dipped
Within the river of his bleeding wounds.
It, as propitious, see, I have reserved,
130 And never hath it left my bloody heart,
Soliciting remembrance of my vow
With these, oh, these accursed murderers,
Which now performed, my heart is satisfied.
And to this end the bashaw I became,
135 That might revenge me on Lorenzo's life,
Who therefore was appointed to the part,
And was to represent the Knight of Rhodes,
That I might kill him more conveniently.
So, Viceroy, was this Balthazar, thy son,
140 That Soliman, which Bel-imperia,
In person of Perseda, murdered,
Solely appointed to that tragic part,
That she might slay him that offended her.

---

1 Acted in the open without expecting to be detected (*OED net* 2b).

Poor Bel-imperia missed her part in this,
145 For though the story saith she should have died,
Yet I of kindness and of care to her
Did otherwise determine of her end.
But love of him whom they did hate too much
Did urge her resolution to be such.
150 And, princes, now behold Hieronimo,
Author and actor in this tragedy,
Bearing his latest° fortune in his fist,   *final*
And will as resolute conclude his part
As any of the actors gone before.
155 And, gentles, thus I end my play.
Urge no more words; I have no more to say.

He runs to hang himself.

KING
Oh, hearken Viceroy! Hold Hieronimo!
Brother, my nephew and thy son are slain!

VICEROY
We are betrayed! My Balthazar is slain!
160 Break ope° the doors; run, save Hieronimo.   *open*

They break in and hold Hieronimo.

Hieronimo, do but inform the king of these events.
Upon mine honor, thou shalt have no harm.

HIERONIMO
Viceroy, I will not trust thee with my life,
Which I this day have offered to my son.
165 Accursed wretch, why stayest° thou him that   *restrain*
Was resolved to die?

KING
Speak, traitor! Damned, bloody murderer, speak!
For now I have thee I will make thee speak.
Why hast thou done this undeserving deed?[1]

---

1 A curious demand, considering that Hieronimo has just explained the events in
  great detail.

VICEROY

170 Why hast thou murdered my Balthazar?

CASTILE

Why hast thou butchered both my children thus?

HIERONIMO[1]

Oh good words!
As dear to me was my Horatio
As yours, or yours, or yours, my lords, to you.
175 **My guiltless son was by Lorenzo slain,**
And by Lorenzo and that Balthazar
Am I at last revenged thoroughly.
Upon whose souls may heavens be yet avenged
With greater far than these afflictions.

CASTILE

180 But **who were thy confederates in this?**

VICEROY

That was thy daughter Bel-imperia,
For by her hand my Balthazar was slain.
I saw her stab him.

KING

               Why speakest thou not?

HIERONIMO

What lesser liberty can kings afford°   *bestow*
185 Than harmless silence? Then afford it me.
Sufficeth° I may not nor I will not tell thee.   *suffice it to say*

KING

Fetch **forth** the **tortures**.
Traitor as thou art, I'll make thee tell.

HIERONIMO

               Indeed,

---

1   The following lines, in distinct font, were replaced in the 1602 quarto by the fifth
of five additional passages, which are printed in Appendix A. The lines in bold
were rearranged and incorporated into the addition by the revising playwright.

Thou mayest torment me as his wretched son
190 Hath done in murdering my Horatio.
But never shalt thou force me to reveal
The thing which I have vowed inviolate.
And therefore, in despite of all thy threats,
Pleased with their deaths and eased with their revenge,
195 **First take my tongue, and afterwards my heart.**

He bites out his tongue.[1]

KING
Oh monstrous resolution of a wretch!
See, Viceroy, he hath bitten forth his tongue
Rather than reveal what we required.

CASTILE
Yet can he write.

KING
200 And if in this he satisfy us not,
We will devise th'extremest kind of death
That ever was invented for a wretch.

Then he makes signs for a knife to mend° his pen.   trim

CASTILE
Oh, he would have a knife to mend his pen.

VICEROY
Here, and advise thee that thou write the troth.°   truth

KING
205 Look to my brother! Save Hieronimo![2]

He with a knife stabs the duke and himself.

---

1 This stage direction is in the 1602 quarto but not 1592.
2 The 1592 quarto attributes this line to the Viceroy. Since the duke (Castile) is the
   King's brother and not the Viceroy's, it makes more sense to attribute the line to
   the King, as Boas does in his edition. This allows the line to be the king's reaction
   as Hieronimo begins the stabbings.

What age hath ever heard such monstrous deeds?
My brother and the whole succeeding hope[1]
That Spain expected after my decease—
Go bear his body hence that we may mourn
210 The loss of our beloved brother's death,
That he may be entombed whate'er befall.
I am the next, the nearest, last of all.

VICEROY
And thou, Don Pedro, do the like for us.
Take up our hapless son, untimely slain.
215 Set me with him, and he with woeful me,
Upon the main mast of a ship unmanned,
And let the wind and tide haul me along
To Scylla's[2] barking and untamed gulf,[3]
Or to the loathsome pool of Acheron,[4]
220 To weep my want for my sweet Balthazar.
Spain hath no refuge for a Portingale.

*The trumpets sound a dead march, the king of Spain mourning after his
brother's body, and the King of Portingale bearing the body of his son.*

ACT 4, SCENE 5

GHOST *and* REVENGE.[5]

GHOST
Ay, now my hopes have end in their effects,
When blood and sorrow finish my desires:
Horatio murdered in his father's bower,
Vile Serberine by Pedringano slain,
5 False Pedringano hanged by quaint device,°   *crafty scheme*
Fair Isabella by herself misdone,
Prince Balthazar by Bel-imperia stabbed,

---

1 All the heirs to the throne.
2 A mythical character who, in Ovid's *Metamorphoses*, was changed below the waist
   to barking dogs, and then transformed into one of the rocks that formed, along
   with Charybdis (a sea monster transformed into a whirlpool), each side of a strait
   deadly to seafarers.
3 Most editors emend 1592's "grief" to 1623's "gulf," which fits more logically with
   references to the sea.
4 The river of sorrow in the classical underworld.
5 See p. 146, note 2.

The Duke of Castile and his wicked son
Both done to death by old Hieronimo,
10 My Bel-imperia fallen as Dido[1] fell,
And good Hieronimo slain by himself.
Ay, these were spectacles to please my soul.
Now will I beg at lovely Proserpine
That by the virtue of her princely doom°   *judgment*
15 I may consort my friends in pleasing sort
And on my foes work just and sharp revenge.
I'll lead my friend Horatio through those fields[2]
Where never dying wars are still inured.°   *habituated*
I'll lead fair Isabella to that train°   *procession*
20 Where pity weeps but never feeleth pain.
I'll lead my Bel-imperia to those joys
That vestal virgins and fair queens possess.
I'll lead Hieronimo where Orpheus[3] plays,
Adding sweet pleasure to eternal days.
25 But say, Revenge, for thou must help or none;
Against the rest how shall my hate be shown?

REVENGE
This hand shall hale them down to deepest hell,
Where none but furies, bugs, and tortures dwell.[4]

GHOST
Then, sweet Revenge, do this at my request:
30 Let me be judge and doom them to unrest.
Let loose poor Tityus[5] from the vulture's gripe,
And let Don Cyprian supply his room.
Place Don Lorenzo on Ixion's[6] wheel,
And let the lover's endless pain surcease.
35 Juno forgets old wrath and grants him ease.

---

1 The queen of Carthage in Virgil's *Aeneid*, who committed suicide.
2 Elysium, where heroes exist pleasantly after death.
3 The poet and musician of myth, whose music had the power to enchant Proserpina in the underworld.
4 Furies (avenging deities), bugs (terrifying objects), and tortures exist in Tartarus, where those suffer whom the gods have condemned.
5 A giant who, for assaulting the goddess Leto, was assigned by Zeus to have his liver forever torn by two vultures.
6 See 1.1.66.

Hang Balthazar about Chimera's[1] neck,
And let him there bewail his bloody love,
Repining at our joys that are above.
Let Serberine go roll the fatal stone
40 And take from Sisyphus[2] his endless moan.
False Pedringano, for his treachery,
Let him be dragged through boiling Acheron[3]
And there live dying still in endless flames,
Blaspheming gods and all their holy names.

REVENGE
45 Then haste we down to meet thy friends and foes,
To place thy friends in ease, the rest in woes.
For here, though death hath end their misery,
I'll there begin their endless tragedy.

Exeunt.

FINIS

---

1   A female monster of myth, who breathes fire and is composed of lion, goat, and
    dragon parts.
2   The mythical king of Corinth, who annoyed the gods with his extreme cleverness
    and was condemned to roll a stone up a hill repeatedly forever.
3   A river of sorrow in the classical underworld; see also 1.1.19, 3.15.3, 4.4.219.

Appendix A: Additional Passages of 1602

The following passages first appeared in the 1602 quarto. See the Note on the Text for further information.

1. First additional passage
(Inserted after 2.5.45.)

Ay me, Hieronimo, sweet husband, speak.

HIERONIMO
He supped with us tonight, frolic and merry,
And said he would go visit Balthazar
At the Duke's Palace. There the Prince doth lodge.
He had no custom to stay out so late.
He may be in his chamber. Some go see.
Roderigo,[1] ho!

Enter PEDRO *and* JAQUES.

ISABELLA
Ay me, he raves, sweet Hieronimo.

HIERONIMO
True, all Spain takes note of it.
Besides, he is so generally beloved,
His Majesty the other day did grace him
With waiting on his cup. These be favors
Which do assure he cannot be short-lived.

ISABELLA
Sweet Hieronimo.

HIERONIMO
I wonder how this fellow got his clothes.
Sirrah, sirrah, I'll know the truth of all.
Jaques, run to the Duke of Castile's presently
And bid my son Horatio to come home.

---

1 No character named Roderigo appears in the play.

I and his mother have had strange dreams tonight.
Do ye hear me sir?

JAQUES
Ay, sir.

HIERONIMO
Well, sir, begone.
Pedro, come hither. Knowest thou who this is?

PEDRO
Too well, sir.

HIERONIMO
Too well, who? Who is it? Peace, Isabella.
Nay, blush not, man.

PEDRO
It is, my lord, Horatio.

HIERONIMO
Ha, ha, Saint James, but this doth make me laugh,
That there are more deluded than myself.

PEDRO
Deluded?

HIERONIMO
Ay, I would have sworn myself, within this hour,
That this had been my son Horatio.
His garments are so like.
Ha, are they not great persuasions?

ISABELLA
Oh, would to God it were not so.

HIERONIMO
Were not, Isabella? Dost thou dream it is?
Can thy soft bosom entertain a thought
That such a black deed of mischief should be done

On one so pure[1] and spotless as our son?
Away, I am ashamed.

ISABELLA
                    Dear Hieronimo,
Cast a more serious eye upon thy grief.
Weak apprehension gives but weak belief.

HIERONIMO
It was a man sure that was hanged up here,
A youth, as I remember. I cut him down.
If it should prove my son now after all—
Say you, say you, light!—lend me a taper—
Let me look again. Oh God,
Confusion, mischief, torment, death and hell,
Drop all your stings at once in my cold bosom
That now is stiff with horror. Kill me quickly.
Be gracious to me, thou infective night,
And drop this deed of murder down on me.
Gird in[2] my waste of grief with thy large darkness,
And let me not survive; to see the light
May put me in the mind I had a son.

ISABELLA
Oh, sweet Horatio. Oh, my dearest son.

HIERONIMO
How strangely had I lost my way to grief.

2. Second additional passage
(Replacing lines 3.2.66–67.)

HIERONIMO
Who, you, my lord?
I reserve your favor for a greater honor.
This is a very toy,[3] my lord, a toy.

---

1 1602's *poor* is typically emended to *pure* from Q7 (1615), to be more in
   keeping with *spotless*.
2 Surround and limit, playing on the familiar idea of girding (putting a belt on)
   a waist and punning on the word *waste*.
3 Trifling matter.

LORENZO
All's one,[1] Hieronimo; acquaint me with it.

HIERONIMO
I'faith, my lord, 'tis an idle thing, I must confess. I ha'been too slack, too tardy, too remiss unto your honor.

LORENZO
How now, Hieronimo?

HIERONIMO
In troth, my lord, it is a thing of nothing,
The murder of a son, or so,
A thing of nothing, my lord.

3. Third additional passage
(Inserted after 3.11.1.)

HIERONIMO
'Tis neither as you think, nor as you think,
Nor as you think. You're wide[2] all.
These slippers are not mine; they were my son
Horatio's, my son, and what's a son?
A thing begot within a pair of minutes, thereabout,
A lump bred up in darkness and doth serve
To ballast[3] these light creatures we call women,
And at nine months' end, creeps forth to light.
What is there yet in a son
To make a father dote, rave, or run mad.
Being born, it pouts, cries, and breeds teeth.
What is there yet in a son? He must be fed,
Be taught to go,[4] and speak. Ay, or yet?[5]
Why might not a man love a calf as well?
Or melt in passion o'er a frisking kid?
As for a son, methinks a young bacon[6]

---

1 Never mind.
2 Wide of the mark.
3 Weigh down.
4 Move about, walk.
5 The second, but shortened, repetition of the proposition, *What is there yet?* (Edwards 125).
6 A pig (by extension).

Or a fine little smooth horse-colt
Should move a man as much as doth a son.
For one of these in very little time
Will grow to some good use, whereas a son,
The more he grows in stature and in years,
The more unsquared, unbeveled he appears,
Reckons his parents among the rank of fools,
Strikes care[1] upon their heads with his mad riots,
Makes them look old before they meet with age.
This is a son. And what a loss were this, considered truly?
Oh but my Horatio grew out of reach of these
Insatiate humors. He loved his loving parents.
He was my comfort and his mother's joy,
The very arm that did hold up our house.
Our hopes were stored up in him.
None but a damned murderer could hate him.
He had not seen the back of nineteen year
When his strong arm unhorsed the proud Prince Balthazar,
And his great mind, too full of honor,
Took him unto mercy, that valiant, but ignoble Portingale.
Well, heaven is heaven still,
And there is Nemesis and Furies,[2]
And things called whips,
And they sometimes do meet with murderers.
They do not always scape; that's some comfort.
Ay, ay, ay, and then time steals on, and steals, and steals,
Till violence leaps forth like thunder
Wrapped in a ball of fire,
And so doth bring confusion to them all.

4. Fourth additional passage
(Forming a new scene between 3.12 and 3.13, replacing the stage
direction at the beginning of 3.13.)

Enter JAQUES *and* PEDRO.

JAQUES
I wonder, Pedro, why our master thus
At midnight sends us with our torches' light,

---

1 Worry.
2 Goddess of vengeance (Nemesis) and three avengers from the underworld
   (Furies).

When man and bird and beast are all at rest,
Save those that watch for rape and bloody murder.

PEDRO
Oh Jaques, know thou that our master's mind
Is much distraught since his Horatio died,
And, now his aged years should sleep in rest,
His heart in quiet, like a desperate man,
Grows lunatic and childish for his son.
Sometimes as he doth at his table sit,
He speaks as if Horatio stood by him,
Then, starting in a rage, falls on the earth,
Cries out, "Horatio! Where is my son Horatio?"
So that with extreme grief and cutting sorrow,
There is not left in him one inch of man.
See where he comes.

Enter HIERONIMO.

HIERONIMO
I pry through every crevice of each wall,
Look on each tree, and search through every brake,
Beat at the bushes, stamp our grandam earth,
Dive in the water, and stare up to heaven,
Yet I cannot behold my son Horatio.
How now, who's there? Sprites? Sprites?

PEDRO
We are your servants that attend you, sir.

HIERONIMO
What make you with your torches in the dark?

PEDRO
You bid us light them and attend you here.

HIERONIMO
No, no, you are deceived, not I, you are deceived.
Was I so mad to bid you light your torches now?
Light me your torches at the mid of noon,
Whenas[1] the sun-god rides in all his glory.
Light me your torches then.

1 When.

PEDRO
Then we burn daylight.

HIERONIMO
Let it be burnt. Night is a murderous slut
That would not have her treasons to be seen,
And yonder pale faced Hecate[1] there, the moon,
Doth give consent to that is done in darkness,
And all those stars that gaze upon her face
Are aglets[2] on her sleeve, pins on her train,
And those that should be powerful and divine
Do sleep in darkness when they most should shine.

PEDRO
Provoke them not, fair sir, with tempting words.
The heavens are gracious, and your miseries
And sorrow makes you speak you know not what.

HIERONIMO
Villain, thou liest, and thou dost naught
But tell me I am mad. Thou liest; I am not mad.
I know thee to be Pedro and he Jaques.
I'll prove it to thee. And were I mad, how could I?
Where was she that same night when my Horatio was murdered?
She should have shone. Search thou the book.
Had the moon shone—in my boy's face there was a kind of grace
That I know, nay, I do know—had the murderer seen him,
His weapon would have fallen and cut the earth,
Had he been framed of naught but blood and death.
Alack, when mischief doth it knows not what,
What shall we say to mischief?

Enter ISABELLA.

ISABELLA
Dear Hieronimo, come in a-doors.
Oh, seek not means so to increase thy sorrow.

---

1 A Greek goddess associated with the moon, night, and witchcraft. Note that
   the quarto reads *he-cat* here, surely a printer's error.
2 Ornamental tags.

HIERONIMO

Indeed, Isabella, we do nothing here;
I do not cry—ask Pedro and Jaques.
Not I indeed. We are very merry, very merry.

ISABELLA

How? Be merry here? Be merry here?
Is not this the place and this the very tree
Where my Horatio died, where he was murdered?

HIERONIMO

Was—do not say what. Let her weep it out.
This was the tree; I set it of a kernel,[1]
And when our hot Spain could not let it grow
But that the infant and the human sap
Began to wither, duly twice a morning
Would I be sprinkling it with fountain water.
At last it grew and grew, and bore and bore,
Till at length it grew a gallows and did bear our son.
It bore thy fruit and mine. Oh wicked, wicked plant!

One knocks within at the door.

See who knock there.

PEDRO

                    It is a painter, sir.

HIERONIMO

Bid him come in and paint some comfort,
For surely there's none lives but painted comfort.
Let him come in. One knows not what may chance.
God's will,[2] that I should set this tree!
But even so, masters: ungrateful servants rear from naught,
And then they hate them that did bring them up.[3]

---

1 Planted it as a seed.
2 An interjection of resignation.
3 A difficult passage obscured further by the quarto's punctuation. *Even so*
   means *in this manner*. The basic sense is the following: Just as a servant born
   into a household can grow up to hate the master who nurtured him, so this
   tree, which I planted and nurtured, grew to do a hateful thing to me, kill my
   son.

Enter the PAINTER.

PAINTER
God bless you, sir.

HIERONIMO
Wherefore, why, thou scornful villain?
How, where, or by what means should I be blest?

ISABELLA
What wouldst thou have, good fellow?

PAINTER
Justice, madam.

HIERONIMO
Oh ambitious beggar, wouldst thou have that
That lives not in the world?
Why, all the undelved mines cannot buy
An ounce of justice. 'Tis a jewel so inestimable.
I tell thee, God hath engrossed[1] all justice in his hands,
And there is none but what comes from him.

PAINTER
Oh, then I see that God must right me for my murdered son.

HIERONIMO
How, was thy son murdered?

PAINTER
Ay, sir, no man did hold a son so dear.

HIERONIMO
What, not as thine? That's a lie
As massy as the earth! I had a son,
Whose least unvalued hair did weigh
A thousand of thy son's, and he was murdered.

PAINTER
Alas, sir, I had no more but he.

---

1 Amassed.

HIERONIMO
Nor I, nor I. But this same one of mine
Was worth a legion—but all is one.[1]
Pedro, Jaques, go in a-doors; Isabella, go.
And this good fellow here and I
Will range[2] this hideous orchard up and down,
Like to two lions reaved[3] of their young.
Go in a-doors, I say.

Exeunt.

The PAINTER *and he sits down.*

Come, let's talk wisely now:
Was thy son murdered?

PAINTER
                    Ay, sir.

HIERONIMO
                              So was mine.
How dost take it? Art thou sometimes mad?
Is there no tricks[4] that comes before thine eyes?

PAINTER
Oh lord, yes, sir.

HIERONIMO
Art a painter? Canst paint me a tear, or a wound, a groan, or a sigh?
Canst paint me such a tree as this?

PAINTER
Sir, I am sure you have heard of my painting. My name's Bazardo.

HIERONIMO
Bazardo, afore God, an excellent fellow. Look you, sir, do you see,
I'd have you paint me in[5] my gallery in your oil colors matted,[6] and

---

1   Never mind.
2   Search.
3   Deprived.
4   "An illusory or deceptive appearance" (*OED* 1c, this cited as earliest instance
    of this meaning).
5   The preposition *in* was omitted in the quarto. Calvo and Tronch introduce
    other possibilities (252).
6   With colors made dull (*OED* 1, this cited as earliest instance of this meaning).

draw me five years younger than I am.[1] Do ye see, sir? Let five years go. Let them go like the Marshal of Spain. My wife Isabella standing by me, with a speaking look to my son Horatio, which should intend to this or some such like purpose: God bless thee, my sweet son. And my hand leaning upon his head thus, sir. Do you see? May it be done?

PAINTER
Very well, sir.

HIERONIMO
Nay, I pray mark me, sir. Then, sir, would I have you paint me this tree, this very tree. Canst paint a doleful cry?

PAINTER
Seemingly,[2] sir.

HIERONIMO
Nay, it should cry—but all is one. Well, sir, paint me a youth run through and through with villains' swords, hanging upon this tree. Canst thou draw a murderer?

PAINTER
I'll warrant you, sir, I have the pattern of the most notorious villains that ever lived in all Spain.

HIERONIMO
Oh, let them be worse, worse! Stretch thine art, and let their beards be of Judas[3] his own color, and let their eyebrows jutty[4] over. In any case, observe that. Then, sir, after some violent noise, bring me forth in my shirt,[5] and my gown under mine arm, with my torch in my hand and my sword reared up thus, and with these words: *What noise is this? Who calls Hieronimo?* May it be done?

---

1   The painting Hieronimo requests in the following lines is remarkable in that it includes movement, sequences of events, dialogue, and even sound.
2   The painter can make it seem like a cry by its external appearance.
3   The betrayer of Christ in the New Testament. Judas' hair was red in medieval popular culture, and the *OED* cites this as the first instance of the compound *Judas color* (C2a).
4   Jut.
5   Nightshirt.

PAINTER
Yea, sir.

HIERONIMO
Well, sir, then bring me forth, bring me through alley and alley,[1] still
with a distracted countenance going along, and let my hair heave up
my nightcap. Let the clouds scowl, make the moon dark, the stars
extinct, the winds blowing, the bells tolling, the owl shrieking, the
toads croaking,[2] the minutes jarring, and the clock striking twelve.
And then at last, sir, starting, behold a man hanging and tottering
and tottering as you know the wind will weave[3] a man, and I with a
trise[4] to cut him down. And looking upon him by the advantage of
my torch, find it to be my son Horatio. There you may show[5] a
passion; there you may show a passion. Draw me like old Priam of
Troy,[6] crying, "the house is afire, the house is afire," as the torch
over my head. Make me curse, make me rave, make me cry, make
me mad, make me well again, make me curse hell, invocate heaven,
and, in the end, leave me in a trance, and so forth.

PAINTER
And is this the end?

HIERONIMO
Oh no, there is no end! The end is death and madness, as I am never
better than when I am mad. Then methinks I am a brave fellow.
Then I do wonders. But reason abuseth me, and there's the torment;
there's the hell. At the last, sir, bring me to one of the murderers.
Were he as strong as Hector,[7] thus would I tear and drag him up
and down.

---

1 Garden passageways.
2 Proverbially, owls were bad omens, and toads were poisonous.
3 To sway back and forth (close to the sense of *OED* 1a or 2), but Q5's *wave* is
   also a possibility.
4 Instantly.
5 Most editors add *show* here, which was omitted in the quarto.
6 The king of Troy and the image of grief; he lost 50 sons in the Trojan War,
   including his beloved son Hector.
7 King Priam's son and Troy's fiercest warrior, who, in the *Iliad*, was killed by
   Achilles and dragged around the city behind his chariot. Given that Hieronimo just described himself as Priam, it is unexpected that he would compare
   himself to Hector's killer.

He beats[1] the PAINTER *in, then comes out again with a book in his hand.*

5. Fifth additional passage
(Inserted after 4.4.172. The lines in bold, here and in the body of the text, are found in the 1592 quarto but rearranged and incorporated into the 1602 quarto by the revising playwright.)

HIERONIMO
But are you sure they are dead?

CASTILE
Ay, slave, too sure.

HIERONIMO
What, and yours too?

VICEROY
Ay, all are dead, not one of them survive.

HIERONIMO
Nay, then I care not. Come, and we shall be friends.
Let us lay our heads together;
See, here's a goodly noose will hold them all.

VICEROY
O damned Devil, how secure[2] he is.

HIERONIMO
Secure? Why dost thou wonder at it?
I tell thee, Viceroy, this day I have seen revenged,
And in that sight am grown a prouder monarch
Than ever sat under the crown of Spain.
Had I as many lives as there be stars,
As many heavens to go to as those lives,
I'd give them all, ay, and my soul to boot
But I would see thee ride in this red pool.

CASTILE
Speak, **who were thy confederates in this?**

---

1 Perhaps Hieronimo acts out the violence he describes in the painting.
2 Carefree, smug.

VICEROY
That was thy daughter Bel-imperia,
For by her hand my Balthazar was slain.
I saw her stab him.

HIERONIMO
Oh good words!
As dear to me was my Horatio
As yours, or yours, or yours, my lords, to you.
My guiltless son was by Lorenzo slain,
And by Lorenzo and that Balthazar,
Am I at last revenged thoroughly,
Upon whose souls may heavens be yet revenged
With greater far than these afflictions.
Methinks since I grew inward with revenge,
I cannot look with scorn enough on death.

KING
What, dost thou mock us, slave? Bring **tortures forth**.

HIERONIMO
Do, do, do, and meantime I'll torture you.
You had a son, as I take it, and your son
Should ha'been married to your daughter, ha, wast not so?
You had a son too; he was my liege's nephew.
He was proud and politic. Had he lived,
He might ha'come to wear the crown of Spain.
I think 'twas so. 'Twas I that killed him.
Look you this same hand; 'twas it that stabbed
His heart. Do you see this hand?
For one Horatio, if you ever knew him,
A youth, one that they hanged up in his father's gardens,
One that did force your valiant son to yield
While your more valiant son did take him prisoner.

VICEROY
Be deaf, my senses, I can hear no more.

KING
Fall heaven and cover us with thy sad ruins.

CASTILE
Roll all the world within thy pitchy cloud.

HIERONIMO

Now do I applaud what I have acted.

Nunc iners cadat manus.[1]

Now to express the rupture of my part,

First take my tongue, and afterward my heart.

He bites out his tongue.

---

1 Now let my dull hand fall (trans. Peter Parisi).

Appendix B: Documents in the Life of Thomas Kyd

1. **From Richard Mulcaster, *Positions, wherein those primitive circumstances be examined, which are necessary for the training up of children, either for skill in their book, or health in their body* (London, 1581), 138–39, 167, 185–86**

[Richard Mulcaster (1531–1611), the most famous educator of the age, headed the Merchant Taylors' School for 25 years until 1586. His two books of educational practice and philosophy, *The Elementary* (1582) and *Positions*, reveal not only his ardent support of crown and country, but also his support for the education of poor children (at least those who show ability), education for girls, and education in a social setting (as opposed to private tutorials for the wealthy). For Mulcaster, a child's interest and aptitude should play a role in deciding whether he or she should receive an education beyond what might now be called elementary school. However, he argues against universal access, since it would create an oversupply of educated citizens. As far as we know, Kyd's entire formal education came from the Merchant Taylors' School during Mulcaster's years. It is impossible to know—but tantalizing to consider—how Kyd, whose play has class and gender inequities at its heart, was influenced by the celebrated headmaster at his school.]

Education for rich and poor

Some doubt may rise here between the *rich* and *poor*, whether all *rich* and none *poor*, or but some in both may and ought to be set to learning. For all in both,[1] that is decided already, No: because the whole question concerneth these two kinds, as the whole commonweal standeth upon these two kinds. If all *rich* be excluded, *ability* would snuff; if all *poor* be restrained, then will *towardness* repine.[2] If *ability* set out some *rich* by private purses for private preferment, *towardness* will commend some *poor* to public provision for public service, so that if neither public in the *poor*, nor private in the *rich* do mar their own market, methink that were best, nay, that will be best, being ruled by their wits to conceive learning, and their disposition to prove virtuous.

---

1 For all rich and poor.
2 The inclination toward learning would feel discontent.

Education for women

When I did appoint the persons which were to receive the benefit of education, I did not exclude young *maidens*, and therefore seeing I made them one branch of my division, I must of force say somewhat more of them. A thing perhaps which some will think might well enough have been passed over with silence, as not belonging to my purpose, which profess the education of boys, and the general train in that kind. But seeing I begin so low as the first *Elementarie*,[1] wherein we see that young *maidens* be ordinarily trained, how could I seem not to see them being so apparently[2] taught?

... And so to prove that they are to be trained, I find four special reasons, whereof any one, much more all, may persuade any their most adversary,[3] much more me, which am for them with tooth and nail. The first is the *manner* and *custom* of my country, which allowing them to learn, will be loath to be contraried by any of her countrymen. The second is the *duty*, which we owe unto them, whereby we are charged in conscience not to leave them lame in that which is for them. The third is their own *towardness*, which God by nature would never have given them, to remain idle, or to small purpose. The fourth is the excellent *effects*[4] in that sex, when they have had the help of good bringing up, which commendeth the cause of such excellency, and wisheth us to cherish that tree, whose fruit is both so pleasant in taste and so profitable in trial. What can be said more? Our country doth allow it, our duty doth enforce it, their *aptness* calls for it, their *excellency* commands it.

Public and private education

I will therefore speak a little of this *private* train,[5] before I pass to the *education* of *gentlemen*. What do these two words import, *private education*? *Private* is that which hath respect in all circumstances to someone of choice, as *public* in all circumstances regardeth everyone alike. *Education* is the bringing up of one, not to live alone, but amongst others (because company is our natural cognizance) whereby he shall be best able to execute those doings in life which the state of his calling shall

---

1 Mulcaster's book in which he lays out an educational philosophy for younger students, especially in reading and writing.
2 Clearly.
3 Most opposed to education for girls.
4 Effectiveness, results.
5 Train of thought on private education, which to Mulcaster meant individual tutoring in a private home.

employ him unto, whether *public* abroad, or *private* at home, according unto the direction of his country whereunto he is born and oweth his whole service. All the functions here be public and regard everyone, even where the things do seem to be most private, because the main direction remaineth in the public, and the private must be squared, as it will best join with that. And yet we restrain *education* to *private*, all whose circumstances be singular to one. As if he that were brought up alone should also ever live alone; as if one should say, I will have you to deal with all, but never to see all. Your end shall be *public*; your mean shall be *private*, that is to say, such a mean as hath no mind to bring you to that end.... For how can *education* be *private*? It abuseth the name as it abuseth the thing.

2. Letter from Queen Elizabeth's Privy Council ordering the arrest of Dutch Church Libel suspects (11 May 1593), *Acts of the Privy Council of England*, n.s., vol. XXIV, ed. John Roche Dasent (London: His Majesty's Stationery Office by Mackie and Co., 1901), 221–22

[This letter, with its chilling call to round up suspects and use torture as needed, came from the Queen's Privy Council and probably led to the death of Thomas Kyd. It was prompted by signs posted in public places in May 1593 by angry Londoners, whose purpose was to intimidate Flemish and French immigrants. Fearing a riot, the Council, in a previous letter, ordered London officials to put a stop to it. When another poster, what's now called the Dutch Church Libel, appeared, the Privy Council issued this much sterner letter authorizing the arrest, search, and torture of suspects. While Kyd likely had no part in these events, he was arrested, imprisoned on charges of atheism, and tortured. While no records exist to show exactly the extent of his injuries, he died a little more than a year later.]

At the Star Chamber, on Friday, being the 11th of May, 1593

Present: Lord Archbishop, Lord Keeper,[1] *Lord Treasurer, Earl of Derby, Lord Buckhurst, Sir Robert Cecil, Sir John Fortescue.*

A letter to Sir R. Martin, Anthonie Ashley, Mr. Alderman Buckle, &c.[2] There have been of late diverse lewd and malicious libels set up within the city of London, among the which there is some set upon the wall

---

1 Sir John Puckering, addressee of Kyd's letters in Appendix B3.
2 Officials of the city of London.

of the Dutch churchyard that doth exceed the rest in lewdness, and for the discovery of the author and publisher thereof Her Majesty's pleasure is that some extraordinary pains and care be taken by the Commissioners appointed by the Lord Mayor for the examining such persons as may be in this case any way suspected. This shall be therefore to require and authorize you to make search and apprehend every person so to be suspected, and for that purpose to enter into all houses and places where any such may be remaining, and upon their apprehension to make like search in any the chambers, studies, chests or other like places for all manner of writings or papers that may give you light for the discovery of the libelers. And after you shall have examined the persons, if you shall find them duly to be suspected and they shall refuse to confess the truth, you shall by authority hereof put them to the torture in Bridewell,[1] and by the extremity thereof, to be used at such times and as often as you shall think fit, draw them to discover[2] their knowledge concerning the said libels. We pray you herein to use your uttermost travail and endeavor, to the end[3] the author of these seditious libels may be known and they punished according to their deserts, and this shall be your sufficient warrant. So &c.

3. Thomas Kyd, Two Letters to Sir John Puckering (1593)[4]

[After Kyd's release from prison in May 1593 and the death of fellow playwright Christopher Marlowe on 30 May, Kyd, desperate to rebuild his social standing, wrote two letters to Sir John Puckering (1544–96), Lord Keeper of the Great Seal, to ask him to intercede on his behalf with his patron, who had apparently found Kyd too much of a liability. The identity of this patron has never been settled, though scholars have advanced Fernando Stanley (Lord Strange), Fifth Earl of Derby (Nicholl 225); Henry Radcliffe, Earl of Sussex (Freeman 34); and Henry Herbert, Earl of Pembroke (Erne 229). Some readers have noted how quick Kyd is in the letters to shift blame to Marlowe, but Marlowe had already been targeted by the Privy Council (in letters dated 18 and 20 May) and was dead at Kyd's writing. What is clear is that Kyd had been frightened by his arrest and torture and was terrified, indeed "utterly undone," by the prospects the ordeal left him, especially if the atheism charges were to trigger further actions.

---

1 A notorious London prison.
2 Reveal.
3 Goal.
4 Transcription in Freeman, *Thomas Kyd* 181–83 (spelling and punctuation modernized for this edition).

In this context, it would not be unreasonable to expect Kyd to shift as much blame as possible to his old chamber mate, Kit Marlowe.]

a. First Letter

At my last being with your lordship, to entreat some speeches from you in my favor to my lord,[1] who (though I think he rest not doubtful of mine innocence) hath yet in his discreeter judgment feared to offend in his retaining me, without your honors' former privity,[2] so it is, now Right Honorable, that the denial of that favor (to my thought reasonable) hath moved me to conjecture some suspicion that your lordship holds me in concerning Atheism, a deadly thing which I was undeserved charged withal, and therefore have I thought it requisite, as well in duty to your lordship and the laws, as also in the fear of God and freedom of my conscience therein, to satisfy the world and you.

The first and most (though insufficient) surmise that ever was therein might be raised of me grew thus: When I was first suspected for that libel that concerned the state,[3] amongst those waste and idle papers (which I cared not for) and which unasked I did deliver up, were found some fragments of a disputation[4] touching that opinion affirmed by Marlowe to be his and shuffled with some of mine (unknown to me) by some occasion of our writing in one chamber two years since.

My first acquaintance with this Marlowe rose upon his bearing name to serve my lord, although his lordship never knew his service but in writing for his players, for never could my lord endure his name, or sight, when he had heard of his conditions,[5] nor would indeed the form of divine prayers used duly in his lordship's house have quadred[6] with such reprobates.

That I should love or be familiar friend with one so irreligious were very rare. When Tullie[7] saith *Digni sunt amicitia quib in ipsis inest causa cur diligantur*[8] which neither was in him, for person, qualities, or

---

1 To ask you to speak on my behalf with my patron.
2 Without your private counsel.
3 The Dutch Church Libel; see Appendix B2.
4 An academic exercise on the topic of the Arian Heresy, which was mistaken for a heretical statement by Kyd or Marlowe. It is reprinted in Boas (cx–cxii).
5 Moral character, in the sense of *OED* 11a.
6 "Squared, agreed" (Marlowe 337, fn 22).
7 Marcus Tullius Cicero (106–43 BCE), Roman statesman and philosopher.
8 Those who in themselves possess the reason why they should be loved are worthy of friendship (trans. Peter Parisi).

honesty, besides he was intemperate and of a cruel heart, the very contraries to which my greatest enemies will say by me.

It is not to be numbered amongst the best conditions of men to tax or to upbraid the dead, *Quia mortui non mordent*,[1] but thus much have I (with your lordship's favor) dared in the greatest cause, which is to clear myself of being thought an atheist, which some will swear he was.

For more assurance that I was not of that vile opinion, let it but please your lordship to inquire of such as he conversed withal, that is (as I am given to understand), with Harriot, Warner, Royden[2] and some stationers in Paul's churchyard, whom I in no sort can accuse nor will excuse by reason of his company, of whose consent if I had been, no question but I also should have been of their consort,[3] for *ex minimo vestigio artifex agnoscit artificem*.[4]

Of my religion and life, I have already given some instance to the late commissioners and of my reverend meaning[5] to the state, although perhaps my pains and underserved tortures felt by some would have engendered more impatience when less by far hath driven so many *imo extra caulas*,[6] which it shall never do with me.

But whatsoever I have felt, Right Honorable, this is my request, not for reward but, in regard of my true innocence, that it would please your lordships so t [...]⁷ the same and me, as I may still retain the favors of my lord, whom I have served almost these six years now, in credit until now and now am utterly undone without herein be somewhat done[8] for my recovery, for I do know his lordship holds your honors and the state in that due reverence, as he would no way move[9] the least suspicion of his loves and cares both towards her sacred majesty, your lordships, and the laws whereof, when time shall serve, I shall give greater instance which I have observed.

As for the libel laid unto my charge, I am resolved with receiving of the sacrament to satisfy your lordships and the world that I was neither

---

1 Because the dead do not bite (trans. Peter Parisi).
2 Thomas Harriot (or Hariot; c. 1560–1621), Walter Warner (1563–1643), and Matthew Roydon (c. 1564–1622), three friends of Marlowe reputed to hold heterodox opinions (Nicholl 80).
3 Had I been in agreement with them (consent), I would have consorted with them.
4 The craftsman recognizes (a fellow) craftsman from the smallest trace (trans. Peter Parisi).
5 Respectful intentions.
6 On the contrary, outside the sheepfold.
7 The manuscript is scraped and unreadable here. Martin suggests *to use* (Marlowe 339).
8 Unless I find some help.
9 Stir up.

agent nor consenting thereunto. Howbeit if some outcast Ismael[1] for want or of his own dispose to lewdness, have with pretext of duty or religion, or to reduce himself to that he was not born unto, by any way incensed your lordships to suspect me, I shall beseech in all humility and in the fear of God that it will please your lordships but to censure[2] me as I shall prove myself, and to repute them as they are indeed, *Cum totius injustitiae nulla capitalior sit quam eorum, qui tum cum maxime fallunt id agunt ut viri boni esse videantur;*[3] for doubtless even then your lordships shall be sure to break [...][4] their lewd designs and see into the truth, when but their lies that herein have accused me shall be examined and ripped up effectually, so may I chance with Paul to live and shake the viper of my hand into the fire[5] for which the ignorant suspect me guilty of the former shipwreck. And thus (for now I fear me I grow tedious) assuring your good lordship that if I knew any whom I could justly accuse of that damnable offence to the aweful majesty of God or of that other mutinous sedition toward the state I would as willingly reveal them as I would request your lordships' better thoughts of me that never have offended you.
Your lordships' most humble and all duties,
Th Kydde

b. Second Letter

Pleaseth it your honorable lordship touching Marlowe's monstrous opinions as I cannot but with an aggrieved conscience think on him or them so can I but particularize[6] few in the respect of them that kept him greater company, howbeit in discharge of duty both towards God, your lordships,[7] and the world thus much have I thought good briefly to discover[8] in all humbleness.

First, it was his custom when I knew him first, and as I hear say he continued it, in table talk or otherwise to jest at the divine scriptures,

---

1 An outcast and hostile person, based on the son of Abraham in Genesis 16.
2 Judge.
3 Since, of all injustice, none is graver than that of those who, at the moment they most deceive, do it so that they seem to be good men (trans. Peter Parisi).
4 The manuscript is unreadable here. Martin suggests *up* (Marlowe 339).
5 In the New Testament, Paul, having just survived shipwreck, shook a snake from his hand without being harmed, thus showing bystanders that he was no criminal and not the cause of the wreck (Acts 28).
6 Identify.
7 The Privy Council.
8 Reveal.

gibe at prayers, and strive in argument to frustrate and confute what hath been spoke or writ by prophets and such holy men.

1. He would report St. John to be our savior Christ's Alexis.[1] I cover[2] it with reverence and trembling, that is, that Christ did love him with an extra-ordinary love.
2. That for me to write a poem of St. Paul's conversion, as I was determined, he said would be as if I should go write a book of fast and loose, esteeming Paul a juggler.[3]
3. That the prodigal child's portion was but four nobles,[4] he held his purse so near the bottom in all pictures, and that it either was a jest or else four nobles then was thought a great patrimony not thinking it a fable.[5]
4. That things esteemed to be done by divine power might have as well been done by observation of men, all which he would so suddenly take slight occasion[6] to slip out as I and many others in regard of his other rashness in attempting sudden privy injuries to men did overslip[7] though often reprehend him for it and, for which god is my witness, as well by my lord's commandment as in hatred of his life and thoughts I left and did refrain his company.

He would persuade with men of quality to go unto the King of Scots whether[8] I hear Royden[9] is gone and where, if he[10] had lived, he told me when I saw him last he meant to be.

4. Thomas Kyd, Dedication to Robert Garnier's *Cornelia* (London, 1594)

[The following document is Thomas Kyd's dedication of his translation of *Cornelia* (first performed in 1573), by Robert Garnier (1544–90). It is not clear why Kyd chose to dedicate the work to nineteen-year-

---

1 Object of homosexual desire, as the boy Alexis is to the Shepherd Corydon in Virgil's Second *Eclogue*.
2 Conceal, screen.
3 A cheat, one who operates the old game "fast and loose" to deceive players.
4 Coins.
5 Here Kyd suggests that Marlowe expressed doubts about the New Testament story of the Prodigal Son.
6 Least opportunity.
7 Overlook.
8 Where.
9 Matthew Roydon (see above, p. 194, note 2).
10 Marlowe.

old Lady Bridget Fitzwalter, Countess of Sussex. Freeman suggests a connection to her father-in-law Henry Radcliffe, fourth Earl of Sussex (*Thomas Kyd* 34), while Erne suggests that Kyd, desperate for support after his recent arrest, wrote the dedication in the hope of finding new patronage (211). Perhaps Kyd thought a translation of a work by the famous French playwright Garnier, especially a play presented in English for private reading rather than for the rough and tumble of the public stage, would be appreciated by an aristocratic lady and potential patron. In any case, beyond the self-effacement conventional in dedications, what comes through is the voice of a man broken by recent events but hopeful enough to promise another work the next summer. Kyd wrote this dedication in the few months between his arrest in May 1593 and its publication in January 1594.]

To the virtuously Noble, and rightly honored Lady, the Countess of Sussex.

Having no leisure[1] (most noble Lady) but such as evermore[2] is travailed[3] with th'afflictions of the mind, than which the world affords no greater misery, it may be wondered at by some, how I durst[4] undertake a matter of this moment, which both requireth cunning,[5] rest and opportunity, but chiefly, that I would attempt the dedication of so rough unpolished a work, to the survey of your so worthy self.

But being well instructed in your noble and heroic dispositions, and perfectly assured of your honorable favors past (though neither making needle's glozes of the one, nor spoiling paper with the other's pharisaical embroidery),[6] I have presumed upon your true conceit and entertainment of these small endeavors,[7] that thus I purposed to make known, my memory of you and them to be immortal.

---

1 Opportunity.
2 Always.
3 Tormented.
4 Dared to.
5 Erudition.
6 A convoluted passage, which means *I know well your honor and your generosity, but I won't bother you with my trifling comments (needle's glozes) on your honor nor waste paper with inflated comments (pharisaical embroidery) on your generosity.* Underlying the language is the metaphor of the needle being too trifling and the embroidery too elaborate to appropriately express anything of value to such a worthy patroness. Kyd chose this metaphor in an age when ladies of standing practiced and appreciated the art of fine needlework.
7 I have been presumptuous to impose on you this unpolished work and its dedication.

A fitter present for a patroness so well accomplished, I could not find, than this fair president[1] of honor, magnanimity, and love. Wherein, what grace that excellent Garnier hath lost by my default, I shall beseech your honor to repair, with the regard of those so bitter times, and privy broken passions that I endured in the writing it.

And so vouchsafe but the passing of a winter's week with desolate Cornelia,[2] I will assure your ladyship my next summer's better travail, with the tragedy of Portia.[3] And ever spend one hour of the day in some kind service to your honor, and another of the night in wishing you all happiness. Perpetually thus devoting my poor self

Your honor's in all humbleness,

T. K.

---

1 Kyd imagines the book itself as the presiding spirit of these values (in the sense of *OED* 1b).

2 Condescend to spend a week reading *Cornelia*.

3 *Porcia* (1568), another play by Garnier.

Appendix C: The Question of Revenge

1. From the Epistle of the Apostle Paul to the Romans, in *The Geneva Bible* (London, 1583)

[England during Elizabeth's reign and during Kyd's lifetime was a Protestant country, and the Bible in English carried enormous weight in public discourse. The following passage in Paul's letter to the Romans (12:10–21) was cited often by those who, like the Elizabethan government, wished to discourage private retribution.]

10 Be affectioned to love one another with brotherly love. In giving honor, go one before another,

11 Not slothful to do service, fervent in spirit: serving the Lord,

12 Rejoicing in hope, patient in tribulation, continuing in prayer,

13 Distributing unto the necessities of the saints: giving yourselves to hospitality.

14 Bless them which persecute you; bless (I say) and curse not.

15 Rejoice with them that rejoice, and weep with them that weep.

16 Be of like affection one towards another: be not high-minded, but make yourselves equal to them of the lower sort. Be not wise in[1] yourselves.

17 Recompense to[2] no man evil for evil; procure things honest in the sight of all men.

18 If it be possible, as much as in you is, have peace with all men.

19 Dearly beloved, avenge not yourselves, but give place[3] unto wrath: for it is written, vengeance is mine: I will repay, saith the Lord.

20 Therefore, if thine enemy hunger, feed him; if he thirst, give him drink, for in so doing, thou shalt heap[4] coals of fire on his head.

21 Be not overcome of evil, but overcome evil with goodness.

2. From Seneca, *Thyestes. Seneca His Ten Tragedies Translated into English*, trans. Jasper Heywood (first century CE; London, 1581)

[The Roman playwright Seneca (4 BCE–65 CE) was celebrated and imitated by Elizabethan writers. This passage illustrates Seneca's ap-

---

1 [*Geneva Bible* note:] That is, in your own conceit.

2 Repay.

3 Give ground.

4 [*Geneva Bible* note:] For either thou shalt win him with thy benefice, or else his conscience shall bear him witness that God's burning wrath hangeth over him.

proach to revenge tragedy, which takes place on a mythical landscape. Here, Atreus, inspired by the story of his father Pelops being slain and fed to the gods, comes up with a plan to exact revenge on his brother Thyestes by arranging a feast at which Thyestes would unwittingly eat his own children. The passage also illustrates Jasper Heywood's fourteen-syllable lines, usually called "fourteeners," a clumsy verse form that was displaced by Marlowe's and Kyd's crisp and powerful blank verse, which ushered in English Renaissance drama.]

Act 2, Scene 1[1]

...

ATREUS
Tell thou which way were best to bring that cruel head to death?

SERVANT
245 Through-pierced with sword, let him be slain and yield his hateful
    breath.

ATREUS
Thou speak'st of th'end, but I him would oppress with greater pain.
Let tyrants vex with torment more;[2] should ever in my reign
Be gentle death?

SERVANT
            Doth piety[3] in thee prevail no whit?

ATREUS
Depart thou hence all piety, if in this house as yet
250 Thou ever wert! And now let all the flock of Furies[4] dire
And full of strife, Erinyes, come, and double brands of fire
Megaera shaking, for not yet enough with fury great
And rage both burn my boiling breast. It ought to be replete
With monster more.

SERVANT
            What mischief new, dost thou in rage, provide?

---

1   This extract is from lines 244–79 of the original play.
2   Let powerful rulers (referring to himself) inflict greater torment.
3   Mercy.
4   Greek goddesses of revenge, also known as the Erinyes, including Megaera
    mentioned two lines below.

ATREUS

255   Not such a one as may the mean of wonted grief abide.[1]
No guilt will I forbear, nor none may be enough despite.[2]

SERVANT
What, sword?

ATREUS
      Too little that.

SERVANT
              What, fire?

ATREUS
                        And that is yet too light.

SERVANT
What weapon then shall sorrow such find fit to work thy will?

ATREUS
Thyestes' self.

SERVANT
          Then ire itself, yet that's a greater ill.

ATREUS
260   I grant, a tumbling tumult quakes within my bosoms low
And round it rolls. I moved am and wot[3] not where unto,
But drawn I am; from bottom deep the roaring soil doth cry,
The day so fair with thunder sounds, and house as all from high
Were rent, from roof and rafters' cracks, and lares[4] turned about
265   Have wried[5] their sight: so be it, so be it, let mischief such be sought,
As ye, O gods, would fear.

SERVANT
             What thing seekest thou bring to pass?

---

1   Not one that most people would be untroubled by.
2   No guilt will I avoid, and yet no action will be enough.
3   Know.
4   Household gods.
5   Turned aside (*OED* 1).

ATREUS

I note what greater thing my mind, and more than wont it was,[1]
Above the reach that men are wont to work, begins to swell[2]
And stayeth[3] with slothful hands. What thing it is I cannot tell,
270 But great it is. Be it so, my mind now in this feat proceed.
For Atreus and Thyestes both, it were a worthy deed.
Let each of us the crime commit. The Thracian house did see
Such wicked tables once. I grant the mischief great to be,
But done ere[4] this. Some greater guilt and mischief more, let ire
275 Find out. The stomach[5] of thy son, O father, thou inspire,
And sister eke.[6] Like is the cause; assist me with your power,
And drive my hand; let greedy parents all his babes devour,
And glad to rent[7] his children be, and on their limbs to feed.
Enough, and well it is devised; this pleaseth me indeed....

3. From "A Sermon against Contention and Brawling" (1547), *Certain Sermons or Homilies Appointed to be Read in Churches in the Time of Queen Elizabeth of Famous Memory* (London, 1687), 143–44, 149, 150

[*Certain Sermons*, or *The Book of Homilies*, was first published in 1547 during the reign of Edward VI (r. 1547–53), under the supervision of his stalwart Protestant bishop Thomas Cranmer (1489–1556). The Elizabethan government endorsed the original twelve homilies and added to the collection, publishing a total of 21 in 1571. The homilies, written to be read aloud in churches to instruct citizens in official theological positions, have since become a gold mine of cultural information about Elizabethan England, albeit from a state-sanctioned perspective. The excerpts below are from Homily 12, which was written in three parts.]

From Part 2

For to speak well against evil, cometh of the Spirit of God, but to render evil for evil, cometh of the contrary spirit. And he that cannot temper, nor rule, his own anger, is but weak and feeble, and rather more like a

---

1 Greater than the usual ideas.
2 Reading *swell* as transitive verb (*OED* 8) yields the basic logic of the passage: *My mind begins to swell a greater thing.*
3 Stops.
4 Before.
5 Passion, desire, but also playing on stomach as a digestive organ, since his plan is to arrange a cannibalistic feast.
6 Too.
7 Tear.

woman or a child than a strong man. For the true strength and manliness is to overcome wrath, and to despise injuries, and other men's foolishness. And besides this, he that shall despise[1] the wrong done unto him by his enemy, every man shall perceive that it was spoken or done without cause. Whereas contrarily, he that doth fume and chafe at it, shall help the cause of his adversary, giving suspicion that the thing is true. And in so going about to revenge evil, we show ourselves to be evil; and while we punish and revenge another man's folly, we double and augment our own folly. But many pretenses find they that be willful, to color their impatience.[2] Mine enemy, say they, is not worthy to have gentle words or deeds, being so full of malice or frowardness.[3] The less he is worthy, the more art thou therefore allowed of God, and the more art thou commended of Christ, for whose sake thou shouldest render good for evil, because he hath commanded thee, and also deserved that thou shouldest so do.

From Part 3

When our infamy, or the reproach that is done unto us, is joined with the peril of many, then it is necessary, in answering, to be quick and ready. For we read that many holy men of good zeal have sharply and fiercely both spoken and answered tyrants and evil men; which sharp words came not of anger, rancor or malice, or desire of vengeance, but of a fervent desire to bring them to the true knowledge of God, and from ungodly living, by an earnest and sharp rebuke and chiding.

...

This zeal hath been so fervent in many good men, that it hath stirred them not only to speak bitter and eager words but also to do things which might seem to some to be cruel, but indeed they be very just, charitable, and godly, because they were not done of ire, malice, or contentious mind, but of a fervent mind, to the glory of God, and the correction of sin, executed by men called to that office. For in this zeal our lord Jesus Christ did drive with a whip the buyers and sellers out of the temple.[4] In this zeal Moses brake[5] the two tables which he had

---

1 Disregard.
2 I.e., those stubbornly set on revenge can find many reasons to justify their lack of patience.
3 Unreasonableness.
4 The story of Jesus driving the money changers out of the temple appears in all four gospels of the New Testament.
5 Past tense of *break*.

received at God's hand, when he saw the Israelites dancing about the calf, and cause to be killed twenty four thousand of his own people.[1] In this zeal Phineas the son of Eleazer did thrust through with his sword Zimri and Cosby, whom he found together joined in the act of uncleanness.[2]

4. From Richard Jones, *The Book of Honor and Arms* (London, 1590), 2–3

[Jones's book represents an alternative mode of thought in Elizabethan culture. Where religious and civil authorities typically express strong opposition to private revenge, Jones expresses impatience with such proscriptions and presents a complex system of honor to guide gentlemen on when to take action against those who have insulted or injured them. At the heart of his discussion is a tension between personal honor, which in certain circumstances demands action to repay an injury, and civil authority, which typically forbids such action in the name of civic order. Richard Jones (fl. 1564–1613) was a London printer who signed the book's preface; the book itself has an anonymous author, though it may be the work of fencing master Vincentio Saviolo (d. 1598/99).]

To the Reader:

True it is, that the Christian law willeth men to be of so perfect patience, as not only to endure injurious words, but also quietly to suffer every force and violence. Notwithstanding, forsomuch as[3] none (or very few men) have attained such perfection, the laws of all Nations, for avoiding further inconveniences, and the manifestation of truth, have (among many other trials), permitted that such questions as could not be civilly proved by confession, witness, or other circumstances, should receive judgment by fight and combat, supposing that God (who only knoweth the secret thoughts of all men) would give victory to him that justly adventured his life, for truth, Honor, and Justice.[4]

Seeing then that all humane laws have permitted the trial of arms, and that every injurious action not repulsed is by common consent of all martial minds holden a thing dishonorable, infamous, and

---

1 Exodus 32.
2 Numbers 25.
3 In consideration that.
4 Jones here describes single combat, which was still legal at this time but not practiced.

reproachful, it cannot be, but at some times and occasions, such questions and quarrels shall arise as necessarily must receive trial by the sword. And Cicero[1] saith, that he who repulseth not an injury, being able, offendeth no less than if he had abandoned his friends, parents and country. By these reasons appeareth that the trial by arms is not only natural, but also necessary and allowable. Notwithstanding, for that the vulgar sort[2] (and many right noble also) be ignorant what are the true causes requiring trial of arms, and what words or deeds are of such quality as ought be repulsed or revenged. I have at the earnest requests and often desires of very honorable friends (by way of abbreviation) reduced into this small volume all causes of quarrel or combat, the nature of injuries and repulses, the equality and disequality of men who may be challenged, and for what respects challenges ought be refused, with many other things in matter of Honor and Arms worthy to be known and considered.

And albeit I am not ignorant that public combats are in this age either rarely or never granted, yet, for that (as is before said) no providence can prevent the questions and quarrels that daily happen among gentlemen and others professing arms, it shall not be amiss, but rather behoveful,[3] that all men should be fully informed what injury is and how to repulse it, when to fight, when to rest satisfied, what is honor and good reputation, how it is gained, and by what means the same is kept and preserved, which was the respect that the Earl Balthazar Castilio in his *Book of the Courtier*,[4] doth among other qualities requirable in a gentleman, specially advise he should be skillful in the knowing of honor and causes of quarrel.

This book doth not incite men to unadvised fight, or needless revenge (as some simple wit may surmise) but informeth the true means how to shun all offences, or, being offended, sheweth the order of revenge and repulse, according unto Christian knowledge and due respect of honor.

5. From William Westerman, *Two Sermons of Assise* (London, 1600)

[An Oxford graduate and member of the clergy, William Westerman (d. 1622) published several sermons and later served as chaplain to the Archbishop of Canterbury, George Abbot (1562–1633). Westerman preached his two sermons at the assize (official session) of jus-

---

1 Marcus Tullius Cicero (106–43 BCE), Roman statesman and philosopher.
2 Commoners, as opposed to noblemen.
3 Useful.
4 Baldesar Castiglione, *The Book of the Courtier* (1528); see Appendix E1.

tices of Hertford, the first of which, *A Prohibition of Revenge*, supplies the passage below. One would' expect a sermon at such a gathering to make a law-and-order argument for leaving revenge to official processes, as Westerman does by analyzing word by word the prohibition against revenge in Paul's letter to the Romans (Appendix C1). He also seems to reinforce his argument with references to the English stage, where the tragedies of revenge, the genre started by Kyd's play, were popular and numerous.]

A Prohibition of Revenge

Are we then beloved of the lord, and of those that are his dear children, though we be maligned and hated, and oppressed of others? O let us keep this haven of refuge and succor open, that when the world is a sea of troubles[1] raging against us, we may shoot ourselves into the same and give back into the comfortable arms of his love. Let us rather lose our longing desire of revenge, than the savor of that lord, by whom we are so dearly beloved.

Thus doth the Apostle[2] sweeten his sharp message, like a lover, giving a *faithful wound* for health and not for hurt,[3] in tender regard to preserve his clients (like a good counselor) in the everlasting possession of their souls by patience. As Paul, so I would all Ambassadors of heavenly peace would keep this note of love, that one string sounding right might serve to set all the other in tune. And thus much for this sweet title: *Dearly beloved*, which I desire of the lord may make such melody in your hearts at this present time that, all desire of revenge and bitter passions of the mind assuaged, you may be transformed into such sincere keepers, counselors, and seekers of peace, that this title may remain forever verified in your souls, *Dearly beloved*. Now followeth the restraint: *avenge not yourselves*. Revenge is a rash proceeding to the punishment of injuries received, without law, without order, without authority. In every private man there be three instruments ready to further this revenge: the heart, the tongue, the hand.

...

The apostle here speaketh in terms of love to all: but how shall we speak? Or what style shall we use to the rufflers[4] and hacksters[5] of our

---

1 Cf. Shakespeare, *Hamlet* 3.1.61.
2 Paul.
3 By challenging his readers for their own good.
4 Rogues
5 Cutthroats.

age? Shall we call them beloved? That were out of fashion with such affectate[1] malcontents that take a pride to be partakers of the curse of Ismael: *that had his hand up against every man, and every man's hand against him* (Genesis 16:12).[2] Shall we call them Christians and so teach them their duty? That name fitteth not the tragical humor, and stage-like behavior of our days, wherein every novice, like a Fury,[3] learns to cry *Revenge*, to offer the stab, to threaten the pistol, and in their advantage not to spare, no, not a brother, but *to strike him as Caine, the first disciple of the devil did Abel*, not a reconciled friend but to wound *him traitorously as Joab did Abner* (2 Samuel 3:17).[4] Alas, how is that precious accompt[5] forgotten which the lord maketh and demandeth of *man and beast, for shedding of man's blood* (Genesis 9:5) with an unprivileged[6] sword and a private anger! What small reckoning is made to deface the image of God or tear the flesh of ourselves as though men were become wolves and dragons to their own kind! Is that valor and fortitude so to fear another man's life that thou canst not live in quiet till thou hast seen his death? Is it manhood to be monstrous and cruel, like the old giants; or savage like beasts of prey?

6. From Ben Jonson, Introduction to *Bartholomew Fair*, *The Works of Benjamin Jonson*, vol. 2 (1614; London, 1640)

[Jonson (1572–1637) was the premier comic and satiric playwright of the Jacobean stage. This passage from *Bartholomew Fair*, delivered by a Scrivener, part of a satirical contract between the author and his audience, illustrates the enduring appeal of revenge tragedy. Jonson sends up those audience members whose tastes are so "constant" that they think of Kyd's *Spanish Tragedy* (Jeronimo) or Shakespeare's *Titus Andronicus* as still the best plays. Also, if the Scrivener is accurate in his estimate of 25 or 30 years since those plays were current (from 1614 when *Bartholomew Fair* was first performed), this would place Kyd's play around 1584–89, which generally agrees with other evidence used to date the play.]

It is also agreed, that every man here, exercise his own Judgment, and not censure by *Contagion*, or upon *trust*, from another's voice, or face,

---

1 Artificial, perhaps like the modern phrases *so-called* or *puffed up*.
2 In the passage of Genesis, Ishmael is cursed to live a life of hostility.
3 Avenging goddesses of Greek myth.
4 Cain killed his brother Abel in jealousy (Genesis 4), and Joab killed Abner in revenge (2 Samuel 3).
5 Reckoning.
6 Unauthorized by the law.

that sits by him, be he never so first, in the *Commission of Wit*: As also, that he be fixed and settled in his censure, that what he approves, or not approves today, he will do the same tomorrow, and if tomorrow, the next day, and so the next week (if need be) and not to be brought about by any that sits on the *Bench* with him, though they indict, and arraign *Plays* daily. He that will swear, *Jeronimo* or *Andronicus* are the best plays, yet, shall pass unexcepted at,[1] here, as a man whose Judgment shows it is constant, and hath stood still, these five and twenty, or thirty years. Though it be an *Ignorance*, it is a virtuous and stayed ignorance; and next to *truth*, a confirmed error does well; such a one the *Author* knows where to find him.

7. Sir Francis Bacon, "Of Revenge," *Essays or Counsels, Civil and Moral* (London, 1625)

[As a philosopher, theorist, aristocrat, and magistrate, Bacon (1561–1626) had a hand in nearly every intellectual endeavor of Elizabethan and Jacobean England. His *Essays*, which he revised and expanded throughout his life, broke new ground in prose style and as a literary form. "Of Revenge," reproduced here as published in the 1625 edition, is an elegant, largely secular, argument against private revenge (the kind most often seen on the English stage), but it did not appear until near the end of the revenge tragedy era.]

Revenge is a kind of wild justice, which the more man's nature runs to, the more ought law to weed it out. For as for the first wrong, it doth but offend the law; but the revenge of that wrong putteth the law out of office. Certainly, in taking revenge, a man is but even with his enemy; but in passing it over,[2] he is superior: For it is a prince's part to pardon. And Solomon, I am sure, saith, *It is the glory of a man to pass by an offence.*[3] That which is past is gone, and irrevocable; and wise men have enough to do, with things present, and to come. Therefore, they do but trifle with[4] themselves that labor in past matters. There is no man, doth a wrong for the wrong's sake, but thereby to purchase himself profit, or pleasure, or honor, or the like. Therefore why should I be angry with a man for loving himself better than me? And if any man should do wrong, merely out of ill nature, why? Yet it is but like the thorn, or brier, which prick, and scratch, because they can do no

---

1 Without exception.
2 Refraining from taking revenge.
3 Paraphrased from Proverbs 19:11, a book traditionally ascribed to Solomon, a Biblical king celebrated for his wisdom.
4 Fool.

other. The most tolerable sort of revenge is for those wrongs which there is no law to remedy. But then, let a man take heed the revenge be such as there is no law to punish. Else, a man's enemy, is still before hand, and it is two for one.[1] Some, when they take revenge, are desirous the party should know whence it commeth. This is the more generous. For the delight seemeth to be not so much in doing the hurt as in making the party repent. But base and crafty cowards are like the arrow that flyeth in the dark. Cosmus Duke of Florence,[2] had a desperate[3] saying, against perfidious or neglecting friends, as if those wrongs were unpardonable: *You shall read* (saith he) *that we are commanded to forgive our enemies; but you never read that we are commanded to forgive our friends.* But yet the spirit of Job[4] was in a better tune: *Shall we* (saith he) *take good at God's hands, and not be content to take evil also?* And so of friends in a proportion. This is certain: that a man that studieth revenge keeps his own wounds green, which otherwise would heal, and do well. Public revenges, are, for the most part, fortunate; as that for the death of Caesar; for the death of Pertinax; for the death of Henry the Third of France;[5] and many more. But in private revenges it is not so. Nay rather, vindicative[6] persons live the life of witches, who as they are mischievous, so end they infortunate.

---

1   Revengers who break the law in the act of revenging are then subject to both private retaliation and the law.
2   Cosimo de' Medici (1389–1464).
3   Hopeless.
4   The central character in the biblical book of Job.
5   Julius Caesar (100–44 BCE) and Pertinax (126–193 CE) were Roman emperors; Henry III (r. 1574–89) was a king of France. All three died by political assassination.
6   Vindictive.

Appendix D: Violence and Entertainment in Elizabethan England

1. From Robert Langham, *A Letter, Wherein part of the entertainment unto the Queen's Majesty at Killingworth Castle in Warwickshire in this summer's progress, 1575, is signified* (1575), 21–24

[This letter was written by Robert Langham (c. 1535–80), a minor figure at court, to describe Queen Elizabeth's progress to Kenilworth Castle for a lavish entertainment put on by her favorite, Robert Dudley, Earl of Leicester (c. 1532–88). R.J.P. Kuin notes that the letter, which was ostensibly addressed to Langham's friend Humphry Martyn, may have been "circulated among a group of friends" (15). Whatever the purpose, the letter captures the delight a spectator would take in what is now considered the cruel practice of bear-baiting, here presented mockingly as a legal proceeding between bears and dogs. Queen Elizabeth herself was said to enjoy bear-baiting, as this letter attests, since the entertainments were designed specifically to please her.]

Thursday, the fourteenth of this July and the sixth day of her majesty's coming, a great sort of bandogs[1] were there tied in the outer court, and thirteen bears in the inner. Whosoever made the panel,[2] there were enough for a quest[3] and one for challenge an[4] need were. A wight[5] of great wisdom and gravity seemed their foreman to be, had it come to a jury. But it fell out that they were roused to appear there upon no such matter, but only to answer to an ancient quarrel between them and the bandogs, in a cause of controversy that hath long depended,[6] been obstinately full often debated with sharp and biting arguments a-both sides, and could never be decided. Grown now to so marvelous a malice that with spiteful upbraids and uncharitable chafings, always they fret, as far as anywhere t'one can hear, see, or smell t'other, and indeed at utter deadly fohod.[7] Many a maimed

---

1 Originally, a dog tied up, but later coming to mean mastiff or bloodhound (*OED*).
2 A deliberative body.
3 Inquest.
4 If.
5 Person.
6 Remained suspended, as in a legal delay (*OED* 7).
7 Deadly feud, seeming "to reflect a popular etymology: foe-hood" (Kuin 92).

member (God wot[1]), bloody face, and a torn coat hath the quarrel cost between them, so far likely the less yet now to be appeased, as there wants[2] not partaker to back them a-both sides.

Well sir, the bears were brought forth into the court, the dogs set to them to argue the points even face to face. They had learned counsel also a-both parts, what may they be counted partial that are retained but a to side:[3] I ween[4] no. Very fierce both t'one and t'other eager in argument: if the dog in pleading would pluck the bear by the throat, the bear with travers[5] would claw him again by the scalp, confess, and, a list, but avoid a could not that was bound to the bar:[6] and his counsel told him that it could be to him no policy[7] in pleading.

Therefore thus with fending and proving, with plucking and tugging, scratching and biting, by plain tooth and nail a to side and t'other such expense of blood and leather was there between them, as a month's licking, I ween, will not recover, and yet remain as far out[8] as ever they were.

It was a sport very pleasant of these beasts, to see the bear with his pink eyes leering after his enemy's approach, the nimbleness and wait[9] of the dog to take his advantage, and the force and experience of the bear again to avoid the assaults. If he were bitten in one place, how he would pinch in another to get free, that if he were taken once, then what shift,[10] with biting, with clawing, with roaring, tossing, and tumbling he would work to wend[11] himself from them, and when he was loose, to shake his ears twice or thrice with the blood and the slaver about his physiognomy,[12] was a matter of a goodly relief.

---

1 Knows.
2 Lacks. The matter is unlikely to be settled because backers exist on both sides, likely in the form of spectators laying wagers.
3 On one side (Kuin 92).
4 Think.
5 A legal term for a formal denial (Kuin 92).
6 The bear wanted ("a list") to avoid the dog, but, being bound to the stake ("bar"), could not.
7 Strategy.
8 As far from agreement.
9 Timing.
10 Action or effort.
11 Turn.
12 Face.

2. From William Harrison, *Description of England. The First and Second Volumes of Chronicles* (London, 1586), 184

[This work by William Harrison (1535–93) is a rare and valuable source of information about everyday life in Elizabethan England. His matter-of-fact descriptions of punishments for malefactors highlight the extreme violence, essentially state-sponsored revenge, that the accused faced in early modern England. They also highlight class inequities, whereby convicted nobility escaped the horror of being drawn, hanged, and quartered and were instead beheaded, a comparably easier death.]

Book 2, Chapter 11: "Of sundrie kinds of punishment appointed for malefactors"

In cases of felony, manslaughter, robbery, murther,[1] rape, piracy, and such capital crimes as are not reputed for treason or hurt of the estate,[2] our sentence pronounced upon the offender is to hang till he be dead. For of other punishments used in other countries we have no knowledge or use, and yet so few grievous crimes committed with us as elsewhere in the world. To use torment also or question by pain and torture in these common cases with us is greatly abhorred, sith[3] we are found always to be such as despise death, and yet abhor to be tormented, choosing rather frankly to open our minds than yield our bodies unto such servile halings[4] and tearings as are used in other countries.[5] And this is one cause wherefore our condemned persons do go so cheerfully to their deaths, for our nation is free, stout, haughty, prodigal of life and blood, as Sir Thomas Smith[6] saith (lib. 2. cap. 25 *de republica*) and therefore cannot in any wise digest to be used as villains and slaves, in suffering continual beating, servitude, and servile torments. No, our jailers are guilty of felony by an old law of the land, if they torment any prisoner committed to their custody for the revealing of his complices.[7]

---

1 Murder.
2 State, commonwealth.
3 Since.
4 Violent draggings.
5 Torture was in fact practiced in England, and Thomas Kyd was one of its victims (see Appendices B2–B4).
6 Author (1513–77) of *De Republica Anglorum* (published posthumously in 1583).
7 Associates.

The greatest and most grievous punishment used in England, for such as offend against the state, is drawing from the prison to the place of execution upon an hardle[1] or sled, where they are hanged till they be half dead, and then taken down and quartered alive, after that their members[2] and bowels are cut from their bodies and thrown into a fire provided near hand within their own sight, even for the same purpose. Sometimes, if the trespass be not the more heinous, they are suffered to hang till they be quite dead. And whensoever any of the nobility are convicted of high treason by their peers, that is to say, equals (for an inquest of yeomen passeth not upon them, but only of the lords of the parliament) this manner of their death is converted into the loss of their heads only, notwithstanding that the sentence do run after the former order. In trial of cases concerning treason, felony, or any other grievous crime not confessed, the party accused doth yield, if he be a nobleman, to be tried by an inquest (as I have said) and his peers. If a gentleman, by gentlemen; and an inferior, by God and by the country, to wit, the yeomanry (for combat or battle[3] is not greatly in use) and being condemned of felony, manslaughter, etc., he is eftsoons[4] hanged by the neck till he be dead and then cut down and buried. But if he be convicted of willful murther, done either upon pretended malice, or in any notable robbery, he is either hanged alive in chains near the place where the fact was committed (or else upon compassion taken, first strangled with a rope) and so continueth till his bones consume to nothing. We have use neither of the wheel nor of the bar,[5] as in other countries; but when willful manslaughter is perpetrated, beside hanging, the offender hath his right hand commonly stricken off before or near unto the place where the act was done, after which he is led forth to the place of execution, and there put to death according to the law.

3. From Philip Stubbes, *The Anatomy of Abuses* (London, 1595), 133–35

[In his *Anatomy*, Stubbes (c. 1555–c. 1610), a zealous Elizabethan moralist, heaps scorn on a broad range of social practices in England. Here, the object of his ire is bear-baiting, a form of entertainment in which a bear was tied to a stake and attacked by large English mastiffs.

---

1 A frame used to drag criminals through the streets to the place of execution.
2 Genitals.
3 Single combat.
4 Soon afterwards.
5 A method of torture or execution called "breaking on the wheel," whereby a victim is bound to a wheel and a heavy bar is used to break the bones of the limbs. This instance of *bar* is cited in *OED* n1 I2b.

Stubbes tells us that people of all ranks filed in to consume this violent form of entertainment, placing bets on the bears or the dogs. He also draws a direct parallel to stage plays, noting that God brought the very same judgment down on theatergoers as on the bear-baiting audience. This is a natural connection since the arenas were very similar, sometimes used for both plays and bear-baiting, and were often located near one another (see illustration, Appendix D4).]

Bear baiting and other exercises used unlawfully upon the Sabbath day in England

These heathenish exercises upon the Sabbath Day, which the Lord would have consecrated to his service, for the glory of his name and our spiritual comfort, are not in any respect tolerable or to be suffered. For the baiting of a bear, besides that it is a filthy, stinking, and loathsome game, is it not a perilous exercise wherein a man is in danger of his life every minute of an hour, which thing, though it were not so, yet what exercise is this meet[1] for any Christian? What Christian heart can take pleasure to see one poor beast to rent, tear, and kill another, and all for his foolish pleasure? And although they bloody be beasts to mankind, and seek his destruction, yet we are not to abuse them, for his sake who made them, and whose creatures they are. For notwithstanding that they be evil to us, and thirst after our blood, yet are they good creatures in their own nature and kind, and made to set forth the glory, power, and magnificence of our God, and for our use, and therefore for his sake we ought not to abuse them. It is a common saying amongst all men, borrowed from the French, *qui aime iean, aime son chien*, that is, "love me, love my dog"; so love God, love his creatures.

If any should abuse but the dog of another man's, would not he who owneth the dog think that the abuse done to his dog resulteth to himself? And shall we abuse the creatures of God, yea, take pleasure in abusing them, and yet think that the contumely[2] done to them redoundeth[3] not to him who made them? But admit it were granted that it were lawful to abuse the good creatures of God, yet is it not lawful for us to spend our golden years in such idle and vain exercises daily and hourly as we do? And some, who take themselves for no small fools, are so far assotted[4] that they will not stick[5] to keep a dozen

---

1 Appropriate.
2 Abuse and humiliation.
3 Accrues, in the sense of *OED* 6c.
4 Made fools of.
5 Hesitate (*OED* v. 15a).

or a score of great mastiffs, to their no small charges,[1] for the maintenance of this goodly game (forsooth)[2] and will not make any bones of twenty, forty, yea an hundred pound at once to hazard at a bet, with "fight dog," "fight bear," "the devil part all "[3] And to be plain, I think the devil is master of the game, bearward[4] and all. A goodly pastime (forsooth) worthy of commendation, and well fitting these gentlemen of such reputation. But how much of the Lord is offended for the profanation of his Sabbath by such unsavory exercises, his heavenly majesty of late hath revealed, pouring forth his heavy wrath, his fearful judgment, and dreadful vengeance upon the beholders of these vanities, and hereafter followeth.[5]

A fearful example of God his judgment upon the profaners of the Sabbath day

Upon the thirteenth day of January last, being the Sabbath day, anno 1583, there resorted an infinite number of people, men, women, and children, of each sort,[6] to those infamous places, where these wicked exercises are usually practiced (for they have their Courts, Gardens, and Yards for the same purpose), and, being all come together and mounted aloft upon their scaffolds and galleries, and in the midst of all their jollity and pastime, all the whole building (not one stick standing) fell down with a most wonderful[7] and fearful confusion. So that either two or three hundred men, women, and children (whereof seven were killed dead) were some wounded, some lamed, and othersome bruised and crushed, almost to death. Some had their brains dashed out, some their heads all too quashed, some their legs broken, some their arms, some their backs, some their shoulders, some one hurt, some another, so that you should have heard a woeful cry, even piercing the skies, parents bewailing their children, children their loving parents, wives their husbands, and husbands their wives, marvelous to have heard. This woeful spectacle and heavy judgment, pitiful to hear of, but most rueful to behold, the Lord sent down from heaven to show unto the whole world how grievously he is offended with those

---

1   At considerable expense.
2   Truly, with a derisive tone.
3   Phrases yelled by spectators during the fight. "Devil part all," an obscure phrase, perhaps means *the fight is on; only the devil can part them.*
4   The bear keeper.
5   Illustrated by the following example.
6   Social rank.
7   Astonishing.

that spend his Sabbath in such wicked exercises, in the meantime leaving his temple desolate and empty. God grant all men may take warning hereby to shun the same, for fear of like or sharper judgment to come.

A fearful judgment of God, showed at the theaters

The like judgment in effect did the Lord show unto them a little before, being assembled at their theaters, to see their bawdy interludes[1] and other fooleries there practiced. For he caused the earth mightily to shake and quaver, as though all would have fallen down, whereat, the people sore amazed, some leapt down from the top of the turrets, pinnacles, and towers where they stood, to the ground, whereby some had their legs broke, some their arms, some their backs, some hurt one where, some another where, and many sore crushed and bruised, but not any but they went away sore afraid and wounded in conscience. And yet can neither the one, nor the other, fray[2] them from these devilish exercises, until the Lord consume them all in his wrath, which God forbid. The Lord of his mercy, open the eyes of the magistrates to pluck down these places of abuse, that God may be honored, and their consciences discharged.

1 A stage play; Stubbes probably has comedy or farce in mind.
2 Frighten.

4. John Norden, Map of London (1593)

[The map below shows how closely associated theater and bear-baiting were. The buildings labeled "bear howse" and "play howse" are strikingly similar in architecture and situated side-by-side on the disreputable south side of the Thames River, beyond the reach of the authority of the city of London.]

Detail showing the bear-baiting house and a playhouse, probably The Rose.

5. The Triple Tree at Tyburn

[In 1571, the infamous Triple Tree was erected at Tyburn, outside of London at a crossroads long used for executions. As Molly Smith points out, more than 6000 victims were hanged here during the reign of Elizabeth, and the culture of spectacle that developed around these hangings was hardly distinguishable from the spectacle of theater, especially in the *Spanish Tragedy* (218). The woodcuts below, though later than Kyd, capture the horror and the theater-like spectacle of these events.]

TYBURN'S TRIPLE TREE.

The coffins.   Javelin men.

An execution at Tyburn about 1680.—From a contemporary print in the Edmund Gardner Collection.

"Tyburn Triple Tree," c. 1882. Image courtesy of the National Archives, UK.

Source unknown; Wikimedia Commons.

Memorial in present-day London that marks the site of the Triple Tree; Wikimedia Commons.

Appendix E: The Social Construction of Women at Court

1. From Baldesar Castiglione, *The Book of the Courtier (The Courtier of Count Baldessar Castilio, devided into four Bookes. Very necessarie and profitable for young Gentlemen and Gentlewomen abiding in Court, Pallace, or Place, done in English by Thomas Hobby* [sic]*)*, Book 3 (1528; London: Printed by John Wolfe, 1588)

[Castiglione's *Book of the Courtier*, published in Italian in 1528, enjoyed great popularity in England, especially in Thomas Hoby's 1561 translation. It takes the form of a series of conversations among Italian courtiers, which, in Book 3, turns to the role of women at court. In this excerpt, Giuliano de' Medici (which Hoby anglicizes to Lord Julian), at Duchess Elisabetta Gonzaga's urging, describes his ideal woman of the court. At the heart of his creation is the idea of *sprezzatura*, a quality that allows court members to display perfect grace, wit, manners, self-control, and charm without a hint of effort.]

Then said the Duchess: pass not your bounds (my lord Julian) but mind the order taken, and fashion the gentlewoman of the palace, that this so worthy a mistress may have him that shall so worthily serve her.

Then the Lord Julian proceeded: for a proof therefore (madam) that your commandment may drive me to assay[1] to do, yea, the thing I have no skill in, I will speak of this excellent woman, as I would have her. And when I have fashioned her after my mind, and can afterward get none other, I will take her as mine own, after the example of Pygmalion.[2]

And whereas the Lord Gasper[3] hath said that the very same rules that are given for the courtier serve also for the woman, I am of a contrary opinion. For albeit some qualities are common and necessary as well for the woman as the man, yet are there some other more meet[4] for the woman than for the man, and some again meet for the man, that she ought in no wise to meddle withal.

---

1 Attempt.
2 In Ovid's *Metamorphoses*, Pygmalion fell in love with a statue that he himself had carved, and the goddess Aphrodite granted his prayer that the statue be brought to life.
3 Another of the courtiers in the conversation.
4 Fitting.

The very same I say of the exercises of the body: But principally in her fashion, manners, words, gestures and conversation (me think) the woman ought to be much unlike the man. For right as it is seemly for him to show a certain manliness full and steady, so doth it well in a woman to have a tenderness, soft and mild, with a kind of womanly sweetness in every gesture of hers, that in going, standing, and speaking whatever she lusteth,[1] may always make her appear a woman without any likeness of man.

Adding therefore this principle to the rules that these lords have taught the courtier, I think well, she may serve her turn with many of them, and be endued with very good qualities, as the Lord Gasper saith. For many virtues of the mind I reckon be as necessary for a woman, as for a man.

Likewise nobleness of birth, avoiding affectation of curiosity, to have a good grace of nature in all her doings, to be of good conditions, witty, foreseeing, not haughty, not envious, not ill tongued, not light, not contentious, not untowardly, to have the knowledge to win and keep the good will of her lady and of all others, to do well and with good grace the exercises comely for a woman.

Me think well beauty is more necessary in her than in the courtiers, for (to say the truth) there is a great lack in the woman that wanteth[2] beauty.

She ought also to be more circumspect, and to take better heed that she give no occasion to be ill reported of, and so behave herself, that she be not only not spotted with any fault, but not so much as with suspicion. Because a woman hath not so many ways to defend herself from slanderous reports, as hath a man.

But for so much as Count Lewis[3] hath very particularly expressed the principal profession of the courtier, and willeth it to be in martial feats, methink also behoveful[4] to utter (according to my judgment) what the gentlewoman of the palace ought to be, in which point when I have thoroughly satisfied, I shall think myself rid of the greatest part of my duty.

Leaving therefore a part of the virtues of the mind that ought to be common to her with the courtier, as wisdom, nobleness of courage, staidness, and many more, and likewise the conditions that are meet for all women, as to be good and discreet, to have the understanding to order her husband's goods and her house and children when she is married, and all those parts that belong to a good huswife,[5] I say that

---

1 Wishes.
2 Lacks.
3 Another courtier in the conversation.
4 Useful.
5 Housewife.

for her that liveth in court, methink there belongeth unto her above all other things, a certain sweetness in language that may delight, whereby she may gently entertain all kind of men with talk worthy the hearing and honest, and applied to the time and place, and to the degree of the person she communeth withal. Accompanying with sober and quiet manners, and with the honesty that must always be a stay[1] to her deeds, a ready liveliness of wit, whereby she may declare herself far wide from all dullness, but with such a kind of goodness, that she may be esteemed no less chaste, wise and courteous, than pleasant, feat conceited[2] and sober, and therefore must she keep a certain mean[3] very hard, and (in a manner) derived of contrary matters, and come just to certain limits, but not to pass them.

This woman ought not therefore (to make herself good and honest) be so squeamish and make wise to abhor both the company and the talk (though somewhat of the wantonest)[4] if she be present, to get her thence, by and by, for a man may lightly guess that she feigned[5] to be so coy to hide that in herself which she doubted others might come to the knowledge of, and such nice fashions[6] are always hateful.

Neither ought she again (to show herself free and pleasant) speak words of dishonesty, nor use a certain familiarity without measure and bridle, and fashions to make me believe that of her that perhaps is not, but being present at such kind of talk, she ought to give the hearing with a little blushing and shamefacedness.

Likewise to eschew one vice that I have seen reign in many: namely, to speak and willingly to give ear to such as report ill of other women, for such as in hearing the dishonest behaviors of other women disclosed, are offended at the matter, and make wise not to credit and (in manner) to think it a wonder that a woman should lead an unclean life, they make proof that since this fault seemeth unto them so foul a matter, then commit it not. But those that go always harking[7] out the loves of others and disclose them so point by point, and with such joy, it seemeth that they envy the matter, and that their desire is to have all men know it, that the like may not be imputed them for a trespass.

And so they turn it to certain laughters with a kind of gesture, whereby they make me to suspect at the very same instant that they take

---

1 Support.
2 With appropriate imagination.
3 Moderation.
4 Most unrestrained or lascivious.
5 Pretended.
6 Coy affectations.
7 Whispering.

great contentation[1] at it. And of this ariseth, that men although to their seeming they give diligent ear to it, for the most part conceive an ill opinion of them, and have them in very small reputation and (to their weening)[2] with these behaviors are enticed to attempt them farther. And many time afterward they run so far at rovers,[3] that purchaseth them worthily an ill name, and in conclusion are so little regarded, that men pass not for their company, but rather abhor them. And contrariwise, there is no man so shameless and high minded, but beareth great reverence toward them that be counted good and honest, because that gravity tempered with knowledge and goodness, is (as it were) a shield against the wanton pride and beastliness of saucy merchants. Wherefore it is seen that one word, a laughter or a gesture of good will (how little soever it be) of an honest woman, is more set by of every man, than all the toys and wanton gestures of them that so lavishly show small shamefastness. And where they lead not in deed an unclean life, yet with those wanton countenances, babbling, scornfulness, and such scoffing conditions, they make me to think they do.

2. **From Juan Luis Vives, *Instruction of Christian Women* (*A verie fruitfull and pleasant booke, called the instruction of a Christian woman. Made first in Latin, by the right famous cleark M. Lewes Viues, and translated out of Latine into Englishe by Richard Hyrde*) (1529; London, 1585), 148–53 [p. 153 misnumbered as p. 143]**

[Juan Luis Vives (1492–1540) was an influential and prolific scholar, born in Spain but more attached to the humanist movement through his Latin writings than to any particular country. He lived in England during the early years of Henry VIII's reign (r. 1509–47). His *Instruction of Christian Women*, published in an English translation by Richard Hyrde in 1529 (which edition is dedicated to Catherine of Aragon), became a popular conduct manual that was reprinted several times throughout the 1500s. In it he advocates for women to be educated, but he also admonishes them to avoid romantic entanglements, as in the following excerpt from the end of Chapter 14, "Of Loving."]

But peradventure[4] the maid is caught already, then must we seek a remedy for the wound, afore it constrain her to do that thing which shall cause her everlasting repentance. First thou mayest be sorry that

---

1 Satisfaction.
2 Supposing.
3 Aimlessly, without purpose.
4 If by chance.

thou hast wittingly thrown thyself into that dungeon. Nor those folks ought to be taken heed unto that say, it lyeth not in their own power to eschew love. For so say some, which excuse their own vice with necessity, as though they had done it against their will. Nor they that so say seem to know the power and nature of love. Also remember this little verse: *love cannot be thrust out, but it may creep out*, whereby we may perceive, that love neither breaketh in violently, nor can be cast out violently. But likewise as it hath by little and little crept in, so by little and little it may be put away again. Therefore, let not thy mind wander. For if it be not kept, it will run thither of it own accord.

Sometime consider thyself, how many things thou hast done foolishly, blindly, and without wit, brain or reason, by the means of love. And how much good time thou hast lost in it, with unprofitable and foolish cares,[1] and lost the occasions of many good deeds. Remember also how thou hast burned, how many things thou hast thought, said, yea, and done, partly foolish, partly mad, yea, and some ungracious. Remember into what misery thou castest thyself like a blind body and what a benefit again thou hast obtained, that hast recovered thy sight, and a purpose and will to come unto better mind again, which thing thou mayest reckon to be a great gift of God, and thyself to be much bounden to him for it.

Therefore set thyself unto some work, and keep thyself from the sight and hearing of the person that thou lovest, and if he come by chance into thy thought, turn thy mind some other way, either with reading or praying, or some good communication, or some honest song, or studying of some merry matter, so that[2] it be clean and honest. And if he whom thou lovest, have any fault or vice, call that oft unto remembrance, and not what virtue and goodness he hath, for there is nobody living, but he hath something that may be dispraised. Therefore let that be had first in remembrance and consider this, that great vices lie hid often under the color of virtue, and many perilous things cloaked under an honest face outward. Beauty maketh folks proud and disdainful; noble birth maketh them stately; riches, intolerable; strength of body, cruel. Therefore consider in thy mind, not what he hath said, that hath liked thee,[3] but what he hath spoken, that disliked thee, as if he hath either done or said aught peevishly, foolishly, foul, horrible, abominable, lewdly, unthriftily, madly, ungraciously, and by that that cometh forth, make conjecture, what lieth hid secretly and closely within. For there is nobody, but he hideth his fault as

---

1 Mental anguish.
2 As long as.
3 That has pleased you.

much as he can and showeth his virtue unto the uttermost, and so the virtue appeareth more than it is, and the vice less.

Moreover, we be deceived with the near similitudes[1] of vices and virtues, when every man laboureth to seem better than he is, and we, unwisely, and after the common opinion, esteem virtues, calling him liberal that is a waster, and him bold that is foolhardy, and eloquent that is a great babbler, and witty, that is unconstant, wherewith young women be oft deceived when they cannot perceive the sooth[2] and judge the man by that which outwardly appeareth. Neither any man goeth to his love, but he setteth himself forth with all his best properties, that he may seem to lack nothing that any man ought to have and, by that means, deceiveth foolish young women, hiding great vices under a thin color of virtue, as birders hide the lime[3] with meat, and fishers the hook with the bait. This a young woman ought to consider before it be too late to repent, lest she begin to wax wise when it shall nothing avail.

And if thou be clean gotten out of love, and healed, and hast recovered thy sight again, then shalt thou see how much thou art bound unto God, that hath taken thee out of thy madness and restored thee unto thy wit. For what virtuous Christian woman, or else Pagan, of any wit or honesty, loved ever any other than her husband. Therefore thou shalt neither desire thyself to be beloved in this wise, neither by ungracious crafts inflame the minds of men, the which fire shall return again unto thyself. Many women rejoice to have lovers, whose hearts they may burn and inflame purposely. O thou ungracious woman, seest thou not, how thou bringest him into the possession of the devil with thy craft, whither thyself shall go also, there to receive thy meed,[4] where ye shall both burn, he for being overcome of the devil, and thou for overcoming him for the devil; ye shall both be paid your wages. Now the Apostle saith, the wages of sin is death.[5]

3. Queen Elizabeth's Armada Speech to the Troops at Tilbury (9 August 1588), in *Elizabeth I, Collected Works*, ed. Leah Marcus et al. (Chicago: U of Chicago P, 2000), 325

[Queen Elizabeth I, who ruled England from 1558 to 1603, delivered this speech to ground troops in anticipation of a Spanish invasion at

---

1 Outward appearances (presumably inaccurate).
2 Truth.
3 Sticky substance used to catch birds; it was a common metaphor, and appears in *The Spanish Tragedy* at 2.1.128 and 3.4.41.
4 Corrupt reward.
5 Saint Paul, in Romans 6:23.

the time of the battle with the Spanish Armada. Though a ground invasion never materialized, the speech became famous. In it, she manages both to acknowledge and to undermine the notion that her gender might limit her as a monarch.]

My loving people, I have been persuaded by some that are careful of my safety to take heed how I committed myself to armed multitudes, for fear of treachery. But I tell you that I would not desire to live to distrust my faithful and loving people. Let tyrants fear: I have so behaved myself under God I have placed my chiefest strength and safeguard in the loyal hearts and goodwill of my subjects. Wherefore I am come among you at this time but for my recreation and pleasure, being resolved in the midst and heat of the battle to live and die amongst you all, to lay down for my God and for my kingdom and for my people mine honor and my blood even in the dust. I know I have the body but of a weak and feeble woman, but I have the heart and stomach of a king and of a king of England too—and take foul scorn that Parma[1] or any prince of Europe should dare to invade the borders of my realm. To the which rather than any dishonor shall grow by me, I myself will venter[2] my royal blood; I myself will be your general, judge, and rewarder of your virtue in the field. I know that already for your forwardness you have deserved rewards and crowns, and I assure you in the word of a prince you shall not fail of them. In the meantime, my lieutenant general[3] shall be in my stead, than whom never prince commanded a more noble or worthy subject. Not doubting but by your concord in the camp and valor in the field and your obedience to myself and my general, we shall shortly have a famous victory over these enemies of my God and of my kingdom.

4. **Lady Arbella Stuart, Letter to King James ("Petition from Lady Arbella Seymour to the King," c. December 1610), *The Life and Letters of Lady Arbella Stuart*, vol. 2, ed. Elizabeth Cooper (London: Hurst and Blackett, 1866), 114–15. Spelling modernized for this edition**

[As a descendent of Henry VII (r. 1485–1509), niece to Mary Queen of Scots (1542–87), and relative of Queen Elizabeth and King James, Lady Arbella Stuart (1575–1615) is about as good a real-life analogue

---

1 Alexander Farnese, Duke of Parma (1545–92), had planned to launch an attack on England from the Netherlands, where he led Spain's war against Dutch Protestants. By signing the Treaty of Nonesuch in 1585, Elizabeth entered England in the war on the side of the Netherlands.

2 Venture, risk.

3 Robert Dudley, Earl of Leicester (1532–88).

to Kyd's Bel-imperia as one can find in early modern England (though only in retrospect, since the main events of Lady Arbella's life happened after Kyd's death). Like Bel-imperia, Lady Arbella was ambitious to be independent, but she encountered insurmountable obstacles. As Sara Jayne Steen observes, "The paradox of the aristocratic woman whose sex signified subordination, but whose class signified authority was more extreme in Stuart's case because of her birth and upbringing. Her letters reflect the tensions among these social forces" (5). In the following letter, Lady Arbella writes to ask the King's forgiveness for her clandestine marriage to William Seymour (1588–1660). As Steen points out, her pleas were unsuccessful. After an adventurous escape in 1611, "cross-dressed like one of Shakespeare's heroines" (68), she was arrested in Calais and returned to London, where she lived in confinement until her death in 1615 (81).]

To King James

I do most heartily lament my hard fortune that I should offend your Majesty the least, especially in that whereby I have long desired to merit of your Majesty as appeared before your Majesty was my Sovereign. And though your Majesty's neglect of me, my good liking of this gentleman that is my husband, and my fortune drew me to a contract[1] before I acquainted your Majesty, I humbly beseech your Majesty to consider how impossible it was for me to imagine it could be offensive unto your Majesty, having few days before given me your Royal consent to bestow myself on any subject of your Majesty's (which likewise your Majesty had done long since). Besides never having been either prohibited any or spoken to for any in this land by your Majesty these 7 years that I have lived in your Majesty's house, I could not conceive that your Majesty regarded my marriage at all, whereas if your Majesty had vouchsafed to tell me your mind and accept that freewill offering of my obedience I could not have offended your Majesty, of whose gracious goodness I presume so much that if it were as convenient in a worldly respect as malice may make it seem to separate us whom God hath joined, your Majesty would not do evil that good might come thereof, nor make me, that have the honor to be so near your Majesty in blood, the first precedent[2] that ever was, though our Princes may have left some as little imitable[3] for so good and gracious a king as your Majesty as David's dealing with Uriah.[4] But I assure myself if it please your Majesty in your

---

1 Marriage.

2 First example (of a king separating spouses).

3 Little to imitate.

4 In 2 Samuel 11, King David arranges for Uriah to be killed in battle so he can have access to Bathsheba, Uriah's wife.

own wisdom to consider thoroughly of my cause, there will no solid reason appear to debar me of justice and your princely favor, which I will endeavor to deserve whilst I breathe. And never ceasing to pray for your Majesty's felicity in all things continue Your Majesty's. A. S.

5. From Elizabeth Cary, *The Tragedy of Mariam, the Faire Queen of Jewry* (London, 1613)

[This closet drama (meant to be read and not staged) revolves around the turbulent marriage of Mariam and Herod the Great, set against a complex political landscape in ancient Jerusalem. Mariam is in the end executed by Herod, having been betrayed by her sister-in-law Salome. Despite her unsavory actions, Salome, in the scene below, strikes a chord of autonomy for women as she boldly insists on a divorce from her husband, the blameless Constabarus. Divorce as Salome describes it, initiated by a woman, would have been unthinkable at the time, yet its articulation in this play suggests that an impulse towards self-actualization for women, however subversive, was alive in Elizabethan London. Cary herself (1585–1639), born Elizabeth Tanfield, was married to Henry Cary, Viscount Faulkland (1575–1633) and circulated in the highest levels of English society. As the scene opens, Constabarus berates his wife Salome, the sister to King Herod, for the private conversation she was having in the preceding scene with her Arabian lover Silleus.]

Act 1, Scene 6

CONSTABARUS
Oh Salome, how much you wrong your name,
Your race, your country, and your husband most?
A stranger's private conference is shame.
I blush for you, that have your blushing lost.
Oft have I found, and found you to my grief,
Consorted with this base Arabian here.
Heaven knows that you have been my comfort chief,
Then do not now my greater plague appear.
Now by the stately carved edifice,
That on Mount Sion makes so fair a show,
And by the altar fit for sacrifice,
I love thee more than thou thyself dost know.
Oft with a silent sorrow have I heard
How ill Judea's mouth doth censure thee,
And did I not thine honor much regard,
Thou shouldst not be exhorted thus for me.
Didst thou but know the worth of honest fame,

How much a virtuous woman is esteemed,
Thou wouldest like hell eschew deserved shame,
And seek to be both chaste and chastely deemed.
Our wisest prince did say, and true he said,
A virtuous woman crowns her husband's head.

SALOME
Did I for this uprear[1] thy low estate?
Did I for this requital beg thy life,
That thou hadst forfeited [to] hapless fate?
To be to such a thankless wretch the wife.
This hand of mine hath lifted up thy head,
Which many a day ago had fallen full low,
Because the sons of Baba are not dead.
To me thou dost both life and fortune owe.

CONSTABARUS
You have my patience often exercised;
Use,[2] make my choler keep within the banks!
Yet boast no more, but be by me advised.
A benefit upbraided forfeits thanks.
I prithee, Salome, dismiss this mood.
Thou dost not know how ill it fits thy place.
My words were all intended for thy good,
To raise thine honor and to stop disgrace.

SALOME
To stop disgrace? Take thou no care for me.
Nay, do thy worst! Thy worst I set not by.
No shame of mine is like to light on thee;
Thy love and admonitions I defy.
Thou shalt no hour longer call me wife.
Thy jealousy procures my hate so deep
That I from thee do mean to free my life
By a divorcing bill before I sleep.

CONSTABARUS
Are Hebrew women now transformed to men?
Why do you not as well our battles fight,
And wear our armor? Suffer this, and then

---

1 Elevate.
2 Habit, practice.

Let all the world be topsy turved quite.
Let fishes graze, beasts swim, and birds descend,[1]
Let fire burn downwards whilst the earth aspires,
Let winter's heat and summer's cold offend,
Let thistles grow on vines, and grapes on briers,
Set us to spin or sew, or at the best
Make us wood-hewers, waters-bearing wights.[2]
For sacred service let us take no rest.
Use us as Joshua did the Gibonites.[3]

SALOME
Hold on your talk, till it be time to end,
For me I am resolved it shall be so:
Though I be first that to this course do bend,
I shall not be the last full well I know.

CONSTABARUS
Why then, be witness heaven, the judge of sins,
Be witness spirits that eschew the dark,
Be witness angels, witness cherubins,[4]
Whose semblance sits upon the holy ark,
Be witness earth, be witness Palestine,
Be witness David's city,[5] if my heart
Did ever merit such an act of thine,
Or if the fault be mine that makes us part,
Since mildest Moses, friend unto the Lord,
Did work his wonders in the land of Ham,[6]
And slew the first-born babes without a sword,
In sign whereof we eat the holy lamb.
Till now that fourteen hundred years are past,
Since first the law with us hath been in force,
You are the first, and will I hope, be last,
That ever sought her husband to divorce.

---

1 Line as emended by Bevington (632).
2 People.
3 In Joshua 9 of the Old Testament, the Gibeonites trick the Israelites into
agreeing to covenant with them; when the trick is revealed, the Israelite leader
Joshua responds by forcing the Gibeonites into servitude as hewers of wood
and bearers of water.
4 Cherubim, an order of angels.
5 Jerusalem.
6 Egypt.

SALOME
I mean not to be led by precedent,
My will shall be to me instead of law.

CONSTABARUS
I fear me much you will too late repent,
That you have ever lived so void of awe.[1]
This is Silleus' love that makes you thus
Reverse all order: you must next be his.
But if my thoughts aright the cause discuss,
In winning you, he gains no lasting bliss.
I was Silleus, and not long ago
Josephus then was Constabarus now.
When you became my friend[2] you proved his foe,
As now for him you break to me your vow.

SALOME
If once I loved you, greater is your debt.
For certain 'tis that you deserved it not.
And undeserved love we soon forget,
And therefore that to me can be no blot.
But now fare ill my once beloved lord,
Yet never more beloved than now abhorred.

CONSTABARUS
Yet Constabarus biddeth thee farewell.
Farewell light creature. Heaven forgive thy sin.
My prophesying spirit doth foretell
Thy wavering thoughts do yet but new begin.
Yet I have better 'scaped than Joseph did,
But if our Herod's death had been delayed,
The valiant youths that I so long have hid,
Had been by her, and I for them betrayed.
Therefore, in happy hour did Caesar give
The fatal blow to wanton Anthony,
For had he lived, our Herod then should live,
But great Anthonius' death made Herod die.
Had he enjoyed his breath, not I alone
Had been in danger of a deadly fall.
But Mariam had the way of peril gone,

---

1 Without deference to Mosaic Law.
2 Lover.

Though by the tyrant[1] most beloved of all.
The sweet faced Mariam as free from guilt
As Heaven from spots, yet had her lord come back,
Her purest blood had been unjustly spilt.
And Salome it was would work her wrack.[2]
Though all Judea yield her[3] innocent,
She often hath been near to punishment.

---

1 Herod.
2 That would have caused her ruin.
3 Consider Mariam.

Appendix F: Spain in Elizabethan Culture

1. From Richard Hakluyt, *A Discourse on Western Planting*[1] (1584), in *History of the State of Maine*, vol. 2, ed. Charles Deane (Cambridge: J. Wilson, 1877), 159–60

[Hakluyt (1553–1616) was the premier English geographer and editor of exploration documents in the Elizabethan age. He argued passionately in favor of an English colonization of North America, partly to block Spain and advance English Protestantism over Spanish Catholicism. Hakluyt did not write the *Discourse* for publication but as a direct appeal in 1584 to Queen Elizabeth and her advisers to pursue the westward expansion of English power. This excerpt is from the summary of his argument that makes up Chapter 20.]

The Spaniards govern in the Indies[2] with all pride and tyranny; and like as when people of contrary nature at the sea enter into galleys,[3] where men are tied as slaves, all yell and cry with one voice, *Liberta, liberta,*[4] as desirous of liberty and freedom, so no doubt whensoever the Queen of England, a prince of such clemency, shall seat[5] upon that firm of America, and shall be reported throughout all that tract to use the natural people there with all humanity, courtesy, and freedom, they will yield themselves to her government, and revolt clean from the Spaniard, and specially when they shall understand that she hath a noble navy, and that she aboundeth with a people most valiant for their defense. And her majesty having Sir Francis Drake[6] and other subjects already in credit with the Symerons,[7] a people or great multitude already revolted from the Spanish government, she may with them and a few hundreths of this nation, trained up in the late wars of France and Flanders, bring great things to pass, and that with great ease; and this brought so about, her majesty and her subjects may both

---

1 To *plant* is to settle a region, to establish colonies.
2 West Indies.
3 A ship propelled by rowers of condemned criminals or slaves.
4 Freedom, freedom!
5 Settle.
6 An English sea captain and explorer, Drake (c. 1540–96) was celebrated by Elizabethans for his attacks against Spanish interests.
7 Maroons, Caribbean slaves who successfully resisted European plantation owners and thrived in remote areas.

enjoy the treasure of the mines of gold and silver, and the whole trade and all the gain of the trade of merchandise, that now passeth thither by the Spaniards' only hand,[1] of all the commodities of Europe; which trade of merchandise only were of itself sufficient (without the benefit of the rich mine) to enrich the subjects, and by customs[2] to fill her majesty's coffers to the full. And if it be high policy to maintain the poor people of this realm in work, I dare affirm that if the poor people of England were five times so many as they be, yet all might be set on work in and by working linen, and such other things of merchandise as the trade into the Indies doth require.

2. **From *A Fig*[3] *for the Spaniard, or Spanish Spirits, Wherein are lively portrayed the damnable deeds, miserable murders, and monstrous massacres of the cursed Spaniard, With a true rehearsal of the late troubles and troublesome estate of Aragon, Catalonia, Valencia, and Portingall, Whereunto are annexed matters of much marvel and causes of no less consequence* (London, 1591)**

[This pamphlet, which appeared in 1591, fits into a tradition of anti-Spanish and anti-Catholic propaganda that started in the 1550s. It plays on and attempts to stoke further the threat many in England felt from the Spanish, especially in the years leading up to and following the English defeat of the Spanish Armada in 1588.]

Now let us see what is and hath been done this year in Portingall.[4] A Portingal gentleman walking in the Roceio[5] of Lisbon, espied a base Castilian of such proud and presumptuous demeanor, so fantasticall in his attire, lofty in his looks, and slow in his pace, (as though he had been treading of measures)[6] could not long bear him, but bearded[7] him, and justled[8] him, whereupon the matter was debated by Stafford law,[9] the Portingall slain, and the Spaniard escaped into the castle. Immediately certain Portingall gentlemen of his familiars swore revenge, and not long since have had their wills. For on S. Matthew's

---

1 Exclusively through the Spaniards.
2 Taxes.
3 A gesture of contempt.
4 Portugal.
5 Rossio Square in Lisbon.
6 To dance in a rhythmic or stately manner (*OED tread* v., 2d).
7 Confronted.
8 Jostled.
9 Settling a matter by delivering a beating with a staff.

Day [21 September] last, finding a crew of Castilians reveling in a brothel house, suddenly set upon, and slew five of them, which caused the other Castilians of the castle to come down in extreme heat of choler, and offer great violence through the city, until the great multitudes of Portingals that were hastily swarmed together, made them betake them to their heels, and ever since more watchfully, and warily guard their castle. The matter being brought in question before the Cardinal[1] (who now a while keepth warm the King of Portingal's seat), and being found that the Spaniards were chief masters of misrule and mischief (as they are always) they were punished severely, but all in vain: for old rancor is not easily forgotten, nor the ancient malice between those two nations lightly forgiven. For it is impossible, and may pass for a paradox to think that those two nations, the Portingall and Spaniard will ever be fully reconciled. For as often as either they shall remember, or their chronicles report the fraudulent feats of false Philip[2] against his neighbor King and kingly nephew Don Sebastion[3] so brave a young prince and only hope of the Portingals, record the damned usurping of the spiteful Spaniards, and miserable exile of Don Anthony[4] lawful and indubitate[5] heir now favored and fostered by her majesty.

3. **From Sir Walter Raleigh,** *A Report of the Truth of the Fight about the Iles of Azores, this last sommer. Betwixt the Revenge, one of her Majesties Shippes, and an Armada of the King of Spaine* **(London, 1591)**

[Few figures were more central to the incipient English Empire than Raleigh (c. 1552–1618), a brilliant writer, soldier, sea captain, explorer, and courtier. In this pamphlet, usually referred to as *The Last Fight of*

---

1 Cardinal Henry. See note 3 below, also see p. 35.
2 Philip II, King of Spain (r. 1556–98).
3 King Sebastian I of Portugal (r. 1557–78). His death in the Battle of Alcacer Quibir in 1578, when he was only 24 years old, created a succession crisis. His uncle, Henry, a Cardinal in the Catholic Church, ruled from 1578 until he died in 1580. Henry's death, and the absence of heirs for both Sebastian and Henry, led to the Portuguese throne being taken over by Philip II of Spain in 1580.
4 António, Prior of Crato (1531–95), who claimed the Portuguese throne after Henry died in 1580. He tried to rule from the island of Terceira (Azores) but was driven into exile by Philip II, taking refuge in England under the protection of Queen Elizabeth. He descended through an illegitimate line from his grandfather Manuel I of Portugal. Philip II was also a grandson of Manuel, through his mother.
5 Undoubted.

the Revenge at Sea, Raleigh inveighs against the Spanish, arguing that their cruelty runs so deep that they even victimize their fellow Europeans and Catholics.]

And if our English Papists do but look into Portugal, against whom they have no pretense of religion, how the nobility are put to death, imprisoned, their rich men made a prey, and all sorts of people captived; they shall find that the obedience even of the Turk is easy and a liberty, in respect of the slavery and tyranny of Spain. What they have done in Sicily, in Naples, Milan, and in the low countries; who hath there been spared for religion at all? And it commeth to my remembrance of a certain Burger of Antwerp, whose house being entered by a company of Spanish soldiers, when they first sacked the city, he besought them to spare him and his goods, being a good Catholic, and one of their own party and faction. The Spaniards answered that they knew him to be of a good conscience for himself, but his money, plate, jewels, and goods, were all heretical, and therefore good prize. So they abused and tormented the foolish Fleming, who hoped that an *Agnus Dei*[1] had been a sufficient target[2] against all force of that holy and charitable nation. Neither have they at any time as they protest invaded the kingdoms of the *Indies* and *Peru*, and elsewhere, but only led thereunto rather to reduce the people to Christianity than either for gold or empery.[3] Whenas in one only island called *Hispaniola*, they have wasted thirty hundred thousand of the natural people, besides many millions else in other places of the *Indies*: a poor and harmless people created of God, and might have been won to his knowledge, as many of them were, and almost as many as ever were persuaded thereunto. The story whereof is at large written by a bishop of their own nation called Bartholome de las Casas, and translated into English and many other languages, entitled *The Spanish Cruelties*. Who would therefore repose trust in such a nation of ravenous strangers, and especially in those Spaniards which more greedily thirst after English blood than after the lives of any other people of Europe, for the many overthrows and dishonors they have received at our hands, whose weakness we have discovered[4] to the world, and whose forces at home, abroad, in Europe, in India, by sea and land, we have even with handfuls of men and ships overthrown and dishonored?

---

1 Literally "lamb of God" (Latin), an object bearing a lamb and a cross, here as a symbol of loyalty to Roman Catholicism.
2 Shield.
3 Empire.
4 Revealed.

Let not therefore any Englishman of what religion soever have other opinion of the Spaniards but that those whom he seeketh to win of our nation, he esteemeth base and traiterous unworthy persons or unconstant fools: and that he useth his pretense of religion for no other purpose but to bewitch us from the obedience of our natural prince; thereby hoping in time to bring us to slavery and subjection, and then none shall be unto them so odious, and disdained as the traitors themselves, who have sold their country to a stranger and forsaken their faith and obedience contrary to nature or religion, and contrary to that humane and general honor, not only of Christians, but of heathen and irreligious nations, who have always sustained what labor soever, and embrace even death itself, for their country, prince, or commonwealth.

Works Cited and Further Reading

Modern Editions of *The Spanish Tragedy*

Boas, Frederick S., ed. *The Works of Thomas Kyd*. Rev. ed. Oxford: Clarendon, 1955.

Cairncross, Andrew S., ed. *The First Part of Hieronimo* and *The Spanish Tragedy*. Lincoln: U of Nebraska P, 1967.

Calvo, Clara, and Jesús Tronch, eds. *The Spanish Tragedy*. London: Bloomsbury, 2013.

Edwards, Philip, ed. *The Spanish Tragedy*. Cambridge, MA: Harvard UP, 1959.

Maus, Katherine Eisaman, ed. *The Spanish Tragedy. Four Revenge Tragedies*. New York: Oxford UP, 1998. 1–91.

Neill, Michael, ed. *The Spanish Tragedy*. New York: Norton, 2013.

Smith, Emma, ed. *The Spanish Tragedy. Five Revenge Tragedies*. London: Penguin, 2012. 1–96.

Primary Works

Achelley, Thomas. *A most lamentable and Tragicall historie, conteyning the outragious and horrible tyrannie which a Spanishe gentlewoman named Violenta executed upon her lover Didaco, because he espoused another being first betrothed unto her*. London, 1576.

Acts of the Privy Council of England. New Series. Vol XXIV. Ed. John Roche Dasent. London: His Majesty's Stationery Office by Mackie and Co., 1901.

Bacon, Francis. "Of Revenge." *Essays or Counsels, Civil and Moral*. London, 1625.

Cary, Elizabeth. *The Tragedy of Mariam, the Faire Queen of Jewry*. London, 1613.

Castiglione, Baldesar. *The Courtier of Count Baldessar Castilio, devided into four Bookes. Very necessarie and profitable for young Gentlemen and Gentlewomen abiding in Court, Pallace, or Place, done in English by Thomas Hobby*. London, 1588.

Chapman, George. *The Revenge of Bussy D'Ambois*. In Maus 175–248.

Chettle, Henry. *The Tragedy of Hoffman*. London, 1631.

Dekker, Thomas. *A Knights Conjuring, Done in Earnest, Discovered in Jest*. London, 1607.

Elizabeth I. "Queen Elizabeth's Armada Speech to the Troops at

Tilbury, August 9, 1588." *Elizabeth I, Collected Works.* Ed. Leah
Marcus et al. Chicago: U of Chicago P, 2000. 325.

*A Fig for the Spaniard, or Spanish Spirits, Wherein are lively portrayed
the damnable deeds, miserable murders, and monstrous massacres of the
cursed Spaniard, With a true rehearsal of the late troubles and troublesome estate of Aragon, Catalonia, Valencia, and Portingall, Whereunto
are annexed matters of much marvel and causes of no less consequence.*
London, 1591.

Foxe, John. *The Second Volume of the Ecclesiaticall Historie, conteining the
Acts and Monuments of Martyrs.* London: Printed by John Day, 1584.

Garnier, Robert. *Cornelia.* Trans. Thomas Kyd. London, 1594.

Hakluyt, Richard. *A Discourse on Western Planting. History of the State
of Maine.* Vol. 2. Ed. Charles Deane. Cambridge: J. Wilson, 1877.

Harrison, William. *Description of England. The First and Second Volumes
of Chronicles.* London, 1586.

Henslowe, Philip. *Henslowe's Diary.* Ed. R.A. Foakes and R.T.
Rickert. Cambridge: Cambridge UP, 1961.

Irace, Kathleen O., ed. *The First Quarto of Hamlet.* Cambridge: Cambridge UP, 1998.

Jones, Richard. *The Book of Honor and Arms.* London, 1590.

Jonson, Ben. *Induction to Bartholomew Fair. The Works of Benjamin
Jonson.* Vol. 2. London, 1640.

——. "To the Memory of My Beloved, the Author Mr. William
Shakespeare, and What He Hath Left Us." *Mr. William Shakespeare's Comedies, Histories, and Tragedies.* London, 1623.

Kyd, Thomas. Letters to Sir John Puckering. In Freeman, *Thomas
Kyd* 181–83.

Langham, Robert. *A Letter, Wherein part of the entertainment unto the
Queen's Majesty at Killingworth Castle in Warwickshire in this
summer's progress, 1575, is signified.*

Leicester's Ghost. In *Leicester's Commonwealth,* by Robert Parsons.
London, 1641.

Lodge, Thomas. *Wits Miserie and the Worlds Madnesse: Discovering the
Devils Incarnat of this Age.* London, 1596.

Marlowe, Christopher. *Tamburlaine the Great, Part One and Part Two.*
Ed. Mathew R. Martin. Peterborough, ON: Broadview P, 2014.

Middleton, Thomas, and William Rowley. *The Changeling.* London,
1653.

Mulcaster, Richard. *The First Part of the Elementarie Which Entreateth
Cheflie of the Right Writing of our English Tung.* London, 1582.

——. *Positions, wherein those primitive circumstances be examined, which
are necessary for the training up of children, either for skill in their
book, or health in their body.* London, 1581.

Nashe, Thomas. "To the Gentleman Students of Both Universities." *Menaphon*, by Robert Greene. London, 1599.

Norton, Thomas, and Thomas Sackville. *The Tragedie of Gorboduc*. London, 1565.

Orders Thought Meete by her Maiestie, and her privie Counsell, to be executed throughout the Counties of this Realme, in such Townes, Villages, and other places, as are, or may be hereafter infected with the plague, for the stay of further increase of the same. London, 1592.

Painter, William. *The First Tome of the Palace of Pleasure contayning store of goodlye histories, Tragical matters, and other Morall arguments, very requisite for delight and profyte*. London: Fleatstrete by Thomas Marshe, 1575.

Raleigh, Sir Walter. *A Report of the Truth of the Fight about the Iles of Azores, this last sommer. Betwixt the Revenge, one of her Majesties Shippes, and an Armada of the King of Spaine*. London, 1591.

Register of the Scholars Admitted into Merchant Taylors' School. Ed. Rev. Charles J. Robinson. Vol. 1. Lewes, UK: Farncombe and Co., 1882.

Sackville, Thomas. "The Complaint of Henry, Duke of Buckingham." *The Last Parte of the Mirour for Magistrates*. London, 1574. Fol. 117–31.

———. "Induction." *The Last Parte of the Mirour for Magistrates*. London, 1574. Fol. 107–17.

Seneca. *Thyestes. Seneca His Ten Tragedies Translated into English*. Trans. Jasper Heywood. London, 1581.

———. *Thyestes. Four Tragedies*. Ed. and trans. E.F. Watling. Baltimore: Penguin, 1966. 41–93.

"Sermon against Contention and Brawling." *Certain Sermons or Homilies Appointed to be Read in Churches in the Time of Queen Elizabeth of Famous Memory*. London, 1687.

Shakespeare, William. *The Norton Shakespeare, based on the Oxford Edition*. 2nd ed. Ed. Stephen Greenblatt. New York: Norton, 2008.

Stuart, Lady Arbella. "Petition from Lady Arbella Seymour to the King." *The Life and Letters of Lady Arbella Stuart*. 2 vols. Ed. Elizabeth Cooper. London: Hurst and Blackett, 1866. 2.114–15.

Stubbes, Philip. *The Anatomy of Abuses*. London, 1595.

Transcript of the Registers of the United Parishes of S. Mary Woolnoth and S. Mary Wollchurch Haw, In the City of London. Ed. J.M.S. Brooke and A.W.C. Hallen. London: Bowles and Sons, 1886.

Vives, Juan Luis. *A verie fruitfull and pleasant booke, called the instruction of a Christian woman. Made first in Latin, by the right famous cleark M. Lewes Viues, and translated out of Latine into Englishe by Richard Hyrde*. Trans. Richard Hyrde. London, 1585.

Webster, John. *The Tragedy of the Dutchesse of Malfy.* London, 1623.

———. *The White Devil.* London, 1631.

Westerman, William. *Two Sermons of Assise.* London, 1600.

Whitelocke, Sir James. *Liber Familicus of Sir James Whitelocke.* Ed. John Bruce, Esq. London, 1858.

Secondary Works

Ardolino, Frank. "'Now Shall I See the Fall of Babylon': *The Spanish Tragedy* as Protestant Apocalypse." *Shakespeare Yearbook* 1 (1990): 93–115.

Baker, Howard. *Induction to Tragedy.* New York: Russell and Russell, 1939.

Barker, William. Introduction to *Positions.* In Richard Mulcaster, *Positions Concerning the Training Up of Children.* Ed. William Barker. Toronto, U of Toronto P, 1994.

Bevington, David, ed. *The Tragedy of Mariam* by Elizabeth Cary. *English Renaissance Drama.* New York: Norton, 2002. 621–72.

Bowers, Fredson Thayer. *Elizabethan Revenge Tragedy, 1587–1642.* Gloucester, MA: Peter Smith, 1959.

Brewer's Dictionary of Phrase and Fable. Centenary Edition, Revised. Ed. Ivor H. Evans. New York: Harper and Row, 1981.

Broude, Ronald. "Revenge and Revenge Tragedy in Renaissance England." *Renaissance Quarterly* 28.1 (1975): 38–58.

———. "Vindicta Filia Temporis: Three English Forerunners of the Elizabethan Revenge Play." *The Journal of English and Germanic Philology* 72.4 (1973): 489–502.

Callaghan, Dympna, and Chris R. Kyle. "The Wilde Side of Justice in Early Modern England and *Titus Andronicus.*" *The Law in Shakespeare.* Ed. Constance Jordan and Karen Cunningham. Early Modern Literature in History. London: Palgrave Macmillan, 2007. 38–57.

Chambers, E.K. *The Elizabethan Stage.* 4 vols. Oxford: Clarendon P, 1923.

Crosbie, Christopher. "Oeconomia and the Vegetative Soul: Rethinking Revenge in *The Spanish Tragedy.*" *English Literary Renaissance* 38.1 (2008): 3–33.

Duthie, George Ian. *The "Bad" Quarto of Hamlet.* Norwood, PA: Norwood Editions, 1975.

Erne, Lukas. *Beyond The Spanish Tragedy.* The Revels Plays Companion Library. Manchester and New York: Manchester UP, 2001.

Fantazzi, Charles, ed. and trans. *The Education of a Christian Woman,* by Juan Luis Vives. Chicago: U of Chicago P, 2000.

Freeman, Arthur. "Marlowe, Kyd, and the Dutch Church Libel." *English Literary Renaissance* 3 (1973): 44–52.

——. *Thomas Kyd: Facts and Problems.* London: Oxford UP, 1967.

Fuchs, Barbara. "Sketches of Spain: Early Modern England's 'Orientalizing' of Iberia." *Material and Symbolic Circulation between Spain and England, 1554–1604.* Ed. Anne J. Cruz. Burlington, VT: Ashgate, 2008. 63–70.

Gurr, Andrew. *Playgoing in Shakespeare's London.* Cambridge: Cambridge UP, 1987.

——. *The Shakespearean Stage, 1574–1642.* Cambridge: Cambridge UP, 1970.

Hillgarth, J.N. *The Mirror of Spain, 1500–1700.* Ann Arbor: U of Michigan P, 2000.

Hotson, J. Leslie. *The Death of Christopher Marlowe.* 1925. New York: Russell and Russell, 1967.

Keene, Derek. "Material London in Time and Space." *Material London, ca. 1600.* Ed. Lena Cowen Orlin. Philadelphia: U of Pennsylvania P, 2000. 55–74.

Kuin, R.J.P., ed. Robert Langham, *A Letter.* Leiden, Netherlands: E.J. Brill, 1983.

McDonald, Russ. "Marlowe and Style." *The Cambridge Companion to Christopher Marlowe.* Ed. Patrick Cheney. Cambridge: Cambridge UP, 2004. 55–69.

Nicholl, Charles. *The Reckoning: The Murder of Christopher Marlowe.* Chicago: U of Chicago P, 1992.

Riggs, David. *The World of Christopher Marlowe.* New York: Henry Holt, 2004.

Smith, Molly. "The Theater and the Scaffold: Death as Spectacle in *The Spanish Tragedy.*" *Studies in English Literature, 1500–1900* 32.2 (1992): 217–32.

Steen, Sara Jayne, ed. *The Letters of Lady Arbella Stuart. Women Writers in English 1350–1850.* New York: Oxford UP, 1994.

Stevenson, Warren. "Shakespeare's Hand in *The Spanish Tragedy* 1602." *Studies in English Literature, 1500–1900* 8.2 (1968): 307–21.

Vickers, Brian. "Identifying Shakespeare's Additions to *The Spanish Tragedy* (1602): A Newer Approach." *Shakespeare* 8.1 (2012): 13–43.

Wilson, Rev. H.B. *The History of the Merchant-Taylors' School.* London: Marchant and Galabin, 1812.

From the Publisher

A name never says it all, but the word "Broadview" expresses a good deal of the philosophy behind our company. We are open to a broad range of academic approaches and political viewpoints. We pay attention to the broad impact book publishing and book printing has in the wider world; we began using recycled stock more than a decade ago, and for some years now we have used 100% recycled paper for most titles. Our publishing program is internationally oriented and broad-ranging. Our individual titles often appeal to a broad readership too; many are of interest as much to general readers as to academics and students.

Founded in 1985, Broadview remains a fully independent company owned by its shareholders—not an imprint or subsidiary of a larger multinational.

For the most accurate information on our books (including information on pricing, editions, and formats) please visit our website at www.broadviewpress.com. Our print books and ebooks are also available for sale on our site.

On the Broadview website we also offer several goods that are not books—among them the Broadview coffee mug, the Broadview beer stein (inscribed with a line from Geoffrey Chaucer's *Canterbury Tales*), the Broadview fridge magnets (your choice of philosophical or literary), and a range of T-shirts (made from combinations of hemp, bamboo, and/or high-quality pima cotton, with no child labor, sweatshop labor, or environmental degradation involved in their manufacture).

All these goods are available through the "merchandise" section of the Broadview website. When you buy Broadview goods you can support other goods too.

broadview press
www.broadviewpress.com

The interior of this book is printed on 100% recycled paper.